"*Body-Oriented Mentalizing in Clinical Practice* is a book borne out of intimate knowledge of how to treat patients with persistent physical symptoms. It is highly recommended for its clear didactic structure, its focus on bodily phenomena in psychotherapy and for its very practical 'Know how' details."

Peter Henningsen, *Professor of Psychosomatic Medicine and Psychotherapy, Technical University of Munich, Germany*

"In this well-written book, the reader will find an extensive theoretical foundation for this multidisciplinary treatment and, importantly, a detailed overview of how to apply this treatment, interspersed with appealing examples. Highly recommended for anyone who guides and cares for people with severe Persistent Physical Symptoms (PPS)."

Henriëtte van der Horst, *Professor Em. of General Medicine, Amsterdam University Medical Center, the Netherlands*, and *former chairman of the Dutch PPS care standard*

"*Body-Oriented Mentalizing in Clinical Practice* describes a pathbreaking adaptation of the therapeutic approach of mentalizing to help patients understand the relationship between their mental and somatic experiences when physical symptoms are persistent. The book includes applications for individual, non-verbal, group, and systemic therapies."

James Levenson, *MD, Rhona Arenstein Professor of Psychiatry, Virginia Commonwealth University, USA*

"This book is one of the most valuable contributions to the particular importance of the body in the mentalization model, both theoretically and practically. Jaap Spaans focuses with the concept of body-oriented mentalization-based therapy on the large group of patients with persistent physical (somatoform) symptoms. This book is a milestone in the improvement of mentalization-based theory and practice for patients with persistent physical complaints, after the body has been forgotten in the discussion of the Theory of Mind."

Ulrich Schultz-Venrath, *Prof. Dr. Med., Professor Emeritus of Psychosomatics and Psychotherapy at Witten/Herdecke University, Germany, working in private practice as psychoanalyst, training group analyst, MBT-Therapist and -Supervisor in Cologne, Germany*

Body-Oriented Mentalizing in Clinical Practice

Body-oriented mentalization-based therapy (B-MBT) helps patients link physical signals to their inner experiences, such as thoughts, emotions, and memories, allowing them to become aware of previously unrecognised bodily sensations and internal responses. This book explores how B-MBT may be used to provide therapeutic support to patients with severe Persistent Physical Symptoms (PPS), formerly also known as Medically Unexplained Physical Symptoms (MUPS).

Chapters present vivid examples of B-MBT in practice and highlight key therapeutic skills for readers to apply to their own work with patients. Divided into three sections, chapters cover:

- An introduction to theory behind B-MBT and PPS.
- A section exploring treatment, including basic interventions, non-verbal therapies, responding to old inner pains, and guidance for encouraging patients to progress towards a balanced lifestyle.
- A section on practical tools for group, systemic and multidisciplinary therapeutic treatments.

Body-Oriented Mentalizing in Clinical Practice is an essential read for any practitioner who wants to learn more about treatment options for patients experiencing severe PPS. It will be of particular interest to (para)medical professionals, mental health specialists and non-verbal therapists.

Tables 5.1, 6.1, 6.2, 8.1, 9.1, A.1, A.2, A.3, A.5.1, A.5.2 and A.5.3 are available as downloadable support materials from www.routledge.com/9781041068617

Jaap Spaans is a senior clinical psychologist and published author. He is the co-founder of the Dutch National Network for Persistent Physical Symptoms. Currently, Jaap supports health care professionals through different services including therapy and supervision.

Body-Oriented Mentalizing in Clinical Practice

Supporting Patients with Persistent Physical Symptoms

Jaap Spaans

Routledge
Taylor & Francis Group

LONDON AND NEW YORK

Designed cover image: © Getty Images, Credit: Maria Mirnaya

First published in English 2026
by Routledge
4 Park Square, Milton Park, Abingdon, Oxon OX14 4RN

and by Routledge
605 Third Avenue, New York, NY 10158

Routledge is an imprint of the Taylor & Francis Group, an informa business

Published in Dutch as 'Lichaamsgericht Mentaliseren: Gids voor de
klinische praktijk' by LannooCampus 2021. The English version is a
translation with revisions and additions.

British Library Cataloguing-in-Publication Data
A catalogue record for this book is available from the British Library

ISBN: 978-1-041-06862-4 (hbk)
ISBN: 978-1-041-06861-7 (pbk)
ISBN: 978-1-003-63748-6 (ebk)

DOI: 10.4324/9781003637486

Typeset in Times New Roman
by Apex CoVantage, LLC

Access the Support Material: www.routledge.com/9781041068617

Contents

About the author

Jaap Spaans (https://orcid.org/0009-0007-3334-9881) is a Dutch senior clinical psychologist, until 2020 affiliated with the highly specialised centre Altrecht Psychosomatiek Eikenboom, Zeist in the Netherlands. He has published books on various subjects such as eating disorders, borderline disorder, midlife, chronic fatigue, unexplained pain, mindfulness and self-regulation. He is one of the founders and, until 2018, was chairman of NALK (https://nalk.info), the National Network for Persistent Physical Symptoms (PPS), the Dutch expertise centre for collaboration of professionals, health care institutions and universities specialised in PPS. He is Editor-in-Chief of the Dutch *Handbook for the Treatment of Somatically Insufficiently Explained Physical Complaints* (MUPS/PPS). Currently, Jaap supports health care professionals through different services including therapy and supervision. Contact: j.spaans@hccnet.nl, https://jaapspaanspsycholoog.nl

Part I

Introduction and theory

Chapter 1

Introduction

1.1 The inner self as a physical experience

We experience the world around us through our bodies. Suppose you are peacefully reading a book and suddenly hear a loud bang. Immediately a physical shock goes through you, your heart rate and breathing speed up. You become alert. In a flash, you think, 'It must be those kids kicking their football at my front door again'. Then the blood rushes to your head, you feel hot and your jaw muscles tighten. You are angry. You rush to the front door and open it to see what is going on. What began as a physical shock ends with you opening the front door in anger.

Our experiences—especially emotional experiences—are fundamentally rooted in our bodily sensations. This is also true of our memories of past emotional experiences. Later, when we think back to that sudden bang, another physical shock goes through us and we feel the blood rise to our head again. Not everyone is aware of signals from their own body and its mental dimensions, such as emotions and thoughts. Some people have never learned to do this, while others temporarily suppress their bodily awareness, for example when they are busy with an important task. As therapists in our practice, we see patients who have difficulty perceiving and making sense of body signals. Our patients do not perceive parts of their body at all, or they do not experience any connection between physical signals and inner experiences. For example, they do not recognise fear or sadness, or there is a lot of unnoticed tension in their body. They can experience symptoms that can be classified as somatic complaints, personality problems, burn-out, persistent mood or anxiety disorders, or eating disorders. By paying close attention to the body in therapy, these patients learn to recognise the workings of the mind, and that emotions and other inner experiences are inextricably linked to the body.

The method of body-oriented mentalization described in this book can be applied to a wide range of patients who find it difficult to make the connection between physical and inner experiences. My expertise and that of my colleagues lies primarily in the area of applying body-oriented mentalizing to the subset of patients with severe Persistent Physical Symptoms (PPS). That's why this book focuses on this group of patients.

DOI: 10.4324/9781003637486-2

1.2 Persistent physical symptoms

PPS are distressing somatic complaints that persist for several months or longer, regardless of their cause. These symptoms occur in the context of somatic diseases, functional somatic disorders, mental disorders and undiagnosed conditions, and are a core problem in a wide range of medical disciplines (Löwe et al., 2024). PPS are physical complaints such as pain, fatigue or dizziness for which adequate medical examination does not reveal a somatic condition that adequately explains the complaint. PPS can also be symptoms associated with a known physical condition such as diabetes, rheumatism or heart disease. In this case, we consider it to be PPS if the complaints are more severe or prolonged, or have a greater impact on functioning than would be expected from the condition.

The term PPS has been used since 2021 and was introduced on a wider international level in 2024 (Löwe et al., 2024). Previously, these complaints were referred to by such diverse terms as psychosomatic syndromes, physically unexplained complaints, poorly understood complaints or medically unexplained physical symptoms.

The symptoms associated with PPS can be very distressing. Many patients with severe PPS are unable to work (fully). Patients seek and undergo all kinds of medical treatments without the desired results. It often takes a long time for health care providers and patients to recognise the problem and receive appropriate help. The physical, mental and social disabilities are particularly evident in patients with (very) severe PPS. They have long-term and multiple symptoms and severe impairments, co-morbidity in terms of psychopathology, personality disorders and/ or somatic conditions. They respond inadequately to treatment in primary and/or specialist mental health and/or somatic care. Appropriate treatment is essential for this group of patients. Strengthening body-oriented mentalizing is an appropriate therapeutic approach for patients in this group who struggle with it.

1.3 The development of body-oriented mentalization based therapy (B-MBT)

The specialist treatment centre for adults with severe PPS, Altrecht Psychosomatiek Eikenboom in the Netherlands, to which the author and co-workers of this book are or were attached, focuses on the group of patients with (very) severe PPS. For many years, this centre has worked with a vision that combines physical and mental experiences. From this perspective, around 2006, it became apparent that what Anthony Bateman and Peter Fonagy (2004) called 'mentalization-based treatment' (MBT) was also relevant to the treatment of patients with (very) severe PPS. Gradually, treatment in our centre began to resemble MBT, but with one clear difference: the focus on the body.

Our first article on the physical aspects of mentalization appeared in 2009 (Spaans et al., 2009). In 2018, the Dutch care standard for PPS (Akwa GGZ, 2018) recognised the importance of B-MBT. The Dutch care standard writes: 'For a subgroup of patients with (very) severe PPS who show no or insufficient recovery in response to evidence-based treatments such as CBT or ACT, body-oriented mentalization based therapy (B-MBT) can be considered. In B-MBT, patients learn to recognise and tolerate their body's signals and to experience connection with inner experiences such as emotions, thoughts, memories, intentions and desires in interaction with others'.

Meanwhile, many hundreds of colleagues have taken a basic course in B-MBT, and (international) lectures and workshops on B-MBT continue to attract great interest. Several health care institutions in the Netherlands now use B-MBT.

1.4 Differences with MBT

Colleagues often ask us 'Isn't B-MBT exactly the same as MBT, just with more consideration for the body?' Broadly speaking, the answer is 'yes'. Therefore, when treating patients with severe PPS, it makes sense to read the books and articles by MBT experts such as Anthony Bateman, Peter Fonagy, Patrick Luyten and Jon Allen and the principles they describe. When we read MBT literature, we can then think of patients with PPS instead of patients with BPS. We can read these inspiring works, follow the MBT teachings and always keep in mind the relevance of bodily sensations. That we see the body as a bridge to the inner self is not inconsistent with MBT thinking.

So why is body-oriented mentalization based therapy described as a separate method in this book? Firstly, the B of B-MBT emphasises that this therapy is primarily intended for patients with severe PPS. While these patients share some characteristics with those with borderline personality disorder, such as problems with emotional regulation, their suffering is primarily physical. B-MBT's emphasis on bodily experience meets the needs of PPS patients and offers more acknowledgment for their symptoms than therapies that focus solely on affect and interaction, such as standard MBT.

Second, MBT emphasises the recognition and acknowledgement of affect and interpersonal affect regulation. Many professionals associate mentalization primarily with these aspects. Terms such as 'body-mentalization' and 'body-oriented mentalizing' emphasise the bodily dimension alongside the affective and interpersonal. Thus, the B in B-MBT reminds us to address the connection between body and inner experience during treatment. It is of the utmost importance that we continue to recognise that the patient's inner self makes itself known through the language of the body. Therefore, we always pay attention to facial expressions, rhythm and tone of voice, breathing, posture, gestures and so on. In short, the B of B-MBT always keeps the body on the agenda.

Patients with severe PPS often also present with unresolved trauma, profound interpersonal problems, and intense difficulties with emotion regulation. Their compelling narratives can focus our attention entirely on verbal psychological methods, in keeping with their tendency to avoid the physical dimension. Conversely, patients who are fixated on physical functioning risk a one-sided physical approach. The B in B-MBT ensures also that we balance attention to both physical and mental experience.

Thirdly, B-MBT differs from MBT in the inclusion of non-verbal therapies such as art therapy, psychomotor therapy, (psychosomatic) physiotherapy, etc. While in MBT non-verbal therapies are a possible addition, in B-MBT they are an indispensable part. In contrast to MBT, B-MBT is therefore much more of a multidisciplinary therapy.

Finally, it is characteristic of B-MBT that, unlike MBT, it also helps patients to develop (physical) activities from within a mentalizing state.

1.5 The psychodynamic tradition in thinking about body and mind

The concept of mentalizing is embedded in a psychodynamic frame of reference. So is the physical side of mentalizing, which has attracted increasing interest in the last decade. The idea that internal phenomena such as thoughts and emotions have a bodily side is not new in psychodynamics. Freud (Freud, 1915) was already convinced that inner experiences such as thoughts have the function of transforming instinctive bodily needs into actions that we take in order to satisfy those needs.

Thoughts give meaning to bodily processes, he believed. Freud assumed that the mind expresses itself entirely and exclusively through bodily signals: 'The ego . . . is first and foremost a bodily ego' (Freud, 1923). If we do not sufficiently acknowledge bodily sensations and desires, their intensity and quantity will increase until a discharge occurs. This economic principle explains why someone who does not recognise bodily signals and the associated thoughts and emotions will experience a lot of bodily arousal and thus bodily discomfort (Freud, 1915).

A view shared by many psychoanalysts is the 'conversion theory' (Freud, 1905): repressed inner conflicts and associated strong negative emotions are expressed symbolically through the body. This can include paralysis of limbs, loss of voice or hearing, or complete physical paralysis with loss of consciousness. The idea that inadequate recognition of body signals and emotions can lead to psychosomatic illness reappeared in the work of the Hungarian American psychoanalyst Franz Alexander shortly after the Second World War.

In the 1960s, the French psychoanalyst Pierre Marty looked at the physical side of mentalizing. He described mentalizing as the mental ability to recognise, interpret and respond to what the body is signalling (Marty, 1968). He also looked at the relational context of mentalizing. For example, he described how unemotional, empty, fantasy-free object relations ('relations blanches') can negatively affect the capacity for mentalizing. This would play a role in the development of psychosomatic complaints (Marty & de M'uzan, 1963).

The French analyst Didier Anzieu helped to clarify in the 1990s the role of early experience of skin and touch in the development of mentalizing capacity. He described this as 'une peau à penser': skin to think with (Anzieu, 1994).

The foregoing describes some of the many reflections and theories from the psychodynamic tradition about the interaction of body and mind and the bodily side of mentalizing. It highlights the history of the current interest in the bodily side of mentalizing in the treatment of PPS (Spaans et al., 2009, 2010, Luyten, Van Houdenhove, et al., 2012).

1.6 About this book

This book offers a vision and treatment method for patients with severe PPS where an inability to body mentalization is apparent. The method can also be applied to (other) psychological conditions where patients find it difficult to make a connection between bodily signals and inner experiences. It is therefore a transdiagnostic method.

This book is intended for professionals from various fields, such as psychologists, psychotherapists, systems therapists, physicians (including psychiatrists, (general) practitioners, rehabilitation specialists, medical specialists (e.g., cardiologists, neurologists, etc.), (specialist) nurses, occupational therapists, physiotherapists, rehabilitation therapists and other allied health professionals. These professionals have very different educational backgrounds and will therefore find different starting points for their field in this book.

This book is not a step-by-step script for therapists, but a comprehensive overview of interventions, considerations and methods to support body-oriented mentalizing. Professionals can integrate their findings from this book into their practice or treatment setting. Additional training, intervision and supervision are recommended for clinical application. While there are similarities between MBT and B-MBT, the differences between the approaches add value, even for those already trained in MBT.

In organising the chapters, we decided to start in Chapter 2 with a brief description of what is important about PPS for reading this book. Here it shows that B-MBT fits in well with recent developments in the field. In Chapter 3, we then describe body mentalization. This chapter describes the physical side of developing the ability to metalize. It also discusses the perpetuating effects of poor body mentalization in PPS and provides a theoretical underpinning for the therapeutic processes of B-MBT.

Part II on treatment begins with the principles of treatment in Chapter 4. The individual basic interventions are presented in Chapter 5. Non-verbal therapy is essential in B-MBT because of its direct focus on physical experience. Chapter 6 deals with two aspects of non-verbal therapy: a) expressing; and b) reflecting on physical and inner experiences. With the basic interventions and the non-verbal approach, patients can reach a basic level of body-oriented mentalizing. As they become aware of what they are physically and mentally experiencing, they may also begin to experience old mental pain. How to deal with this is discussed in Chapter 7. This involves responding to emotional pain related to past painful relationships and traumatic events. It is typical of B-MBT that a therapy focusing on awareness of body and mind also includes behavioural instructions. Chapter 8 describes how we can help patients move from a body-mentalizing mode to activities in a well-measured manner.

Part III of this book describes a number of application areas in which the methodological considerations described in Part II recur: group therapy (Chapter 9), systemic therapy (Chapter 10), and multidisciplinary treatment (Chapter 11). Chapter 11 also covers training and intervision. This chapter also describes how team members can use body-oriented mentalizing in contact with each other for the benefit of both effective treatment and team member job satisfaction.

NB: Throughout this book the therapist is written about and referred to as 'he'. Instead, the reader can equally well read 'she'. When referring to a patient in a general sense, we also use 'he'. This can also be read as 'she'. This is to maintain consistency throughout the book. It does not imply an emphasis on the importance of a particular gender of therapists or patients.

Chapter 2

Persistent physical symptoms

Before describing body-oriented mentalizing as a treatment method in the follow-ing chapters, we first briefly discuss the physical problems experienced by patients that are the focus of this book: persistent physical symptoms (PPS). We outline those aspects of PPS that are relevant to understanding what is described in the rest of the book. We use the term PPS because it has a broad consensus across different health care sectors and in the international scientific and clinical literature.

2.1 Terminology

Frequently reported persistent physical symptoms include chronic back pain and headaches, chronic fatigue, abdominal and gastrointestinal complaints. Depend-ing on the context, other terms have been used in recent decades to describe such complaints:

- Medically unexplained somatic symptoms
- Functional Somatic Syndromes
- Body-Mind Disorders
- Psychogenic complaints
- Psychosomatic complaints
- Functional symptoms
- Somatoform disorders
- Somatic symptom disorders

Many therapists, scientists and patients feel that many of these terms overemphasise 'what is psychologically wrong' or 'what is somatically insufficiently explained'. But they don't think that's the problem. It rather is the long-term physical symp-toms associated with distress and functional limitations that is at the heart of the problem.

Since 2024, there has been increasing international agreement on the use of the term PPS. They are defined as distressing somatic complaints that persist for several months or longer, regardless of their cause. These symptoms occur in the context of somatic diseases, functional somatic disorders, mental disorders and undiagnosed

DOI: 10.4324/9781003637486-3

conditions, and are a core problem in a wide range of medical disciplines (Löwe et al., 2024). They may be symptoms with which no somatic disease can be associated after adequate medical examination. However, it can also be symptoms of a physical condition, where the symptoms are more severe or prolonged, or more disabling, than would be expected from the condition. Psychological factors affecting a medical condition may play a role (Levenson, 2008). Of course, social factors can also have their impact here.

Often, persistent physical symptoms are not specific to the organ systems involved in the primary condition, and subjective symptom burden correlates poorly with the severity or stage of the underlying disease (Conway et al., 2011; Hansen et al., 2022).

Six stable clusters of interrelated symptoms have been repeatedly described in clinical and general population samples, namely clusters of general, cardiopulmonary, gastrointestinal, musculoskeletal, nervous system and urogenital symptoms (Burton et al., 2020; Senger et al., 2022). Medical specialists typically characterise PPS that are somatically insufficiently explained as a functional somatic syndrome, such as chronic fatigue syndrome, fibromyalgia, non-specific low back pain, tension headache, irritable bowel syndrome and functional movement disorder.

In mental health care, disorders are classified according to the Diagnostic and Statistical Manual of Mental Disorders (DSM). In the previous version (DSM-IV-TR; American Psychiatric Association, 1994), symptoms similar to PPS were classified as somatoform disorders. In the current DSM-5 (American Psychiatric Association, 2014), symptoms that fall under PPS are usually classified as somatic symptom disorders or related disorders. The following disorders are distinguished:

- Somatic symptom disorder
- Sickness anxiety disorder
- Conversion disorder (functional neurological symptom disorder)
- Psychological factors affecting other medical conditions
- Factitious disorder
- Other specified somatic symptom and related disorder
- Unspecified somatic symptom disorder or r elated disorder

Sickness anxiety disorder and factitious disorder are different from the other disorders in this category, and PPS is not part of it. That is because they do not necessarily have obvious physical symptoms. In these disorders, the focus is on anxiety, obsessions or deliberately producing, feigning or exaggerating symptoms.

Somatic symptom disorder is the most common disorder within this category. Its main feature is dysfunctional coping with physical symptoms: disproportionate and persistent thoughts about the severity of symptoms and/or persistently high levels of anxiety about health and symptoms and/or spending excessive time and energy on symptoms or health (American Psychiatric Association, 2014). The DSM-5 introduced a different view of explained and unexplained physical symptoms that is different from what was common up to and including DSM-IV. A positive criterion, a maladaptive response to physical symptoms, was chosen instead of the previous negative criterion that symptoms had to be inadequately explained somatically. This dropped the distinction between somatically explained and somatically unexplained symptoms, and moreover abandoned the artificial separation between body and mind (Tak & van Geelen, 2017). Patients with somatically explained physical conditions, such as heart disease or diabetes, may meet the criteria for a somatic symptom disorder if they have excessive thoughts or feelings about their condition or related excessive behaviours.

2.2   Prevalence

The proportion of PPS that cannot be attributed to a recognised disease is estimated at 20-26% in the general population (Creed et al., 2011), 40% in primary care (Olde Hartman et al., 2013) and 35-53% in specialist care (Creed et al., 2011). Of all patients visiting a GP, 16% have severe PPS (De Waal et al., 2004). PPS is more common in women than in men (Steinbrecher & Hiller, 2011). Back pain, headache, abdominal pain and fatigue are among the most commonly reported symptoms by patients in western primary care, accounting for up to 50% of all consultations (Kroenke, 2003).

2.3   (Very) severe PPS

A subgroup of patients suffers from (very) severe PPS. This group is characterised by (van der Boom & Houtveen, 2014):

- Prolonged and multiple symptoms
- Severe limitations in functioning (ADL's, social, work)
- Comorbidity in terms of psychopathology, personality disorders, somatic conditions
- Insufficient effect of previous treatment in primary and/or specialised mental health and/or somatic care
- Complications and iatrogenic damages
- Difficulties in communication and lack of agreement in caregiving relationships

In the Netherlands, (very) severe PPS is mainly treated in specialist mental health care. If the symptoms are too complex for specialist mental health care, or if treatment is unsuccessful, referral to highly specialised mental health care is indicated as a next step (den Boer et al., 2017). In these centres, after a comprehensive intake, outpatient, individual or group, day or residential treatment is offered. The treatment is tailored to the specific symptoms, perpetuating factors and underlying problems. There often is a choice of:

- Cognitive behavioural therapy
- Acceptance and Commitment Therapy (ACT)

- Body-oriented Mentalization Based therapy (B-MBT)
- Trauma therapy
- Sensorimotor Psychotherapy

During treatment, diverse professionals work intensively together such as doctors, psychiatrists, psychologists, physiotherapists, psychomotor therapists, occupational therapists, art therapists, nurses and social workers. Pharmacotherapy is used to treat co-morbid psychiatric disorders as well as pain. As much attention as possible is also given to any neglected somatic comorbidity. These highly specialised mental health care institutions also offer consultations and second opinions, and conduct scientific research on the results of their treatments.

The case study of the fictitious Mrs Schutte presented in box 2.1 illustrates the problems of patients with (very) severe PPS who are eligible for B-MBT.

Box 2.1   Case study: A long journey from therapist to therapist

Mrs Schutte is a 49-year-old group worker with a long history of unexplained physical complaints such as collapsing, chronic fatigue, back pain and abdominal cramps. From childhood, Mrs Schutte tried not to be a burden to anyone, including her parents, as her brother, who was three years older, had severe behavioural problems and had difficulty keeping up at school. Later in her own family, 'helping others' also came in handy, as both her husband and children had health problems. Mrs Schutte kept the family going and also worked part-time as a group worker in a home for young people with mental health problems. Mrs Schutte rarely let her feelings be heard. Seven years ago, a series of stressful events occurred in rapid succession: a conflict with a colleague, a bicycle accident, a reorganisation at work and her husband's hospitalisation for heart bypass surgery. She then developed severe symptoms of fatigue, pain in her neck, shoulders and back, and cramping in her abdomen. The GP first prescribed medication and she went to see a physiotherapist, but her condition worsened. She became depressed, sometimes thought of suicide, collapsed regularly and was unable to work. The internist, neurologist and gastroenterologist could find no explanation for the symptoms.

A journey of many years from therapist tot therapist followed, involving psychologists, an occupational therapist, a hypnotherapist, a psychosomatic physiotherapist and alternative therapies such as acupuncture, aromatherapy and Reiki. When individual cognitive behavioural therapy failed, her GP referred her to a rehabilitation centre for intensive treatment. She was admitted for a day treatment with no apparent results. The rehabilitation doctor referred her through the GP to the highly specialised psychosomatic mental health centre. On admission, it was immediately noticeable that Mrs Schutte talked about her physical complaints in a rambling and unemotional way. The tendency not to focus on her own body and mind was so obvious and persistent that a six-month day clinic treatment based on B-MBT was indicated.

2.4 The biopsychosocial model

Theoretical models of PPS always offer limited explanations because of the complexity of neurobiological processes, the inseparability of body and mind, and the interconnectedness of the individual and the environment. In addition, the boundary between disease and health is not always sharp. In recent decades, an impressive number of biological, psycho-physiological and (bio)psychosocial explanatory models for the onset and persistence of PPS have been developed, partly based on scientific research. These models are often based on one or a few causal factors. Examples include perceptual-cognitive models, cognitive theories, behavioural models, psycho-physiological models, attachment and mentalization models, emotion regulation theories, personality models, trauma models, dissociation theories, memory theories, resilience models, social theories, etc.

Each of these generic theories provides limited explanations. However, it is essential to maintain a broad perspective. Rather than seeking a single cause, PPS should be viewed as a multi-factorial phenomenon influenced by unique somatic, psychological and social factors for each patient (Spaans & van der Boom, 2017). The biopsychosocial model offers a personalised framework to understand the onset and persistence of PPS, identifying how these factors interact. For example, low back pain (biological) may trigger thoughts like 'my day is ruined', leading to depression (psychological) and cancelled social plans (social). Explaining these interactions to patients can enhance treatment motivation, showing that even if somatic improvement is limited, changes in psychological or social domains can improve quality of life or even influence biological factors. This model also aids in identifying vulnerabilities across three key areas when creating a treatment plan:

- Predisposing factors are often long-standing or genetic characteristics or past experiences that make a person vulnerable to the onset or chronicity of symptoms.
- Triggering factors precipitate the onset of symptoms.
- Maintaining factors maintain or intensify symptoms.

This creates a matrix of interacting risk factors. Combined with the biological, psychological and social factors mentioned earlier, a matrix of interacting aetiological factors can be constructed (see Table 2.1 for a few examples of each).

Table 2.1 Examples of risk factors for the development of PPS.

	Biological	Psychological	Social
Predisposing	genetic predisposition long-term somatic illness early physical or sexual abuse	early psychological trauma personality traits insecure attachment style	long-term family and relationship problems dealing with illness in the family emotional neglect
Triggering	acute somatic disease physical accident physical exhaustion	psychosocial problems intense unmanageable emotions inner conflict	drastic social events such as: illness in family, moving house, divorce, death of loved one
Maintaining	inactivity overactivity loss of physical condition	movement anxiety catastrophising thoughts failing to recognise body signals and emotions	stigmatisation loss of work and income little social support

Distinguishing between the various factors in the individual patient is essential for treatment. Therapy will focus as much as possible on the personalised combination of predisposing, triggering and maintaining factors in their interrelationship.

2.5   Maintaining factors in relation to B-MBT

As (very) severe PPS is characterised by the symptoms lasting a long time, the perpetuating factors that maintain or exacerbate the symptoms are of particular importance for both explanation and treatment. Among the maintaining factors often mentioned in the international literature are also factors that are related to a deficient capacity for body-oriented mentalization. These include difficulties in perceiving, experiencing and interpreting body signals and emotions; and attachment problems and dysfunctional interactions with loved ones (Casius et al., 2016; Janssens et al., 2017). These factors form the focus of Body-oriented Mentalization Based Therapy.

2.6   Treatment of PPS

For the group of (very) severe PPS, such as somatic symptom disorder, it is generally assumed that the best-suited approach is stepped care with close cooperation of primary care, a somatic specialist and mental health care professionals operating on the basis of a biopsychosocial model (Henningsen, 2018). Henningsen and colleagues (2007) described that patients with functional somatic syndromes benefit more from treatment with active participation, such as exercise and psychotherapy, than those that involve passive physical measures, including injections and operations. The same can be assumed for patients with (severe) PPS.

Looking at the effects of therapeutic methods in the treatment of PPS, cognitive behavioural therapy (CBT) occupies a prominent place; it is currently the best researched and most widely used treatment method. The positive results of CBT are often still modest (Spaans & van der Boom, 2018), and therefore CBT is not a panacea. A significant proportion of patients with severe PPS do not respond adequately to CBT. These patients show little or no improvement with evidence-based treatments like second-generation CBT (van der Boom & Houtveen, 2014). This highlights the need to consider alternatives such as B-MBT—particularly when body mentalization is impaired (Akwa GGZ, 2018; Feldmann-Sinnige et al., 2023; Houtveen et al., 2015). In general, there is growing attention in literature and clinical practice for body-oriented mentalization in the treatment of severe PPS. One of the inspiring examples is the description of mentalization in patients with somatoform disorders/somatic symptom disorders in *Mentalizing the Body* (2023) by Ulrich Schultz-Venrath.

There is also broad agreement that a non-verbal experiential approach using, for example, psychosomatic physiotherapy, art therapy, music therapy, occupational therapy, or psychomotor therapy is essential as part of the treatment of PPS. An important theme in non-verbal therapies is body awareness. As non-verbal therapies can act as a booster or perpetuator of more verbal therapies, it seems to be recommended to combine verbally oriented therapies with non-verbal therapies (Akwa GGZ, 2018). Non-verbal therapies play also an important role in B-MBT.

2.7   Conclusion

In this chapter we have looked at the target group that is central to this book: patients with PPS. It turns out that PPS is common in general or specialist practice. CBT occupies a prominent place in the treatment. A subgroup of patients suffer from (very) severe PPS, which constitutes the problem lasting a long time along with many co-morbidities and severe impairments. In this group of patients, the factors that maintain or exacerbate symptoms are particularly important for recovery. Factors related to poor body mentalization appear to play a strong maintaining role. Based on this, together with positive clinical experience and research data (see Section 4.2), it seems important to consider B-MBT as a therapy for (very) severe PPS when body mentalization is impaired.

Chapter 3

Body-oriented mentalizing

3.1 What are body mentalization and body-oriented mentalizing?

3.1.1 The concept

The term 'body mentalization' refers to the ability to experience a connection between bodily signals and inner experiences, such as emotions and thoughts. The concept helps to clarify the problems of patients with severe persistent physical symptoms (PPS). These patients appear to have difficulty with body mentalization, especially when experiencing physical complaints and stress. Research shows that patients with severe PPS have difficulty perceiving body signals and linking them to inner experiences. For example, they no longer realise that tense muscles are related to anger. Subic-Wrana concludes that in patients with somatic-symptom disorder, both body awareness and mentalizing ability are impaired. Previously, they were often called 'alexithym', indicating a limited ability to articulate emotions and bodily experiences. They perceive emotions selectively, have difficulty recognising and naming emotions, and have difficulty distinguishing between emotions and physical sensations (Subic-Wrana et al., 2010; Waller & Scheidt, 2004). Body mentalization is a useful concept for dealing with these issues.

Body mentalization is a form of mentalization, defined by Fonagy and Target (1996) as 'the capacity to understand behaviour of self and others in terms of underlying mental states, such as thoughts, feelings, desires, and intentions.' It involves understanding that both our own actions and those of others are driven by internal mental processes, allowing us to make sense of behaviour and navigate social interactions effectively. A mentalizing attitude is not only focused on one's own body and emotion regulation. It is also an everyday compassionate attitude aimed at mutual affective attunement and cooperation with others. Fonagy and Target's description has been used in the context of borderline personality problems with much emphasis on emotions and interaction (Fonagy & Target, 1996). However, in order to mentalize, it is a prerequisite that people can pay attention to what they feel in their bodies (Nicolai, 2017a). This ability is particularly challenging for patients suffering from severe PPS (Waller & Scheidt, 2006).

DOI: 10.4324/9781003637486-4

The physical aspect of mentalizing was already evident in earlier descriptions of the concept of mentalization, such as by Pierre Marty (1968), who defined it as a mental ability to identify, interpret and respond to bodily expressions. In mentalization theory, recognising the bodily expressions of affect (e.g. sweaty hands as a sign of anxiety) is considered a basic expression of mentalizing. A heightened level of mentalization is indicated by an awareness of the interpersonal context of emotions (e.g., experiencing feelings of insecurity in the presence of someone who does not take you seriously). So the ability to identify body expressions of affect is a prerequisite for attaining higher levels of mentalization (Choi-Kain & Gunderson, 2008).

Mentalization can be seen as a multi-dimensional concept that includes affective, interpersonal and physical aspects. Breaking the concept down into its dimensional elements may be helpful to patients. Studies and our clinical impression suggest that patients with severe PPS experience their bodies as dysfunctional, have difficulties in recognising and understanding the body, and act (dysfunctional) on this basis (Spaans, 2017). In these patients, the bodily side of mentalizing can be particularly problematic: it is difficult for them to derive emotions from bodily sensations, especially negative emotions (Dendy et al., 2001; Oldershaw et al., 2011; Stonnington et al., 2013). Body sensations are interpreted one-sidedly or unrealistically, which can perpetuate physical and emotional problems. In addition, many of these patients appear to have negative beliefs about their own emotions (Hambrook et al., 2011). It therefore seems important to consider the physical dimension of mentalizing in patients with severe PPS.

In the context of severe unexplained physical symptoms we defined body-oriented mentalizing (body mentalization) as the ability to perceive and be receptive to one's own and others' body signals and to experience a connection with mental states (Spaans et al., 2009, 2010). We developed this definition with a view to clinical practice in PPS treatment to emphasise the relevance of a therapeutic process that focuses on the body to strengthen mentalizing. Our definition emphasises receptivity—opening up to body signals—because this is how awareness of inner experiences often begins in therapy. It forms the basis of B-MBT as described in this book.

To understand and treat functional somatic disorders, Luyten, Van Houdenhove, et al. (2012) used the term 'embodied mentalizing'. They defined it as the capacity to see the body as the seat of emotions, wishes and feelings, and the capacity to reflect on one's own bodily experiences and sensations and their relationships to intentional mental states in the self and others. They see mentalizing as largely rooted in the body (e.g. 'I feel crumpled' or 'I float with happiness') and partly determined by biological factors. However, the definition leaves little room for the fact that patients with PPS may be in a state in which mentalizing is not yet possible at all: the so-called body state (Schultz Venrath, 2023). Or as Jurist (2022, p. 200) formulates this state: The body is not a receptacle for unwanted mental life; it informs and supports mental life.

Our definition of body-oriented mentalizing (body mentalization) (Spaans et al., 2009, 2010) allows more room for the possibility that patients with PPS can be in a body mode (see Section 3.1.2) where mentalization is not yet possible. Patients with PPS, when in the body mode, react impulsively to body signals (e.g. that the body feels cold), but hardly recognise them. In a next phase of (not) mentalizing, they can learn to recognise the body signals and reflect on them (I feel cold). In yet another next phase of (not) mentalizing, they learn to recognise the associated inner experiences (I miss someone and that feels cold). By bringing awareness to bodily sensations and signals and reflecting on the emotional meaning, they learn to regulate emotions and their physical aspects.

In this book, the term 'body mentalization' refers to the psychological ability and mental process, while 'body-oriented mentalizing' stands more for the skill as addressed in therapy. Nicolai (2017a) describes the bodily side of mentalizing simply as 'observing what is happening in your body and understanding what emotions are being expressed in it.' Other simple descriptions are:

- To understand the language of the body
- Keeping body and mind in mind
- Recognising that the body is the seat of emotions, desires and feelings
- Paying attention to body and mind and how they are connected
- Engaging with the inner self with attention to the body
- Focusing on how the inner self is expressed through the body
- Seeing the connection between body signals and emotions

3.1.2   Modes and dimensions of (non-)mentalizing

Modes of (non-)mentalizing

Fonagy and Bateman (2006) describe three modes of non-mentalizing that occur when someone has difficulty understanding and regulating mental states in themselves and others:

- Teleological mode: Behaviour and intentions are judged exclusively on the basis of visible, physical outcomes. Inner experiences are not seen as explanatory or relevant. For example: 'If you loved me, you would be here now'.
- Equivalence mode: Inner experiences are equated with reality on a one-to-one basis, with no room for alternative perspectives. Feelings and thoughts are experienced as absolute truths, which can lead to intense anxiety or rigidity of thought. For example: 'I feel worthless, so I am a worthless person'.
- Pretend mode: There is a disconnection between inner experience and external reality. Thoughts and feelings are not taken seriously. This can lead to superficial or distant communication. For example, someone talks about intense pain without any affective involvement.

Schultz-Venrath (2023) suggested that the three previous modes should be extended by introducing *the body mode* as the earliest. From a developmental psychology perspective, the body mode is defined by the fact that the infant does not experience his body and psyche as separate until about nine months. Instead, it is primarily concerned with bodily and skin sensations. The body mode is part of the non-verbal, largely unconscious interaction that is differentiated by posture, gesture, touch, facial expression, gaze, voice and speech melody and helps to understand PPS and somatic symptom disorders and other body-related disorders.

The body mode of mentalization can also be reflected in the other non-mentalizing modes—the teleological mode, the equivalence mode and the pretend mode. This implies that bodily signals and experiences in these three modes can be processed in an often limited or distorted way.

- Teleological mode and the body: In this mode only what is physically concrete, visible and tangible is experienced. For example, a patient will only believe that a therapist cares about them if the therapist performs a physical action, such as putting a hand on the patient's shoulder.
- Equivalence mode and the body: Here the internal physical experience is taken as absolute truth. A patient who feels physical tension may interpret this as undeniable evidence of imminent danger.
- Pretend mode and the body: In this mode there is a disconnect between physical sensations and emotional meaning. A patient may talk about intense physical discomfort without any affective charge or connection to their own experience.

By also acknowledging the physical aspects in the teleological, equivalence and pretend modes, one avoids an overly fragmented or rigid interpretation of someone's physical and mental functioning.

Dimensions of body mentalization

To clarify neurological and therapeutic processes, mentalizing can be described in terms of a number of interrelated polarities (Lieberman, 2007; Luyten & Fonagy, 2015). These also apply to body mentalizing and are briefly described in the following section.

- Controlled (explicit) vs. automatic (implicit)

The most important dimension is that of automatic (implicit) versus controlled (or explicit) body mentalization. In many cases, body mentalization in everyday life manifests itself in implicit, unconscious, intuitive processes that can be expressed physically (e.g. through 'sensing'). Without thinking about it, people notice that the hairs on the back of their necks stand up when they're listening to someone's story. This rapid, unreasoned, non-verbal, automatic process has a strong bodily side. Body signals are therefore a gateway to (implicit) mentalizing. In therapy, we explicitly encourage body mentalization with questions such as 'What thoughts are going through your mind now that you have back pain?' or 'What emotions are you experiencing now that you are tired?' This conscious body mentalization is related to the controlled, slow, reflective process of explicit body mentalization. The difference between implicit and explicit body mentalization can be compared to the difference between automatic and conscious breathing. We usually breathe implicitly: unconsciously, without thinking about it. In breath therapy we consciously focus our attention on breathing and it becomes an explicit process.

• Self vs. Other

We can apply body mentalization to ourselves in order to become aware of our own state (including our physical experiences). We can also focus it on others to assess their state (including their bodily experiences). The two aspects of 'self' and 'other' are closely related. The ability to body mentalize about oneself is highly dependent on the ability to body mentalize about others. An imbalance between the two will seriously affect the quality of body mentalizing. A large group of people with PPS are very concerned about the fate of others. They adopt a caring attitude towards others without paying attention to their own physical and mental state. The focus is on the other person. Therapy might teach them to pay attention to their own physical experience and mental condition. However, there is also a subgroup of patients with PPS who are more focused on their own physical and mental state, where therapy could focus on the other side of the problem: the other person.

• Cognitive vs. affective

Body mentalization involves the ability to name, recognise and reason about bodily states and internal reactions (in oneself or others)—the cognitive aspect. When we ask patients to focus their attention on a particular way of thinking or to change their perspective, we are appealing to this cognitive side of mentalizing. However, body mentalizing can also focus more on emotions. People then try to feel and understand their own and others' emotions. It is closely related to the ability to feel empathy for others.

A significant proportion of individuals diagnosed with PPS experience difficulty in processing their own emotions, suggesting a need for emphasis on the affective aspect of body mentalization. However, in cases where patients with PPS frequently find themselves overwhelmed by emotions due to their physical condition, a focus on the cognitive dimension of body mentalization could be beneficial.

• Internal vs. external

Internal body mentalization involves gaining insight into one's own and others' bodies and minds by paying attention to one's own inner lives and bodily sensations. External body mentalization, on the other hand, seeks to gain insight into one's own and others' minds through external features (e.g. information on social media, test scores, or behaviours and bodily expressions of self and others).

Everyone is either externally or internally focused when body mentalizing. Many PPS patients focus on external factors for their physical and mental well-being. They are sensitive to what somatic/medical experts say and focus exclusively on examination results and diagnoses. In their case, the focus of the therapy may be mainly on their inner signals. If the opposite is true, patients are locked in their physical complaints and no longer pay attention to external issues, then therapy should focus on external mentalization.

In therapy, we can use the four dimensions described here to make well-considered decisions about interventions. For example, do we help the patient focus more on themselves and pay more attention to their own bodily signals and affects and their behaviour towards others (focus: self, affective and external)? The therapist might ask: 'What behaviour and physical signals did you notice about yourself during the argument? And what did you feel?' The focus can also be on the other dimensions, cognitive and internal. The therapist might then ask: 'What did you notice about his body language? What do you think was going through his mind at that moment?'

3.2   Attachment and body mentalization

3.2.1   The interconectedness of attachment and body mentalization

In line with the principles of MBT (Bateman & Fonagy, 2006), we believe that the capacity for body mentalization is embedded in the nature of the relationships people have with significant others. This is where John Bowlby's (1988) attachment theory comes in, which posits a universal human need to form close, affective relationships. Thus, the nature of the attachment relationship significantly determines the nature and intensity of the mentalization of bodily signals. The reverse is also relevant: the intensity of body mentalizing determines the nature and intensity of the attachment relationship. Attachment theory suggests that people in an attachment relationship have a mutual influence on each other. Mutual affective involvement requires the ability to distinguish between bodily signals and internal experiences of self and others. Through body mentalization, people learn in interaction to understand and distinguish the other person's bodily expression and mind from their own.

3.2.2   The role of the body in the development of attachment and mentalization

John Bowlby (1973) defined the attachment system as a fundamental psychobiological system. In order to enhance the survival of the species, humans have a biologically determined drive to seek closeness to a specific other in times of tension, fear, fatigue, despair and illness (Bowlby, 1951). A secure interaction between educators and children is the basis from which one discovers and develops the world and oneself. The quality of the attachment relationship between caregiver and child is predictive of the child's development. A lack of attachment can lead to problems in a number of areas including learning, relating and regulating emotions.

In his early work, Bowlby emphasised the internal working model of attachment (the cognitive representation of attachment relationships) without making connections to bodily processes. He saw attachment experiences mainly as generating an abstract system of expectations. In his later work and in the attachment theories of later colleagues (modified attachment theory), a body-centred perspective was adopted. He hypothesised that the original motor of the attachment process from the child to the caregiver is the experience of the child's body (such as its movements). This allows it to control the caregiver's responses. This is primarily a bodily, sensorimotor experience. Bowlby (1969) argues that the mind is never completely free of these primary generating physical forces.

Fonagy and Bateman (2019) suggest that the child's first experience of mentalization is experiencing body mentalization ('embodied mentalization'). Babies learn to recognise their own bodily responses and affects in secure attachments through the gestures, facial and vocal reflections of the caregiver (Gergely, 2007). In the first physically determined phase of life, the baby expresses emotions through physical arousal. As the early childhood caregiver recognises the emotions in this and engages in the process of affective mirroring with the baby, later on in the first year of life the child is able to express them through primary emotions such as joy or fear.

For an adequate affective mirroring process, it is important that the caregiver empathises adequately with the child's inner world, senses needs ('attuning') and reflects ('mirroring') these. Here it is essential that the caregiver clearly emphasises ('marks') his mirroring as a mirroring of the child's inner world and not of his own inner world. Marked mirroring is also not just mirroring, but addressing the child with overly emphatic facial expressions and intonation. This means that the parent wants to make something clear to the child about themselves (Nicolai, 2017a). With magnified mirroring of the child's physical expression, the caregiver evokes the child's curiosity. For example, a mother may shake her head and say in a high-pitched voice, 'You don't like that, do you?' when the child indicates that she doesn't want to eat something. This shows that she understands what the child is feeling and that this has a name. If the caregiver does not sufficiently adopt this 'pedagogical stance', does not sufficiently and clearly empathise, the child will not feel understood and secure, and mentalization will not develop sufficiently. Shai and Belsky (2011) use the term 'parental embodied mentalization' to describe the physical aspect of mentalization between caregiver and child. They also emphasise the importance of strong affective mirroring by the parent of the child's physical expression. If there is too little parental body mentalization (parental embodied mentalization), the child remains cut off from its 'real' own physical and mental experiences. They experience them as an 'alien self' (Fonagy & Target, 2000).

In summary, because the caregiver clearly mirrors the child's physical expression and the mental state it represents, the child is able to experience his or her own body with all its associated emotions and to distinguish it from the physical experiences of others. The caregiver understands, tolerates and connects to the child's physical expression and the mental state that underlies this. In early development, the regulation of physical arousal and emotion is a dyadic process. In this process the reciprocal psycho-physiological processes of the caregiver and the child are aligned (Schmeets & van Reekum, 2007).

3.2.3   The role of the body in self-development

That the body has a fundamental place in the development of the self is expressed by Fonagy et al. (2002) in their model of self-development. The physical self, the ability to feel and recognise one's own body as a starting point for perception and action, develops in the first months of the child's development. The implicit experience of the body as part of the self forms the basis for later explicit mentalization in the form of emotional awareness. The starting point for the development of the self, resulting in the ability to reflect on oneself and others, lies in the beginning of the first phase of the development of the physical self.

At first the baby's response is primarily physical (not mental). The child develops an awareness of him/her own body through external cues such as the caregiver's touch and voice. In early sensory interactions, physical touch is one of the first routes by which the development of the bodily self takes place (Crucianelli & Filippetti, 2018). The nature of the caregiver's touch determines how the baby experiences his or her own body. In the last two decades, the importance of affective touch has received increasing attention in psychology and neuroscience. Such attuned, slow, gentle touch is thought to support the development of the bodily self (McGlone et al., 2014). Shai and Belsky (2011) emphasise that parents' mentalization of the body ('embodied mentalization') is initially non-verbal and implicit. That is, babies 'find their inner selves in the arms of their caregivers.' Winnicott (1960) describes the importance of holding and physical handling. Holding the child involves the caregiver's unspoken communication: 'You can trust me because I know what you need. I care about you, and I want to give you what you need'. Physically, skin-to-skin contact, such as the hand on the stomach or the nipple in the mouth, is central as the first forms of psychological containment, mentally taking care of the child (Bion, 1970). It is in this intimate, physically emotional relationship with the caregiver that the first experiences of body mentalization (embodied mentalization) take place (Fotopoulou & Tsakiris, 2017). In this first physically determined phase of life, the baby expresses emotions through limbic arousal. As the caregiver recognises emotions in this and engages in the process of affective mirroring with the baby, the child can learn to express him/herself later in the first year of development through primary emotions such as joy or fear.

However, the bodily self also develops through information from within, from one's own physiological state such as restlessness, fatigue or pain (Craig, 2010). The child implicitly experiences his/her own bodily state and changes in it, such as the difference between lying on its back and lying on its stomach, in order to move on to action. The baby also learns in the first stage of life that it has a physical effect on others, just as others have an effect on him/her. The baby realises that he/she can move his/her arms and legs and that the caregiver can grasp and move his/her arms and legs. The baby also experiences itself in relation to others in the room and feels whether or not there is physical contact with the caregiver. At this early stage of development, the baby also notices that he/she can physically affect objects (Verfaille, 2018).

Building on the development of the physical self, the social self develops from three months onwards, seeking well-matched emotional reflection with the caregiver through eye contact, facial expressions and vocalisations (Fonagy et al., 2002). At nine months, the teleological self begins to develop (goal-oriented thinking with particular interest in the physically perceivable world). After one and a half years, the intentional self emerges in the toddler (learning about one's own and others' wishes, feelings and thoughts). From the fourth year, the representational self emerges. This is when children can reflect on themselves and others and recognise that their feelings and (physical) desires are personal and not the same as reality. They can then reflect on their thinking and develop a 'theory of mind'. This also creates the autobiographical self, being able to reflect on the self over time.

3.2.4   The role of the body in the development of emotional processing

Gradually, without being aware of it, the child first learns to channel bodily arousal by expressing affects that are the first traces of emotions ('proto-emotion', see Elster, 1999). Later, with sufficient mirroring by the caregiver, the child will become aware of more and more emotions. The psychoanalyst and cognitive scientist Wilma Bucci (1997) describes in her multiple code theory how emotional information processing develops in the child. Initially, there is only the implicit perception of bodily sensations. Affects (emotionally tinted, involuntary bodily reactions) are at first mainly sub-symbolic: implicit and sensory (mainly through feeling). They are expressed in movement and behaviour, for example a child's movement towards the breast. The caregiver and child then share emotions without words, such as being happy and laughing together.

The next stage is to arrive at a cognitive representation or symbolisation of affect. The symbolic representations of how the child experiences emotions are initially non-verbal (as in pictures) and later become verbal. In the non-verbal, symbolic representation of emotions, conscious and unconscious (dream) images play an important role. These images are symbolic adaptations of the original affect. The child dreams of a monster as an expression of the emotion of fear. The symbolic images are metaphors, fantasies and memories associated with the bodily affect. Fonagy et al. (2002) refer to the emotions as 'mentalized affect' because the transition has been made from bodily to psychological.

In the next stage, when symbols become verbal and the child can verbalise emotions, Bucci considers emotions to be feelings. The child is then able to tell a story that matches the emotions. This is part of conscious feeling and speaking. These developmental stages of emotion processing outlined by Bucci can also still be recognised in adults.

From a developmental psychology perspective, before we experience feelings we first sense bodily signals such as the accelerated beating of the heart. These bodily signals lead to a limbic sensation (I feel restless), which carries the affect (the first physical traces of an emotion). Then, through symbolic representations and memories, emotions emerge. We then learn to consciously put words to them and to talk about our emotions with others.

3.2.5   Attachment styles

Children learn to view themselves and the world based on repeated experiences of the availability of caregivers when they ask for support, help or comfort. They develop internal working models and mental representations of themselves and others. These internal working models of attachment are centred on two key questions. The first is whether a child learns, through daily interactions with caregivers, to see themselves as capable and worthy of the love and support of others. The second is whether a child learns to rely on others as a source of support and comfort in times of (emotional) distress. If the caregiver provides the necessary security for the young child, the child will develop the expectation that the caregiver is and will always be available. This develops a sense of basic security, an internal working model of secure attachment and a secure attachment style.

Through years of reinforcement and support, internal working models of attachment become automated. They begin to guide behaviour in later social and intimate relationships and emotion regulation. Based on new, current attachment experiences, people can then adjust internal working models of attachment in both positive and negative directions. However, change is not easy; basic patterns are formed in an implicit way and try to maintain their internal consistency: 'Today's glasses are coloured by experience.' (Zevalkink, 2007)

Brennan and her colleagues (1998) suggested that two basic dimensions can be identified in adult attachment patterns: anxiety and avoidance. People who score high on anxiety worry about whether their partner will be available, responsive, attentive, and so on. People who score high on avoidance tend not to trust or open up to others. Securely attached people score low on both dimensions. Those who score high on either anxiety or avoidance tend to rely on secondary attachment strategies in response to primary activation of the attachment system. They deactivate or hyperactivate their attachment system in an attempt to cope with intimacy (Cassidy & Kobak, 1988). People with an 'anxious style', who also have a high need for closeness ('preoccupied style'), are prone to a hyperactivating strategy. They have learnt from previous experiences with caregivers to maximise their attachment needs at the expense of their own autonomy. Even in non-threatening situations, people with a hyperactivating strategy show a lot of (negative) emotion and attachment behaviour in an attempt to bind and keep the other person close. A hyperactivating strategy leads to an exaggerated, inaccurate perception of physical and emotional signals in oneself and others. What is striking for the hyperactivating strategy is an expressive way of communicating emotions and ('subtly') addressing others in an attempt to enable effective (co-)regulation of emotions and bodily sensations. There is little awareness of one's own emotions or behaviour. This strategy can be combined with an excessive focus on the body or a particular part of the body that is affected, whereby one can quickly become overwhelmed by symptoms and the emotions associated with them. For example, explaining pain, fatigue or paralysis to these patients does not come across well as they focus on the symptom and affect rather than the cognitions. The hyperactivating attachment strategy is also characterised by frequent hyperarousal with negative affectivity, anxiety and corresponding sympathetic activation. This is accompanied by increased muscle tension and heart rate, and a tendency to flee or fight.

People with an avoidant attachment style use a deactivating strategy. This strategy is characterised by avoiding contact. The need for attachment is denied as a defence against the pain of deeper unmet needs. Based on the belief that others cannot be trusted anyway, one has learned to recognise and express few or no emotions. There is a compulsive autonomy or counter-dependency. One has to and wants to do everything on one's own. These patients deny the importance of attachment relationships and emotions when they have physical complaints. They deny the importance of attachment relationships and emotions when experiencing physical complaints. They tend to rationalise away physical complaints: 'Everybody has something sometimes'. They assume in advance that others will not help them: 'The doctor probably doesn't have time or will write another prescription that won't help me'. These patients also ignore physical signs that indicate a need for contact with others or support from loved ones. Non-verbal communication is restrained, with little facial expression, little eye contact, frequent turning away from others and few emotional features in voice use. The deactivating attachment strategy is characterised by activation of the parasympathetic nervous system with (somatic) dissociation, slowed heart rate and movement, and reduced sensory activity (Dozier & Kobak, 1992).

Patients may also have developed inconsistent strategies in which they alternate between hyperactivating and deactivating strategies. These inconsistent strategies first develop in childhood as adaptive strategies to inconsistencies in the availability of attachment figures (Luyten & Fonagy, 2019). For example, the caregiver is the source of safety, love and care, as well as abuse and neglect. Studies of patients with severe unexplained symptoms or PPS (e.g. somatoform disorder (DSM-IV) or a somatic symptom disorder or related disorder (DSM- 5)) show that many of them have an insecure attachment style. There is an overrepresentation of the deactivating attachment strategy (Kooiman & Koelen, 2012). However, the hyperactivating ones, such as the preoccupied and disorganised styles, also occur in this group (Waller et al., 2004). The insecure attachment strategies may be adaptive in the short term: they initially seem to restore psychological and physical balance. In the long term, however, they can lead to tension, irritation and even rejection by others,

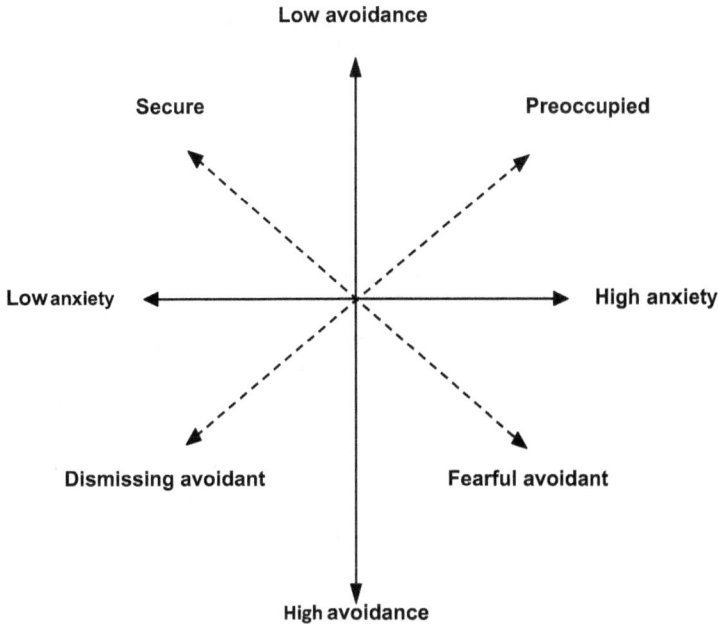

Figure 3.1 Two-dimensional and four-category model of attachment (Bartholomew & Horowitz, 1991).

Source: Copyright © 2015 by American Psychological Society. Reproduced with permission from Fraley, R. C. et al. (2015). Are adult attachment styles categorical or dimensional? A taxometric analysis of general and relationship-specific attachment orientations. *Journal of Personality and Social Psychology, 109*(2). https://doi.org/10.1037/pspp0000027

including professional caregivers. This leads to an intensification of tensions and physical symptoms, with either more explicit and implicit requests for help and high care consumption, or increased avoidance and refusal of care. Both deactivating and hyperactivating or disorganised attachment strategies appear to be associated with forms of reduced (body) mentalization (Kooiman & Koelen, 2012). For the treatment of PPS, it is important to be aware of the possible ongoing effects of these attachment styles and the associated diminished body mentalization.

Combining two dimensions, the anxious and avoidant attachment dimension, can also lead to a classification of four attachment styles (Bartholomew & Horowitz, 1991, see Figure 3.1). These styles are also characteristic of how patients seek help for long-term physical complaints:

1. The safe, secure or autonomous style: The person has little tendency to be anxious or avoidant in relationships. One is sure of oneself and has no doubts about others; one views interactions with others with confidence. In the case of

physical complaints, the person is able to ask for help appropriately and to use and benefit from it autonomously.

2. The insecure, dismissing, avoidant style: One has little anxiety in relationships, but is prone to avoidance. One is sure of oneself but has doubts about others. By deactivating the need for attachment, one seeks independence from others. In the case of physical complaints, people will try to find a solution for these themselves.

3. The insecure, fearful avoidant style: There is a great fear of intimacy. Although there is a desire for social and intimate relationships, there is a tendency to avoid them for fear that the other person will reject, harm or hurt you. One doubts oneself and the other person. In the case of physical complaints, one does not ask for help, but does not trust one's own solutions.

4. The insecure, preoccupied (or ambivalent) style: There is a strong need for closeness, but also a fear that the other person will not be able to meet the strong need for care and closeness, and doubts as to whether one is nice enough or important enough for the other person. In the case of physical complaints, one may persistently ask for help and use a demanding or claiming attitude to force care or support.

Bartholomew and Horowitz's classification of the four attachment styles can be used in therapy to help patients identify their attachment style. In severe PPS, the dismissive avoidant and fearful avoidant styles are common. However, when using a classification such as Bartholomew and Horowitz's, we should be careful not to place people too rigidly into one of these styles; many variations on the four styles are possible. Within the combination of the high/low anxiety and high/low avoidance polarities, individual differences in attachment can also be represented dimensionally.

3.2.6   Epistemic trust and mistrust

Insecure attachment styles are associated with epistemic mistrust, a lack of openness to learning from others in new situations. Fonagy and Allison (2014) define epistemic trust as openness to social knowledge that is personally relevant and has generalizable meaning. Epistemic trust allows people to receive social knowledge that enables them to navigate through the social environment. It maximises the benefits of cooperation with others. Through epistemic trust when cooperating with others, we give others insight into our inner selves and are able to use our social imagination benignly and constructively (Fonagy & Bateman, 2019).

In patients with PPS, epistemic mistrust may manifest itself in a variety of interactional problems and stressors associated with PPS. For example, in the absence of objective somatic abnormalities, patients may experience little recognition for their symptoms and limitations (Newton et al., 2013). Inadequate communication between patient and caregiver, such as a physician, may also play a role (Weiland et al., 2012). Patients with PPS also often experience a lot of social pressure. They are influenced by all kinds of social stigma about health, for example from people in their immediate environment, employers, health care institutions and insurance companies. For example, patients may perceive themselves as failures or abnormalities. This is often due to the prejudice that well-being and a healthy body are possible for everyone, at any time, if they put enough effort into it (Dehue, 2014). The unpredictability of PPS can also put patients in a constant position of having to defend themselves or negotiate (De Wilde, 2015).

Within the family, PPS is often accompanied by problems in interacting with loved ones; patients find it important to be taken seriously by those around them (de Drachler et al., 2009). On the one hand, the physical symptoms are of concern, but in the long term, suspicion and overburdening of family members can also occur. The alternation between sympathy, care, security and closeness on the one hand and suspicion, distance and hostility on the other creates stress and affects the well-being of the patient, but also of partners and all family members (Enzlin & Pazmany, 2006). In this atmosphere, a lack of trust in each other quickly develops.

The concept of 'epistemic trust or distrust' can help to better understand interpersonal problems that occur in the case of PPS. Epistemic distrust occurs primarily in an avoidant or disorganised attachment style, which we see in PPS patients with symptoms that are difficult to explain (Waller & Scheidt, 2006). These patients may oscillate between overconfidence and extreme distrust of others, or epistemic hypervigilance. They're constantly on guard and question the motives behind someone's opinions and advice. These patients are also often desperate and then see a therapist as their last resort, while being full of epistemic mistrust. It is therefore not surprising that these patients' relationships with health care professionals are often turbulent and characterised by both idealisation and devaluation (Luyten & Fonagy, 2019). Extremely high and low expectations alternate. Patients may react quite unexpectedly to a well-intentioned comment or gesture from the therapist, with increased distrust, stress and multiplication of physical complaints. They usually do not have enough trust in a therapist to explicitly share what they are experiencing in the therapeutic contact.

3.3   The neurobiology of body mentalization, attachment and stress

The neurobiology of body mentalization covers a wide field. For the purposes of this book, we will select a few aspects, which are described in the following sections.

3.3.1   The body-oriented approach in light of the structural make-up of the brain

B-MBT has a body-oriented focus in which non-verbal therapies are an indispensable part. Non-verbal therapies are characterised by physical experience, action and the use of creativity and expression. This approach stimulates different brain processes than the more verbal approach that is also part of B-MBT. To clarify this difference, MacLean's model of the triple brain can be helpful. This model suggests that although the brain functions as an integrated whole, it is made up of parts that are hierarchically organised as a result of evolution (MacLean, 1990).

In the brainstem, the evolutionary oldest part, sensory, proprioceptive and homeostatic inputs from the body enter and sensorimotor experiences are processed. In the middle part, the limbic system (including the hippocampus, amygdala and hypothalamus), sensorimotor experiences are processed, and unconscious emotional processes take place. The evolutionarily most recent higher level, the neocortex (new cerebral cortex), contains cognitive functions, including the integration and coordination of experiences and processes from the older parts of the brain. Part of the neocortex, for example, is the somatosensory cortex, in which the homunculus, a 'map' of the body, resides This part of the brain helps to localise pain and sensations in the body, while the (emotional) perception of the complaints and strength of the signal is influenced by processes in the limbic system mentioned earlier.

Processes in the lower parts of the brain are fast and beyond our conscious awareness. Processes in the cortex are relatively slow and conscious. The hierarchical organisation of our brain has different directions of information processing: top-down or bottom-up, and the interaction between the two. Here, implicit body-mentalizing, which is unconscious, non-verbal and non-reflective, activates older brain circuits (limbic system and brainstem) that rely heavily on sensory behavioural information (Fonagy & Luyten, 2009; Satpute & Lieberman, 2006). Body-oriented mentalizing and its use of non-verbal therapies provide opportunities for a bottom-up learning process in addition to top-down learning: from the body to emotions and to conscious cognitions.

3.3.2   The neurobiological link between attachment, stress regulation and mentalization

In securely attached individuals, stress usually leads to a search for closeness to attachment figures, either real or internal, which results in a reduction of stress (Luyten, Van Houdenhove, et al., 2012). There now seems to be sufficient scientific evidence for the link between secure attachment experiences, mentalization capacity and effective stress regulation (Kooiman & Koelen, 2012). This is seen in the role of neurotransmitters in attachment. Neuropeptide oxytocin, for example, has been shown to promote attachment, mentalization and stress regulation (Fonagy & Luyten, 2009; Neumann, 2008). Attachment between the baby and the parent involves an interaction between oxytocin and dopamine, known as cross-talk (Ebert & Brüne, 2018). Secure attachment is therefore pleasurable. Activation of the attachment system in securely attached people, in addition to activation of the mesocorticolimbic dopaminergic reward system, leads to down-regulation of the amygdala and neuroendocrine stress regulation systems such as the HPA (hypothalamic-pituitary-adrenal axis, also known as the stress axis) and sympathetic nervous systems. Down-regulation of these systems produces relaxation. In insecure attachment, on the other hand, activation of the attachment system leads to activation of the stress systems and downregulation of the reward system (Luyten & Fonagy, 2015).

Based on this explanation, Kooiman and Koelen (2012) concluded that in patients with (severe) insufficiently explained symptoms, there is indeed a sub-group with insecure attachment, which is associated with reduced mentalization and increased autonomic nervous system activity. As body mentalization is an aspect of the multidimensional concept of mentalization, we can assume that the ability for body mentalization is also positively associated with secure attachment and effective stress regulation. We should note immediately that these findings should not lead to far-reaching causal conclusions such as 'insecure attachment and low body mentalizing ability cause PPS'. At most, we can assume that persistent physical complaints increase stress, which may further disturb already existing limitations in attachment and body mentalization (Luyten, Van Houdenhove, et al., 2012). This impaired ability for body mentalization can then lead to physical complaints, creating a vicious circle (see also Section 3.5). Thus, impairments in body mentalization and insecure attachment styles may be both consequences and causes of long-term severe PPS.

3.3.3 Neural systems involved in body mentalization

Attachment leads to activation of neural systems involved in body mentalization. The brain regions involved are:

- Lateral and medial prefrontal cortex
- Lateral and medial parietal cortex
- Medial temporal lobe
- Rostral anterior cingulate cortex (Fonagy & Luyten, 2009; Lieberman, 2007)

Luyten and Fonagy (2015) focus on the four polar dimensions of mentalizing (see also Section 3.1.2) when describing the main characteristics of the polarities and hypothesising about the associated brain circuits: automatic (implicit) and controlled (explicit); internal and external; self and other; cognitive and affective:

Automatic (implicit) mentalizing. *Features:* Unconscious, parallel, fast processing of social information that is reflexive and requires little effort, focused attention, or intention; therefore, prone to bias and distortions, particularly in complex interpersonal interactions (i.e. when arousal is high). *Neural circuits*: Amygdala, basal ganglia, ventromedial prefrontal cortex (VMPFC), lateral temporal cortex (LTC), dorsal anterior cingulate cortex (dACC).

Controlled (explicit) mentalizing. *Features:* Conscious, verbal, and reflective processing of social information that requires the capacity to reflect consciously and deliberately on and make accurate attributions about the emotions, thoughts, and intentions of the self and others. Relies heavily on conscious control and language. *Neural circuits:* Lateral prefrontal cortex (LPFC), medial prefrontal cortex (MPFC), lateral parietal cortex (LPAC), medial parietal cortex (MPAC), medial temporal lobe (MTL), rostral anterior cingulate cortex (rACC).

Internal mentalizing. *Features:* Understanding one's own mind and that of others through a direct focus on the mental interiors of both the self and others. *Neural circuits:* Medial frontoparietal network (more controlled).

External mentalizing. *Features:* Understanding one's own mind and that of others based on external features (such as facial expressions, posture and prosody). *Neural circuits:* Lateral frontotemporoparietal network (more automatic).

Self vs. others mentalizing. *Features:* Shared networks underpin the capacity to mentalize about the self and others. *Neural circuits:* Shared representation system (more automatic) versus mental state attribution system (more controlled).

Cognitive vs. affective mentalizing. *Features:* Mentalizing may focus on more cognitive features (more controlled), such as belief-desire reasoning and perspective taking, versus more affective features (more automatic), including affective empathy and mentalized affectivity (the feeling and thinking-about-the-feeling) *Neural circuits:* Cognitive mentalizing involves several areas in prefrontal cortex; affectively oriented mentalizing seems particularly related to the VMPFC.

All these mentioned neural circuits work together to enable the mind to, among other things, check reality, activate the embodied self (comparable to the physical self, see Section 3.2.3), experience relationships as meaningful, take perspective and think imaginatively (Debbané & Nolte, 2019).

Luyten and Fonagy (2015) highlight how, in situations of increasing 'arousal' or stress, automatic mentalization increases via posterior cortical and subcortical systems. At relatively low levels of arousal, prefrontal systems can stimulate explicit, controlled mentalizing. This is important in patients with severe PPS, who react with stress when physical symptoms worsen and appear to lose the capacity for explicit, controlled body-oriented mentalizing.

3.3.4 Recent neurobiological and neurocognitive findings on bodily aspects of mentalizing

Mentalization of the body ('embodied mentalization' or 'body mentalization') has now been the subject of several neurobiological publications. Debbané and Nolte (2019) argue that the circuits shown in Section 3.3.3, in their mutual alignment, are also capable of activating the embodied self. The embodied self, comparable to the physical self (see Section 3.2.3), allows us to align our thinking, feeling and acting with our own physical experience. This is important for people with severe PPS. They may be able to push aside many unwanted physical sensations and physically experienced emotions by focusing on short-term solutions. As a result, they have difficulty aligning their thoughts and feelings with their physical experiences.

Body mentalization is related to recognising and understanding other people's physical signals. This is also accentuated by the neurobiological finding that the more body-focused frontoparietal system (mirror neurons) is involved in understanding the physical expression of others (van Overwalle & Baetens, 2009).

Further research into the functioning of the insula, the brain region between the temporal and frontal lobes, may shed light on body mentalization. This area contains a map of the inner world. When the insula is dysfunctional, people have a limited ability to perceive physical aspects of themselves and therefore have difficulty perceiving emotions (Nicolai, 2017a).

Fotopoulou and Tsakiris (2017) place the bodily aspect of mentalization (embodied mentalization) within a neurocognitive framework. From there, they define it as the brain process by which primary sensorimotor and multisensory signals form predictive cognitive models. These cognitive models allow us to orient ourselves spatially, affectively and cognitively to our environment. These models represent hypothetical, dynamic and generative processes that we constantly update by receiving bodily error signals in new situations. This process of integrating bodily signals takes place from our very first interactions between baby and caregiver and continues throughout development in adulthood.

Debbané and Nolte (2019) hypothesise that our brains are designed to build predictive models of the world using their own bodily signals. Therefore, children's brains must first learn to make a fundamental distinction between self and non-self causes for sensations. This means that the baby must first learn to distinguish between self and non-self (others) (Friston, 2017). It must also learn to distinguish between what is physical and what is emotional (Schore, 2011), the first signs of body mentalization.

That the distinction between self and others underlies not only the development of the self but also body mentalization is an interesting topic for further neurobiological and neurocognitive research. It fits with the recent development of studies on the neurobiological aspects of self-development in infancy (Cittern et al., 2018) and throughout development into adulthood (Debbané & Nolte, 2019).

3.4 Assessing capacity for body-oriented mentalizing

As yet, there are only a few simple screening instruments that can validly and reliably measure capacity for mentalization, and in particular body-oriented mentalizing, in people with PPS. Problems in this area include that self-reporting is problematic when mentalizing capacity is low, as individuals need these mentalizing skills to answer questions about mentalizing (Fonagy et al., 2016). Patients with PPS also have problems interpreting their body cues, which can make it difficult to complete a questionnaire on body mentalization. There are also problems with the administration of instruments. Structured interviews such as the Adult Attachment Interview, (AAI) could be combined with an assessment of reflective capacity using the Reflective Functioning Scale (RFS) (Taubner et al., 2011). However, this method of measurement is very time consuming and laborious.

For scientific research on the effects of B-MBT in PPS, Feldmann-Sinnige et al. (2023) operationalised the concept of body-oriented mentalizing with two separately described elements, namely body awareness and mentalizing. Patients' body awareness was measured by the Multidimensional Assessment of Interoceptive Awareness (MAIA-2) and mentalizing by the Mentalization Questionnaire (MZQ). These instruments were found to be sufficiently valid and reliable. This combination of instruments seems suitable for measuring progress on these two outcome measures in groups of patients undergoing B-MBT. This allows conclusions to be drawn about the general effectiveness of B-MBT (see also Section 4.2). However, these instruments seem less suitable for individual screening related to treatment. 'This is probably because, on the one hand, these modes of non-mentalizing are context-dependent and do not occur stably over time; on the other hand, they sometimes intermingle with another mode.' (Schultz Venrath, 2023)

For clinical practice, a relatively simple way to assess body-oriented mentalization skills might be to use a direct observation instrument. Experienced clinicians could use such an instrument to assess the behaviour of patients with severe PPS (Huisman, 2017). We recommend the development of such an instrument and research into its applicability, validity and reliability.

Until additional screening tools are developed for clinical practice, the best approach is to use questions that aim to evoke bodily mentalization in the here and now. For example, the therapist can ask, 'What emotion are you experiencing with this pain in your back?' However, questions should also relate to mentalization in current and past attachment relationships and how the patient may be mentalizing how they experience symptoms and complaints in this context, e.g. 'What do you experience inside when your partner touches your painful arm?' and 'Do you have any idea what goes on inside him when he does that?' Using the characteristics of the non-body mentalizing modes (see Section 3.1.2, Section 5.1.1 and Appendix A.3), the therapist can get an idea of the limitations the patient has in terms of body-oriented mentalizing. In our experience, at least several observations during different therapies with different therapists and at different levels of distress are needed to get a reasonably reliable impression of the capacity for body-oriented mentalizing in the context of therapy.

3.5   Perpetuating effects of impaired body mentalization

A multi-factorial explanatory model is preferred in order to take the broadest possible view of (severe) PPS (see also Chapter 2). The biopsychosocial model is widely recognised as a fruitful multi-factorial explanatory model of the problem for each patient. Within the three domains of biological, psychological and social, factors such as physical exhaustion, trauma or a relationship problem are inventoried for each patient. These factors are of a predisposing, precipitating/provoking or persistent/maintaining nature (Spaans & van der Boom, 2017).

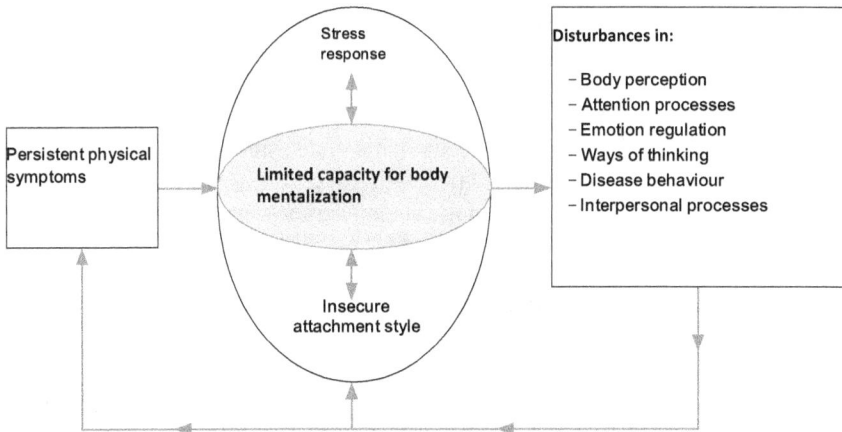

Figure 3.2 The perpetuating effect of impaired body mentalization.

Source: Author's own creation ©Spaans, 2020

As mentioned before, we are cautious about assuming that deficient body mentalization is the main triggering or predisposing psychological factor for PPS. There is still too little scientific support for this due to a lack of prospective studies (Luyten, 2014). In patients with severe PPS, we suspect that early and later negative life events may well play a role in long-term disturbances in the stress system, attachment and mentalization. However, the influence of disturbed body mentalization is mainly felt as a perpetuating factor of physical symptoms.

Therefore, for treatment purposes, we pay particular attention to disturbed body mentalization, related attachment style and stress response as a result of experiencing distressing PPS. In this context, Luyten (2014) points out that patients with PPS are often quite capable of reflecting on symptoms and their impact on themselves and relationships. However, this is no longer possible once stress increases and physical complaints intensify, at which point the perpetuating effect of deficient body mentalization sets in. This is illustrated in Figure 3.2. This figure makes it clear that the experience of (an increase in) distressing long-term persistent symptoms can go hand in hand with a reduction in body mentalization, which is associated with a stress response and an insecure attachment style (Kooiman & Koelen, 2012).

Inadequate body mentalization manifests itself in a variety of disturbances (Figure 3.2), such as:

- *Impaired perception of the body,* such as not recognising bodily signals of emotions and stress, but only perceiving biological signals.
- *Disturbed attentional processes,* such as one-sided attention to biological processes; excessive attention to bodily sensations, or conversely avoidance of

them, which can lead to somatoform dissociation: the disappearance of emotionally charged bodily sensations from consciousness.

- *Impaired emotion regulation,* such as difficulty in (re)identifying and regulating emotions, resulting in distressing negative emotions and stress.
- *Distorted ways of thinking,* such as rumination and catastrophising, or reducing the body to a (dysfunctional) machine, with excessive adherence to and search for biological theories and physiological explanations.
- *Inappropriate disease behaviour,* such as over- or under-activity, unhealthy lifestyles, exceeding one's own limits, excessive doctor visits and medication use.
- *Dysfunctional interpersonal processes,* such as conflict, communication problems and mutual misunderstanding.

These behavioural, cognitive, emotional and social factors lead to increasing physical symptoms, more disturbed body mentalization, stress and anxiety. This creates a vicious cycle of perpetuating physical symptoms.

3.6   Theoretical reflections on explicit therapeutic processes

The recovery of body-oriented mentalizing skills (see Chapter 4 onwards) develops in the context of a close therapeutic relationship between patient and therapist. In the safety of the therapist's presence, the patient learns to focus attention on and reflect on bodily processes and inner experiences (especially emotions). The patient learns how people are interconnected by influencing each other's physical and mental states. The next sections of this chapter discuss some other relevant theoretical aspects of B-MBT therapeutic processes: focusing attention, awareness of body and emotions, reflection and interpersonal influence.

3.6.1   Focusing attention

Focusing attention is one of the most powerful tools in body-oriented mentalizing. We ask our patients to focus their attention on their own and others' bodily signals, behaviours, thoughts, feelings, tendencies and so on. This is the process of mindfulness: 'awareness developed by consciously paying attention to experiences that we do not normally pay attention to.' (Kabat-Zinn, 1990)

Mindfulness is a process of paying attention to whatever the object of attention may be: a flower, one's own breathing, thoughts or emotions. Mindfulness refers to the whole panorama of what we can experience in the present moment. It can be compared to standing in a dark room with a spotlight to see what that room is. The beam of light, regardless of where it is focused, can be compared to attention (mindfulness). In body mentalization, the spotlight is focused mainly on certain objects in this imaginary dark room: physical and inner experiences. Body mentalization could therefore be seen as mindfulness focused on the body and mind.

There are differences in the role of focusing attention in B-MBT and mindfulness therapy. For example, mindfulness therapy is about the 'here and now' experience, whereas in body mentalization we also focus on the recent past. Mindfulness therapy focuses on becoming aware of the impermanence of personal experience and learning to let go of it. Body-oriented mentalizing is more about exploring the unconscious aspects of one's own and others' physical and mental experiences in order to learn about their psychic depth. Another notable difference is the role of interaction. Mindfulness therapy is mainly concerned with one's own (intra-psychic) attentional processes, whereas B-MBT is also concerned with other people's (inter-psychic) attentional processes.

By attention, Brown (2004) means not only the focused conscious perception of the environment and ourselves, but also the cognitive processes within the individual's attention system. He described how the attention system works in PPS. He distinguished between an unconscious, primary attention system, which uses primary representations and impressions to control behaviour in a rapid and highly efficient way. This is an automatic, spontaneous, intuitive process that the individual experiences with self-evident validity. For example, without thinking, people do not drink coffee when they have a stomach ache.

In addition, there is a secondary attention system that then consciously adjusts actions and cognitions with long-term goals in mind ('Let me have coffee now anyway, because I have a long day ahead of me and could use some energy'). The primary attention system is the realm of implicit or automatic body mentalization, while the secondary system is more the realm of explicit or controlled body mentalization.

In severe PPS, according to Brown, particularly inadequate primary representations ('the pain will never go away') force a biased selection of information (e.g. only perceiving body signals as pain). Inadequate mentalization of the body does not allow bodily experience (including the experience of bodily symptoms) to be adequately adjusted in the light of conscious mental processes. Thus, the primary attention system directs the experience of distress towards spontaneous and absolute black-and-white perception. In body-oriented mentalizing therapy one learns to become aware of the signals from the primary attention system. One then learns to evaluate them self-consciously and to decide whether or not to follow spontaneous impulses based on the primary attention system. For example, the primary attention system sends a person the feeling 'stay in bed because you don't feel well'. Recognising this signal as an implicit message, a conscious thought from the secondary attention system, such as 'if I get up, I will feel better later', may decide to get up anyway.

3.6.2 Body awareness

The capacity for body mentalization involves the ability to be aware of our own and others' bodily signals and the inner experiences associated with them. We are able to perceive our bodies and thus sense what emotions we are having and what we are thinking. This includes body signals on the surface of the body (such as shoulder pain) or inside the body (such as a rumbling in the abdomen), in smaller (such as localised pain in the hand) or larger areas of the body (such as stiffness in the lower body). It may also involve the global state of the body (such as a feeling of discomfort) or global changes in the body (such as an increase in fatigue or temperature). It may also involve the recognition of somatic and kinaesthetic needs, such as hunger, the need to be touched or to move, which may be related to underlying mental states, such as a negative mood. Body awareness is primarily about being aware of the signals and meanings of the body. In short, it is about understanding the language of the body. Body awareness, as defined by Mehling et al. (2011), is our ability to subjectively perceive our own body and its parts. Through body awareness we become aware of the position, movement and tonus of organs, limbs, joints and tendons, the feeling of 'heaviness' in some parts of the body, and the fatigue or alertness of muscles. According to Mehling et al. (2011), body consciousness also includes interoception, the ability to perceive stimuli from within one's own body. Through interoception, we have a subjective sense of the internal state of our body, including emotions.

Body awareness, according to Van der Maas et al. (2015), is not only about perceiving one's own body, but also about being sensitive and attentive to bodily signals and emotions. It does not involve the rigid monitoring of bodily signals, the top-down cognitive process. This compulsive evaluation of bodily sensations based on appearance or physical condition tends to limit awareness of one's own body. Body awareness is the willingness to experience and tolerate bodily impulses and sensations as they are, even the less pleasant experiences such as pain, fatigue or loss of function in a leg. Body awareness is also the ability to act in a self-conscious way while being open to the signals and messages from our body. It also means being receptive to less familiar bodily sensations and inner experiences that are not directly under one's control or that one cannot yet assign meaning to.

The body awareness of people with PPS is often severely impaired. People are particularly aware of physical complaints and less aware of 'normal', non-complaint related body signals, such as a normal increased heart rate, normal accelerated breathing, and normal muscle pain on exertion (Houtveen, 2009; Schaefer et al., 2012). People will soon interpret normal bodily signals associated with physical activity as complaints. Limited body awareness can be a consequence of a long history of physical complaints. After years of physical symptoms, the view of the body is narrowed. It is also possible that a subgroup of patients with PPS may have had limited body awareness before (Lind et al., 2014). As a result of trauma or problems in development and upbringing, contact with the body and the ability to understand body signals may have been insufficiently taught or developed, increasing the likelihood of developing PPS.

A significant subgroup of people with severe PPS struggle with a disturbed relationship with their body as part of a poor body image. As a result, they do not accept their physical symptoms and do not adapt to them appropriately. For this reason, for these patients it is important in therapy to (re-)find the right connection to their own body. Kalisvaart et al., (2012), call this connection to the body 'body relatedness'. They investigated what patients with severe PPS and their therapists understood by body relatedness: 'What do you think are the most important things a patient needs to learn about their body?' After analysing the data, patients seemed to see body relatedness as: being aware of the body and self by understanding, accepting and adapting to bodily cues. They also saw relatedness as respecting and regulating the body and trusting and respecting themselves and being autonomous. Patients with severe PPS and their therapists saw recognising, experiencing and understanding body signals as the most important treatment goal (Kalisvaart et al., 2012).

3.6.3 Awareness of emotions

Being aware of emotions is part of body mentalization. An emotion is an inner experience such as joy, fear, anger or sadness that can be triggered by a particular situation or can occur spontaneously. Emotions can be classified according to types such as pleasant/unpleasant, but also to intensity and degree of awareness. The types of emotions can be reduced to some basic emotions such as anxious, angry, happy, sad and ashamed, of which other emotions are derivatives or mixtures. We can experience emotions consciously, but we can also be unaware of them (such as unconscious fear and anxiety), leading to automatic, rapid reactions.

According to Frijda (1988), emotions serve as a signal to tell us that a certain event is important to us, either positively or negatively. He assumes that emotions arise because people consider certain events to be beneficial or detrimental to their own interests. He characterises emotions on the basis of their action tendency (for example, the action tendency of love is to seek closeness, that of fear is to run away). When we are aware of the action tendencies of emotions, we are faced with the choice of how to express that emotion. For example, when giving a talk, you may be nervous and want to walk away, but decide to stay. Emotions also accompany physical reactions, such as posture or facial expression, and physical activity. Emotions are also always part of physical processes such as changes in neurotransmitters, hormones and brain activity, muscle activity, changes in heart rate and circulatory processes.

Nicolai (2017a) distinguishes between affects (unconscious, bodily reactions to external stimuli), emotions (partly conscious and partly unconscious reactions to stimuli) and feelings (emotions to which we actively assign verbal meaning). Affects, according to Nicolai, are involuntary bodily responses to internal or external stimuli. They are aroused automatically, like trembling with fear in the face of great danger. Affects come naturally from deep within: 'I wanted the ground to swallow me up' or 'I have a knot in my stomach'.

Affects are the first expressions of an emotion, the so-called 'proto-emotion', a (subtle) physical expression that you are not yet fully aware of (Elster, 1999). It is only when these physical proto-emotions are perceived as emotions by themselves or others that they can be recognised as such. We can also forget them.

They can remain unconscious even though they have a strong influence on our bodily functioning. In this context, Damasio (2010) speaks of subtle background emotions, which are still difficult to put into words, that strongly determine us. They drive us to a fight-or-flight response that is implicit and mainly physical. These deeper, implicit emotions form the background to other, more conscious emotions such as anger, sadness, happiness and fear, and directly influence bodily processes.

Emotions are affects that we can partly think about and feel. They are partly conscious and partly unconscious. Emotions are usually represented in symbolic non-verbal images and memory images. When we share these images with others through words, the emotion can become conscious. In becoming aware of emotions, feelings arise.

Feelings are emotions that we have consciously given a personal verbal meaning. We can think about them and consciously express them in words and images. For example, when we feel joy, we first experience a tendency to jump. We suddenly remember how we used to jump for joy as a child, and so joy arises as an emotion. When we notice this and talk to others about it, 'I'd like to hop, I'm so happy', we have feelings of joy. (Recognising) emotions also involves a cognitive appraisal ('I'm not allowed to be angry') (Allen et al., 2008). This appraisal then guides further awareness of the emotion and determines what one does with one's anger or sadness. Our awareness of emotions affects how much influence they can have on us and others.

Emotional awareness begins with reading your own and others' emotional body language. Body language is non-verbal communication through physical signals. We can read other people's body language from their facial expressions, posture, gestures, eye movements, use of voice, touch and use of space. Through unconscious body language, people implicitly communicate their emotions and attitudes. By attuning to the posture, gestures, body language, tone of voice and breathing of others, we can come into direct contact with a deeper emotional layer of the other person. This is the basis of contact, good rapport, empathy and understanding with another person (Rutten-Saris, 1990). This emotional and bodily exchange with others in turn has an emotion-regulating effect and can improve the quality of relationships.

Emotions are revealed not only through bodily signals and non-verbal language, but also through conscious and unconscious (dream) images. The transition from experiencing physical signals to experiencing emotions is the area of transition from non-symbolic or sub-symbolic language to symbolic language. For example, dreaming of a deep hole can symbolise the fear of falling and failing. Dreaming of what it is like to fly symbolises the feeling of being free. Emotional awareness in therapy is therefore not only a matter of focusing on physical signs and expressions, but also of asking for symbolic images. In this way we learn to recognise emotions, including emotional conflict and ambivalence, to give emotional meaning to our relationships and to regulate our emotions.

3.6.4 Reflection

Reflection is the mental activity in which one's own bodily signals, thoughts, sensations and memories are the subject of contemplation. Reflection includes the metacognitive aspect of being able to observe one's own mind. In many European languages, 'meta' is a prefix meaning 'concerning the subject itself'. Metahumour is humour about humour, metacognition is thinking about thinking. The metacognitive aspect of body mentalization is that adults are able to think at a higher level about their own body, thinking, feeling, remembering, with a certain amount of objectivity. One is aware of one's own subjectivity.

The term reflection emphasises the more explicit side of body mentalizing: the conscious, body-oriented mentalizing that is part of therapy. This involves observation, awareness of one's own physical and mental experience, rather than thought processes such as analysis or rationalisation. Reflection goes hand in hand with an awareness of subjectivity. When we reflect on our physical experiences, thoughts and feelings, we realise that they are personal, they are different for everyone. We realise that what we perceive, feel and think is not necessarily the true state of affairs. We may feel ill, but that does not necessarily mean we are ill. Reflection is mental work in which we make an effort to check 'is this the external factual reality or is it my subjective experience?'

Reflection also means knowing the difference between oneself and the bodily sensations and inner phenomena. This capacity for perspective is accompanied by the ability to experience distance from one's own physical or mental experiences. One does not unite with what one is experiencing, one does not fuse with it, but always remains aware of being the observer of one's own physical or mental reaction. In reflection we engage the perceiving part of ourselves. This is what Ormont et al. (1964) call the 'observing ego'. This is the part of us that does not feel, act or make decisions. It only perceives what there is to perceive. It is like a camera that records without judgement. It never weighs any thought, gesture or action on the scale of right or wrong, sane or insane, good or bad. It is a psychic entity separate from what we perceive.

3.6.5 Intersubjectivity

Body mentalization has a strong social aspect. It is part of what happens between people. It is the ability to perceive one's own and others' bodily signals, to be receptive to them, and to experience a connection with mental states (Spaans et al., 2009, 2010). It enables us to open up to the physical expression and inner response of others. Body mentalization is the ability to read the inner life of others by paying attention to their bodily expressions, just as others can do for us. We see someone at a bus stop pacing and looking at their watch and interpret this as someone who is in a hurry and hoping the bus will arrive soon. The innate ability to learn from others is partly because we interpret others' behaviour on the basis of 'theory of mind' (Baron-Cohen, 1991): if someone is shaking and sweating, they might be anxious. We can apply this ability to self-awareness: are my hands shaking and am I sweating? Then I might be anxious.

Using 'theory of mind' we can understand, for instance:

- Other people experience physical symptoms such as pain or tiredness differently from us.
- Our perceptions and thoughts about our physical condition are personal.
- Others can get an impression of how we feel on the outside, but they cannot know for sure because the inside is not directly observable.
- Misunderstandings with others, for example about our physical condition, arise because everyone has their own perspective.

The starting point for body mentalization is intersubjectivity: mutual influence is inescapable (Friedman, 1988). Every bodily response and associated inner response is somehow connected to and influenced by the bodily and mental responses of others. Through body-oriented mentalization we experience reciprocity: that we are influenced by each other. This makes us aware that we are social beings. Humans have a primarily social disposition, which is also biologically anchored. Our brains seem to be highly social. The social brain hypothesis suggests that human thinking evolved as a means of surviving and reproducing in large and complex social groups (Dunbar, 1998). The brain has learnt to adapt to others in the group and has learnt to understand physical expression, thoughts and emotions of others.

Body-oriented mentalization allows us to form close affective relationships. We can communicate in words and gestures about our deeper inner experiences and show empathy for those of others. We are able to move into the inner state of the other person and empathise with it. Empathy is about feeling the other person and at the same time knowing that what we are experiencing is related to the other person's condition, not our own.

3.7   Conclusion

In this chapter we have seen what the concept of bodily mentalization involves: the ability to perceive and be receptive to bodily signals, both from oneself and from others, and to experience a connection with mental states. This also describes the explicit skill, body-oriented mentalizing, that patients can strengthen in therapy. A subgroup of patients with severe PPS have limitations in their ability to mentally relate to their body, especially when they experience severe tension and physical discomfort. There are several polar dimensions to body mentalization, such as controlled versus automatic, self versus other, cognitive versus affective and internal versus external. We have seen how the tendency to body mentalize arises in a secure attachment to the caregiver when there is strong affective mirroring. In this way, a physical self develops first, from which the child can develop socially. We also considered the different attachment styles that can develop. We distinguished between deactivating and hyperactivating attachment styles as insecure attachment styles, both of which can be found in patients with severe PPS.

Attachment and (body) mentalization seem to be rooted in our neurobiology. This underlines the social brain hypothesis: human thinking evolved to enable us to survive and reproduce in large social groups. The brain has learnt to adapt to others in the group and to understand their body language, including their thoughts and emotions, in order to better work together. A subgroup of patients with severe PPS react to physical discomfort with stress and a reduction in body awareness, in which an insecure attachment style plays a role. The limitation in body mentalization then leads to numerous emotional, cognitive, behavioural and social consequences that perpetuate the PPS problem.

Finally, five therapeutic processes in B-MBT were briefly explained theoretically. These were: focusing attention, body awareness, emotional awareness, reflection and interpersonal influence.

What B-MBT looks like in practice is covered in Part II, where we will begin with explaining the principles of treatment.

Part II

Treatment

Chapter 4

General characteristics and principles of B-MBT

4.1 Brief description of the therapy

Body-oriented mentalization based therapy (B-MBT) is based on 'mentalization-based treatment' (MBT) for patients with borderline personality disorder developed by Bateman and Fonagy (2006). The aim of B-MBT is for patients with severe PPS, like patients with borderline personality disorder, to learn to mentalize. However, the focus in B-MBT is much more body-oriented: patients learn to recognise and tolerate bodily signals from themselves and others, and to experience a connection with inner experiences such as emotions, intentions, thoughts, memories and desires. B-MBT emphasises the relevance of a therapeutic process that focuses on the body to strengthen mentalization and the possibility that patients are in a body mode where mentalization is not yet possible. Compared to MBT, B-MBT not only pays more attention to the non-verbal aspects of the patient's functioning; non-verbal therapies are also an explicit part of the treatment. Furthermore, there is more attention to developing physical activities.

A therapist provides a safe, therapeutic relationship that is physical, attentive, reflective, affective and interpersonal. The therapist checks whether the patient is in a mentalizing state (mode). If the patient stops body-oriented mentalizing, the therapist intervenes to encourage it. The similarities or differences in the patient's and therapist's bodily signals and inner experiences can be explicit topics in therapy. Much of the therapeutic work takes place in the therapeutic relationship. As therapists, we form an emotional bond with our patients. Within this safe context, patients are given the opportunity to change. In contact with us, they learn to notice physical signals, emotions and thoughts that they were previously unable, unwilling or not allowed to notice.

4.2 Scientific effect studies

Until now, there has been little scientific research on the effects of body-oriented mentalizing in PPS. No randomised controlled trials (RCTs) or meta-analyses are available. Houtveen et al. (2015) investigated the effectiveness of an intensive

DOI: 10.4324/9781003637486-6

clinical and part-time day treatment with multidisciplinary B-MBT for severe PPS, as described in this book, at the highly specialised centre Altrecht Psychosomatiek Eikenboom in the Netherlands. The study included 183 patients. The B-MBT approach was combined with some components from *Acceptance and Commitment Therapy (ACT)* that are completely compatible with B-MBT principles. This was a prospective, observational study with a long follow-up of two years and a large number of patients. Several follow-up measurements were made. This study did not use a control group, but a multilevel analysis was able to show that the effects found were the result of the treatment. Treatment was found to be effective even in the most severe cases of PPS, and improvements continued for up to two years after treatment. Significant improvements in (somatic) complaints, quality of life and medical costs were also found in the long term.

Houtveen et al. (2025) examined changes and change points during and after in-patient multidisciplinary B-MBT for severe PPS at the Altrecht Psychosomatiek Eikenboom centre in the Netherlands. The B-MBT treatment again included some ACT components compatible with B-MBT principles. Fifty-five in-patients were included. There was no control group, but observational Routine Outcome Monitoring (ROM) data were analysed using two-phase, multiple-lag mixed model regression analysis to examine changes during and after treatment. This study observed increases in mental and physical health and decreases in symptoms of psychopathology during and after the treatment, with delayed improvements for some outcomes.

Feldmann-Sinnige et al. (2023) investigated whether body-oriented mentalization, the presumed working mechanism of B-MBT, actually improves during treatment. They investigated this again in the intensive (in-patient and part-time day treatment) B-MBT treatment at the highly specialised centre Altrecht Psychosomatiek Eikenboom. This study included 51 patients. The concept of body-oriented mentalizing was operationalised by two separately described elements, namely body awareness and mentalizing. Both body awareness and mentalizing improved significantly, resulting in a large effect size.

It can be concluded that that there is some scientific evidence to support considering B-MBT for patients with PPS who have difficulty with body-oriented mentalizing. Further research with higher-quality designs, such as randomised controlled trials, is desirable, as well as research on subgroups that benefit more or less from B-MBT. N=1 studies could also make a substantial contribution, especially in clarifying the effects of different B-MBT interventions in a given patient profile.

4.3 Target group

B-MBT is a transdiagnostic treatment model that is suitable for various forms of PPS and 'somatic symptom disorder and related disorders'. It focuses on the inability to body-oriented mentalize as a sustaining factor. If the patient's behaviours and expressions reveal an inability to body-oriented mentalizing, we may consider B-MBT, especially if previous evidence-based treatments such as cognitive behavioural therapy have proved insufficiently effective. Thus, B-MBT may be a particularly effective therapeutic tool in the subgroup of patients with (very) severe PPS. These patients struggle with chronic and multiple symptoms, severe physical and psychosocial impairments, comorbidity of somatic diseases and psychological disorders (van der Boom & Houtveen, 2014). B-MBT can also be used for other severe psychological problems where patients find it difficult to make a connection between physical signals and inner experiences. Examples include patients with symptoms of personality problems, burn-out, persistent mood or anxiety disorders, or eating disorders.

In formulating contraindications to B-MBT treatment, we should consider a severe mental or psychiatric crisis, current severe psychosocial stress (e.g. legal proceedings, current divorce, domestic violence), inadequate language skills, too low a level of intelligence, excessive drug or alcohol use or excessive use of addictive and damping substances such as opioids and/or benzodiazepines. In consultation with the referrer or general practitioner, one may set up a programme to make the necessary changes in these areas first.

4.4   Treatment setting

B-MBT is suitable for both individual and group therapy and for both in-patient and out-patient treatment. Techniques from B-MBT can also be used in all types of therapy for PPS to integrate body-oriented mentalization into treatment. The author and contributors to this book have experience in both intensive clinical and part-time day treatment, as well as outpatient treatment in a highly specialised treatment setting.

B-MBT aims for a high degree of multidisciplinary collaboration between professionals (such as doctors, psychiatrists, psychologists, physiotherapists, psychomotor therapists, occupational therapists, art therapists, nurses and social workers). It is highly recommended that they are trained in B-MBT and integrate aspects of this approach into their therapy. They should see body-oriented mentalization as a meaningful common thread throughout their therapy that helps them to achieve an attentive, sensitive, reflective, flexible way of working with patients (also see Chapter 11). The components of B-MBT therapy described in this book, such as individual therapy, group therapy, systems therapy and non-verbal therapy, can also be given as stand-alone therapies. In those cases, coordination with other service providers is important so that care is provided from a shared perspective.

4.5   The treatment plan

We apply B-MBT on the basis of a clear treatment contract which, in addition to a brief description of the problem, includes a clear description of the form of treatment. A clear form of treatment includes a pre-agreed goal, duration and a clear structure that the patient agrees to. As part of the problem, we also mention the problematic interaction patterns (attachment styles) that have been discussed with the patient. To maximise involvement in the treatment plan, we formulate it in collaboration with the patient, so that the formulation is in line with a shared vision of the problem by the patient and the clinician. The patient's vision is particularly reflected in the formulation of likely perpetuating factors in PPS, such as making too-high demands, not paying enough attention to body signals, using an insecure attachment style or avoiding valuable activities.

4.6   The therapeutic stance

Because B-MBT is about the interaction between patient and therapist, the therapeutic stance is the catalyst of the therapeutic process. The therapist offers the patient a safe interaction in which he provides opportunities to explore own body signals and inner experiences. Bowlby (1988) compares the role of the therapist to that of a caring, reliable, attentive and empathic mother or father who provides a safe base from which the child dares to explore the world. The pillars of therapeutic contact formulated by Rogers, namely unconditional acceptance, empathy and genuineness (Rogers, 1951) are also part of B-MBT.

Bateman and Fonagy (2004) emphasise the joint search process in the therapeutic stance. They compare it to looking together for directions bent over a map. Therapist and patient explore what is happening in the body and mind of the patient and therapist. They keep 'body and mind in mind' together. The therapist clearly takes the initiative in this process and will not wait so long or be so silent that the patient goes beyond his tolerance zone of 'arousal' (see Section 4.8.8.).

In B-MBT the therapist is not an all knowing expert. Rather, the therapist is a compassionate, 'non-knowing' person involved, who is open to and accepts his own and others' physical and inner experiences. A not-knowing therapeutic attitude refers to the acknowledgement that mental states are opaque by definition. The not-knowing attitude is also characterised by curiosity and open doubt, so that multiple perspectives can be considered. For example, the therapist might ask, somewhat naively, 'Is that so?' or 'I don't know either, and wonder: could it also be different?'

We combine our attitude of not knowing with an expert attitude concerning body-oriented mentalization and PPS. This balance is important. Otherwise, our not-knowing stance may confuse the patient as being 'without knowledge or insight'. We can use a 'not-knowing mentalizing attitude' in a way that makes it clear that while we are experts, we can also expand our knowledge through what we experience in therapy. The therapist's attitude is also a transparent model, thinking out loud and being open about his own body signals and inner experiences. Self-disclosure is a core element that of course always is in the service of the treatment process. The therapist is also open to feedback from the patient and shows that the patient's perspective is valuable. He will admit mistakes, he explores differences in perspective and acknowledges when he has slipped into a non-mentalizing mode: 'I notice that I automatically start to offer you solutions without first reflecting on what I am experiencing in my body and my mind'. By naming his own non-mentalizing moments aloud, the therapist again sets an example for the patient. Given its body-oriented nature, B-MBT requires therapists to relate to patients with familiarity when addressing bodily sensations. This also requires the therapist to be familiar with his own physicality.

4.7   Education

Both education about PPS and body-oriented mentalizing are components of treatment. It is preferable to give the education in groups (see also Section 9.2). Education about PPS can include providing knowledge about symptoms, mechanisms of maintenance, treatment interventions and self-help interventions. As PPS focuses on physical symptoms, knowledge of how the body works and the interaction between body and mind is also part of the education. Education about the body is also important because misunderstandings about the body can lead to the perpetuation of PPS. For example, many people have been taught at home that tension is a sign of weakness, that when you are tired you should go to bed and that pain is a sign that something is broken.

It may be necessary to explain how the various physiological control systems work and interact. For example, the digestive system, the musculoskeletal system, the processing of pain stimuli and stress systems such as the hypothalamic-pituitary-adrenal axis can be explained (Branch et al., 2017). Explanations of the sympathetic and parasympathetic nervous systems and the effects of prolonged stress on the immune system are also useful. We can also explain stress responses such as fight/flight/freeze, types of stressors, the physical manifestations of stress and the interplay between emotions and the stress system.

In explaining bodily processes we also look at the physiology of the attachment system and body mentalization. This includes the influence of early childhood trauma and neglect on the stress system and mentalization. Our mental state and closeness to others activate or deactivate the nervous system, depending on the attachment style. This can cause us to calm down in times of intense stress through the emotional closeness of others or, on the contrary, to become even more stressed by this closeness.

Patients with PPS may get the idea that when physical processes are explained, it is all about reductionist, monocausal explanations. They may draw conclusions such as 'it's all about stress' or 'it's because I'm thinking wrong'. To avoid this, we should always place our explanations in a broader biopsychosocial perspective. We should explain that there are always multiple physical, psychological and social factors at play (Branch et al., 2017). We can describe how emotions (such as anger), thoughts (such as 'I don't accept this tiredness') and social behaviours (such as not letting people know about your symptoms) can interact and be related to physical symptoms (such as experiencing more and more pain (Tak et al., 2017).

The difficulty of separating emotions and bodily symptoms may, for example, be clarified using the example of the overlap between physical and emotional pain.

We can focus on the interaction between physical and emotional pain (Eisenberger et al., 2003; Eisenberger & Lieberman, 2004). We can also explain which emotions are associated with which physical signs, like anger with an increase in temperature, trembling muscles and increased heart rate.

Because many people with PPS have a one-sided, obsessive focus on physical symptoms, it is useful to explain that health is more than the absence of physical symptoms. For example, health is made up of the quality of daily functioning: social functioning, well-being, sense of purpose, mental functioning and physical functioning (Huber et al., 2011). To experience health, we try to maintain a balance between all these aspects. This is how we develop the resilience to cope with setbacks, such as long-term physical complaints.

It can be very helpful to use metaphors or visuals in education (Tak et al., 2017). One example is the metaphor of the full bucket: when there are too many stressors, the bucket overflows and someone experiences symptoms. Another example is the bank account as a metaphor for exhaustion: if you ask too much of yourself, you can end up on the bank in the red. Another common metaphor is the pressure cooker: if you don't express your feelings, you'll be under a lot of pressure. Before starting B-MBT, it is advisable to educate patients about what body-oriented mentalizing is, how poor body-oriented mentalization can perpetuate physical symptoms, and what the treatment entails. For example, the text in the appendices (see Appendix A.1) can be used in the form of a leaflet.

4.8 Principles of treatment

4.8.1 Starting from the unity of body and mind and the biopsychosocial model

In B-MBT we assume that body and mind are inseparable. Psychological and physiological processes are like two sides of the same coin. Phenomena such as stress, anger, fear, but also fatigue and pain reflect physiological processes and vice versa. We can consider this view against the background of the biopsychosocial model, which is widely accepted in medicine and the social sciences (see Section 2.4.2). The therapist therefore always keeps an eye on what is happening in the physical, mental and social domains. Patients learn to recognise when a bodily signal, such as a heavy feeling in the abdomen or sweaty hands, is related to an emotion such as sadness or shame. They also learn to recognise what meaningful others have to do with experiencing these emotions. We also look at the biopsychosocial model in terms of the patient's functioning inside and outside the sessions. This means, for example, that if patients suddenly experience more physical discomfort, we always ask ourselves what developments are taking place in the psychological and social arenas outside the therapy sessions. What inner tendencies does a patient feel when facial pain suddenly worsens? How does this affect communication with their partner?

4.8.2 Standing still and focusing on the body and the mind

The basic principle of B-MBT is that action is stopped in order to focus on what patients are experiencing in the here and now in terms of bodily sensations and inner experiences in themselves and others. Attention to the body is central to the idea that it is essential for our self-regulation and interpersonal functioning. By consciously attending to bodily signals from oneself and others, awareness of unrecognised bodily sensations and inner experiences begins.

This includes focusing on physical symptoms such as headaches, fatigue or signs of loss of a physical function. Part of 'paying attention to body and mind' is reflection. One observes one's own body and mind from a meta-position. This reflection assumes that everyone has a mind that expresses itself through the body and through behaviour. We use reflections on body and mind especially when patients no longer mentalize in a body-oriented way. The therapist is therefore always alert to the patient's non-mentalizing modes: the body, teleological, equivalence or the pretend mode (see Appendix A.3). Although we focus attention on the whole spectrum of internal experience, particular attention is paid to the noticing of affects and emotions (see also Section 3.6.3). After all, a large group of patients with PPS have difficulty in making sense of their own or others' emotions.

4.8.3 Interaction in a safe relational context

In B-MBT we assume that people naturally learn body-oriented mentalizing within safe affective relationships. Therefore, during treatment, learning about one's own and others' physical and mental responses takes place within a safe therapeutic relationship. Reciprocal communication between patient and therapist is therefore central to B-MBT. The patient and therapist exchange views. This requires the therapist to be a safe key figure for the patient (Hafkenscheid, 2014). To this purpose, the therapist adopts a predictable, relaxed, supportive, empathic and hopeful attitude. He is involved, transparent and active. The aim is to achieve optimal emotional safety by providing a 'holding environment' that includes clear boundaries, containment, growth factors and predictability (see Winnicott, 1960, among others). The premise is that people experience their own and others' bodily signals and inner states mainly in moments of genuine contact. This requires therapists to be aware of the degree and quality of contact they experience with their patients.

Daniel Stern (2004) emphasised the importance of mentalizing in the interaction between patient and therapist with the term 'moments of meeting'. In a 'moment of meeting' there is an intersubjective exchange that is affective and healing. It requires the therapist to truly engage with the patient in the here and now. In doing so, the therapist gives a specific, authentic and transparent response that bears the therapist's personal signature (Wallin, 2010). To achieve a healing personal encounter and effective and lasting change, it is not so much verbal expression, rationalisation or explanation that is crucial. According to Stern, while words can lead to cognitive understanding, they can also cause the experienced reality to lose completeness or richness. For a 'moment of meeting', a sensitive, mutual, emotional exchange is much more important. Here the therapist is not afraid to bring in his own bodily signals and inner experiences. Of course, the therapist only does this when it enhances the therapeutic process and helps the patient to experience a connection with his or her own body signals and inner experiences. That the interaction between patient and therapist is central, the interpersonal method, should be explained to the patient as early as possible in the treatment, either orally or in writing (preferably both).

4.8.4   Non-verbal approach

B-MBT consists of a combination of verbal and non-verbal interventions. Non-verbal interventions can be incorporated into talk therapy or offered separately during physiotherapy, psychomotor therapy, art therapy or other body-oriented therapies (see Chapter 6). These therapies have the advantage that, unlike verbal interventions, they help to promote the process of body-mentalization through bottom-up learning processes from body to emotion to conscious cognition and feeling.

4.8.5   Focus on current and recent experiences

Talking about distant past experiences in therapy, such as analysing childhood, can carry the risk of pseudo-mentalization. Patients then rationalise and find explanations for inappropriate behaviour, such as 'my tendency to avoid sport is because of my mother's overprotective attitude in my childhood'. No matter how correct this explanation may be, the search for a suitable explanation does not guarantee that body-mentalization will increase in the here and now. We therefore do not focus on the distant past, but on situations in the therapy room in the present moment and on very recent experiences outside the therapy room. These are situations that the patient (still) really can experience in the therapy room. The therapist then engages the patient in a thoughtful and clarifying exploration of the situation.

4.8.6   Connecting the topic of conversation with body-oriented mentalizing

During an B-MBT session, a variety of topics related to PPS problems may come up. Common themes are:

- Coping with physical limitations and boundaries
- Feeling misunderstood
- Lack of support
- Feeling ignored
- Conflicts with others
- Experiencing opposition

- Assertiveness
- (Lack of) emotional closeness with others
- Experiencing loss
- Daring to express emotions
- Dealing with loved ones

The therapist takes care to make the topic personal by asking about very recent personal experiences: 'When was the last time you felt obviously ignored?' The therapist then looks to see if the patient communicates this in a body-oriented mentalizing way, for example by saying, 'I felt ignored by you (the therapist) just now when you looked at your watch. Then I feel the blood rise to my head and I get angry'. As soon as the patient does not body mentalize (e.g. by telling an elaborate, general, emotionless story), the therapist will continue to stimulate body-oriented mentalizing. As far as possible, the therapist maintains a balance between the content-related discussion and the process of body-oriented mentalizing.

We also consider whether the problem we are talking about with the patient is somehow occurring in the session. For example, if the theme is 'going beyond physical boundaries', we can look at whether the session is actually too long for the patient and whether he needs a long time to recover from it. We should also be alert to whether the theme discussed is occurring in the current interpersonal relationship. If so, we can name it or ask about it (e.g. 'Do you feel ignored by me?' or 'Do you have the courage to tell me when you don't like something?'). In this way the therapist looks for traces of the problem discussed in the current session and in the current mutual contact. When discussing these, the therapist again pays attention to whether the patient mentalizes in a body-oriented way.

4.8.7 Responding to attachment style

The therapist responds to the attachment style: the interpersonal patterns that are activated when the patient enters into relationships with others. An exploration of problematic interaction patterns takes place as early as possible, for example in the pre-therapy phase or the first phase of treatment. Therapist and patient look at 'what can go wrong' in relation to the therapist, other patients and therapy as a whole. This can help to prevent early withdrawal and avoidance behaviour. The therapist can also provide information about different attachment styles. This can be done, for example, by discussing the results of instruments such as the Experiences in Close Relationships-Revised (ECR-R) questionnaire (Kooiman et al., 2013). In this way we can reach a consensus with the patient on his or her attachment style. Although recognised interpersonal patterns have their origins in childhood and early attachment relationships, these origins are not the focus of B-MBT. The therapist is more concerned with identifying attachment patterns as they emerge in the here and now of treatment sessions and in the patient's current daily life.

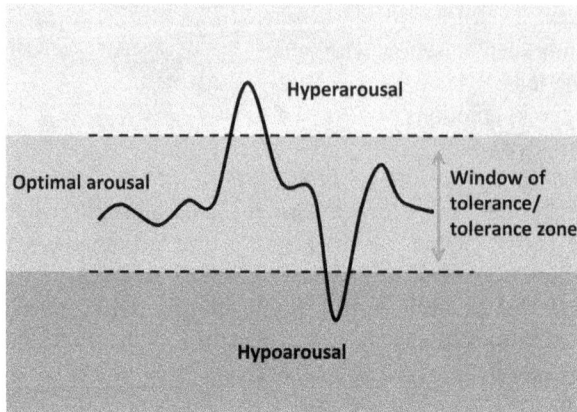

Figure 4.1 The tolerance zone, 'window of tolerance' according to Siegel (1999).
Source: *Adapted from Siegel (1999) ©Spaans (2020)*

4.8.8   Taking the 'window of tolerance' into account

The therapist monitors the patient's tolerance zone ('window of tolerance', Siegel, 1999), the zone of safe 'arousal' between hyperarousal and hypoarousal (see Figure 4.1). The patient also learns to identify these. This is important because too much or too little activation of the autonomic nervous system reduces the ability of body mentalization. The patient's tension should be neither too high nor too low, 'forging iron when it is lukewarm'. Hyperarousal can occur with worsening physical symptoms, intense emotions or strong activation of the attachment system.

With hyperarousal, for example, the therapist will use stress-, arousal- or symptom-regulating interventions. These may include responding empathically, shifting attention to cognitions rather than emotions, exploring and clarifying together where the strong emotional arousal is coming from, or teaching the patient to 'count to 10'. Other regulating exercises and advices include:

- Physical rest or moderate physical exertion/sports
- Performing (increased) movements such as arm waving or stamping
- Muscle relaxation exercises
- Breathing exercises
- Focusing attention on the feet on the floor or other 'grounding exercises'
- Getting some fresh air
- Orientation exercises
- Practicing yoga or Tai Chi
- Tapping (tapping on acupressure points (van der Kolk, 2014)
- Various mindfulness exercises such as a body scan, mindful breathing or mindful exercise (such as mindful walking or mindful running)
- Visualising a 'safe place'

These techniques help patients managing arousal, stress and emotion: helping them return to their window of tolerance. At the same time, the therapeutic relationship itself plays a key role in emotional regulation. This is known as *co-regulation*: the process by which one person's regulated, attuned presence helps another person to stabilise their internal state. When the therapist remains calm and grounded, this has a direct impact on the patient's nervous system, supporting emotional safety and restoring the capacity to mentalize.

In addition to our co-regulation, we continue regulating exercises until a level of arousal is reached where the sense of safety and control seems sufficient. Then the patient is also able to reflect on his current physical and mood state and we can move on to basic body-oriented mentalizing interventions (see Chapter 5). In hypoarousal, on the other hand, the therapist brings in emotional material to achieve the minimum level of arousal necessary for a learning process. One of the goals of body-oriented mentalization is to widen the window of tolerance.

The idea with these regulating interventions is for the patient to become more and more independent, using exercises that they can do themselves. The therapist can also use body awareness here by asking the patient to be aware of the level of stress or arousal and express it in a number between 0 (no tension) and 10 (a lot of tension). If the patient needs comfort or protection, we can also use self-regulation by asking them to put an arm around themselves, listen to some pleasant music or take a warm foot bath.

Many a patient with severe PPS experiences not only temporary excessive stress or physical symptoms during B-MBT treatment, but a continuous high level of physical symptoms and limitations. Then we are forced to constantly combine B-MBT with body regulation interventions. Here we can use B-MBT in combination with:

- Fitness exercises
- Movement and postural exercises
- Meaningful activity building (see Chapter 8)
- Exercises to overcome fear of movement
- Relaxation exercises
- Massage
- Advice on personal hygiene and sleep
- Advice on setting limits to emotional overload.

However, we will combine interventions that focus on regulation of arousal, symptoms, emotions and stress always with interventions that focus on body-oriented mentalizing as much as possible. There should always be a balance between regulation and mentalization. See also Section 6.7.3.

4.8.9 *Starting from the opacity of the mind*

Body-oriented mentalizing, like mentalizing, is inherently uncertain. Internal states expressed by the body are opaque, changeable and often difficult to determine, even for the person themselves (Fonagy & Bateman, 2019). This means that body-oriented mentalizing is prone to error or inaccuracy. We must assume that we can never know with certainty what is going on in the patient's mind. Therefore, in our efforts to read our own minds or the minds of others, we will regularly get it slightly wrong. For example, this may involve small misjudgements of one's own emotions that someone also corrects himself: 'I'm not really angry, I'm more disappointed'. It can be a misjudgement of someone else's inner state, which is corrected by feedback from that person: 'I'm not feeling anxious as you think, I'm more tense'. So not only will we as therapists not know for sure what is going on in the patient, we may never know better than the patient (Allen et al., 2008). Body-oriented mentalizing is therefore a process of finding, through trial and error, the right understanding of bodily experience and the inner life of oneself and others. This involves bodily and inner experiences of which the patient is not yet fully aware, partly because of the opacity of the mind.

4.8.10   Addressing trauma and transference

During therapy, when patients begin to pay attention to body signals and are able to open up to their own inner world, painful memories of trauma may surface. Besides physical trauma like sexual abuse or a car-accident, B-MBT focuses on relational trauma like emotional neglect (see Chapter 7). The therapist helps the patient to focus his or her attention on the trauma and the associated physical and mental reactions. At the same time, the patient remains aware of the here and now, in the safe presence of the therapist (dual awareness, Ogden & Fisher, 2017). We assume that relational patterns (attachment styles) based on previous interactions with significant others, such as former caregivers, will be repeated in therapy (see Chapter 7). Transference and counter-transference are obvious phenomena that the therapist makes space for so that the patient can become aware of the recurring patterns.

4.8.11   Simple interventions

The aim of interventions is to be compatible with the patient's capacity for body mentalization. The longer or more complex the interventions, the less likely they are to be compatible with this capacity. Interventions should be particularly simple and brief at times of high intensity of physical symptoms, emotional arousal or high stress. This is when the capacity for body-oriented mentalizing is likely to be low. So we avoid long sentences and say, for example, 'Where exactly is the pain now?' or 'How do you experience your fatigue now?'

4.8.12   Mentalizing in case of inadequate illness behaviour and increasing physical symptoms

The therapist refrains as much as possible from offering solutions, working on short-term symptom reduction, making interpretations and prescribing different behaviour or a different way of thinking or feeling. B-MBT is process-oriented, which means that we see therapy as an ongoing process aimed at (re)integrating bodily sensations, thinking and feeling. A long-term effect can be a reduction in symptoms, but also a better quality of life. We validate current physical and inner experiences as they are, without giving the message that things should be different. In this way, the therapist communicates that the patient's physical and inner experiences really do matter. By mentalizing rather than solving problems in a somatic way, patients learn to relate to their problems differently and to deal with their physical complaints in a healthier way.

However, it is not always possible to avoid giving health-promoting behavioural advice, for example when patients are engaging in behaviour that is directly damaging to their physical health, such as overexertion. We should, when behavioural advice is necessary, address both the physical and psychological response to the advice given. Behavioural counselling may also be needed to bring the patient back into his or her tolerance zone of arousal. Even if the patient is able to mentalize in a body-oriented way later in treatment, we may also advise them to gradually build up activities. In doing so, we ensure that the patient performs these behaviours from a mentalizing mode, i.e. with awareness of their own and others' bodily signals and inner experiences.

4.8.13   Shifting focus over the course of therapy

At the beginning of therapy, as patients are often still looking for a somatic solution, more attention is given to the physical complaints and experiences. Patients then learn the connection between physical sensations and underlying mental states. Gradually the focus of therapy can shift from somatic to emotional, from non-verbal to verbal, and from the therapeutic relationship to current intimate relationships and situations outside the therapy room. During this process we also have to move back and forth between the polarities inner/outer, self/other and cognitive/affective. The choice of intervention stays also highly dependent on the attachment strategy, the current ability to mentalize (see Section 5.5) and the nature of the contact. Throughout the entire course of therapy, we must ensure that the patient remains aware of his or her bodily sensations, to avoid the possibility of the patient appearing to progress psychologically while deteriorating physically.

4.9   Conclusion

Knowledge of general treatment characteristics and principles is necessary for a fruitful use of the interventions described in the following parts of the book. The treatment interventions relate to the broad group of patients with (very) severe PPS who have difficulty making a connection between body signals and inner experiences. When giving B-MBT, it is important to consider the appropriate treatment setting, the treatment plan, the therapeutic relationship and the role of education. Together with the 13 treatment principles described in this chapter, they form the basis for all types of intervention. Inadequate attention to the treatment principles can lead to B-MBT interventions that may be correct in themselves but are, for example, poorly timed or poorly linked to the actual interaction with the patient. It is like playing a piece of music: you play the right notes, but with too little feeling for the intended musical atmosphere (Bateman & Fonagy, 2006).

If, during therapy, we are no longer sure what to do, the first thing to do is to 'stand still and pay attention to body and mind'. In other words, if we are very unsure about what to do, we can stop the conversation and reflect on the patient's and our own current physical and inner experiences. Or we can go back to when the conversation was still in a mentalizing mode and reflect on what the patient and ourselves were experiencing physically and internally at that time. In the following chapter on basic individual interventions, this principle is, for example, translated into the interventions 'stop and stand still' and 'stop and go back' (see Section 5.2.16 and Section 5.2.17).

Chapter 5

Individual basic interventions

In B-MBT, a number of individually oriented techniques form the basis of clinical practice. They can be recognised in any form or application of body-oriented mentalization. The basic techniques can be summarised by the acronym MEET:

M = Mode (of mentalizing) recognizing
E = Exploring body signals and inner experiences of the patient
E = Exploring by the therapist of one's own body signals and inner experiences and being transparent about them
T = Triggering mutual exchange of body signals and inner experiences

These basic interventions form a whole. They are always used in conjunction with each other. Promoting body-oriented mentalizing is therefore often a matter of 'recognising the mode' and 'exploring the patient's body and inner experiences' and 'exploring one's own body and inner experiences as a therapist and being transparent about them' and 'initiating exchange'. Interventions should also take into account the mode of (non-)body-oriented mentalizing: body, teleological, equivalence or pretend mode (see Section 5.5 in this chapter).

5.1 Recognising mode of (non-)mentalizing

5.1.1 Identifying the patient's mode of body mentalization

The therapist always assesses whether the patient is still mentalizing their own and other people's bodily and inner experiences. The explicit side of body-oriented mentalizing addressed in therapy focuses on verbalising what the patient is experiencing physically and emotionally, such as 'I can feel the muscles in my hands and my jaw tightening. I am angry'. Language is therefore an important medium: finding words, phrases and stories to accompany physical sensations and inner experiences.

The capacity for body-oriented mentalizing is manifested in the accurate, rich, affective and flexible use of language to articulate one's own and others' bodily signals and inner experiences. Here the verbal expression matches what the

DOI: 10.4324/9781003637486-7

body is expressing. We therefore look at the correspondence between verbal and non-verbal expression in the patient. We also look at whether the patient recognises and tolerates body signals and inner states and experiences their interrelationships, even if they are unpleasant or painful. Does the patient recognise that bodily sensations and inner experiences are personal and not 'factual truths', even under heightened stress? Huismans (2017) explored how experienced clinicians believe body mentalization can be detected in patients. She asked them: 'How do you see or experience that a patient is body mentalizing?' Some of the categories of observable characteristics of patients who are in a body-oriented mentalizing mode are:

1. Notice physical signs and inner experiences.
2. Accept and tolerate physical cues and inner experiences.
3. Demonstrate congruence between non-verbal and verbal expressions.
4. Use thoughtful, inquisitive, non-judgemental verbalisations of body cues and inner experiences.
5. Demonstrate the ability to talk about the physical and inner experiences one is having in the moment.
6. Use verbalisations that link physical signals and inner experiences.
7. View one's own and others' physical and inner experiences from different perspectives and be open to the views of others.
8. Showing interest in other people's bodily signals and inner experiences, and how they interact with one's own bodily signals and inner experiences.

For a more comprehensive overview of the main signs of body mentalization, see Appendix A.2. In identifying non-mentalization, the therapist distinguishes four types of non-mentalization of the body. The body, teleological, equivalence and pretend mode (also see Section 3.1.2). There is a certain hierarchy within these body-oriented non-mentalizing modes, depending on the degree to which someone is capable of body-oriented mentalizing. In general, these modes form a continuum, ranging from the most rudimentary (body mode) to the more refined (but still flawed) forms of mental representation (pretend mode):

Body mode: The patient experiences physical sensations in a concrete, literal way, without being able to integrate them into a broader psychological or social context. There is no reflection on the experience; the physical sensation *is the* reality. The person cannot, for example, imagine that stress or emotions play a role. With a pounding heart, one reacts automatically based on the physical sensation, without further interpretation. One calls the hospital without any awareness of one's own inner world.

Teleological mode: The patient experiences only a tangible, physical, material reality that affects physical symptoms. No attention is paid to the inner experiences or to the connections between physical symptoms and the mind. The patient is mainly interested in diagnoses and short-term solutions such as medication. He may adopt a compelling or even manipulative attitude with a lack of compromise: no substitute, no alternative to the desired goal, is accepted ('If you don't give me your phone number, I never will see you again'!).

Equivalence mode: The patient equates the inner experience with the physical reality. He takes inner experiences too literally. For example, equating mental pain with physical pain. The equivalence mode can be seen, for example, when the patient is overwhelmed by painful emotions or physical experiences, has no words for them, experiences only one reality, becomes confused, suspicious, which can lead to many misunderstandings in communication. Magical thinking can also be seen as part of the equivalence mode: 'I am guilty, therefore my body is punishing me with this pain'.

Pretend mode: Inner experiences that accompany a physical sensation (such as sadness in the case of back pain) are not experienced in a fully conscious way: with a grim expression on their face, patients tell an unemotional story about their pain. Inner experiences may be repressed, denied, dissociated, projected or rationalised away. This can be seen, for example, in the excessive use of 'clichéd', 'canned' words and stories or, on the contrary, in elaborate, overly flowery narratives, excessively detailed reporting and analysis, talking about 'there and then', talking about 'others', talking about external circumstances or a body posture that does not match what is being said.

Thus, in the four different modes of non-mentalizing, the limited body-oriented mentalizing, with its associated experience of and response to physical complaints, can emerge in a different way each time (Table 5.1).

Table 5.1 Example of experiences of and responses to physical complaints in different modes of non-mentalizing.

	Body mode	Teleological mode	Equivalence mode	Pretend mode
Experience of physical complaint	Physical complaint is perceived as pure physical reality.	Physical complaint acknowledged but must be clearly proven and resolved.	Physical complaint acknowledged but interpreted as an absolute truth, with no room for alternative explanations.	Physical complaint is acknowledged, but without real engagement or inner experience.
Mentalizing	Absent; physical complaint not placed in broader context.	Limited; concrete actions or external evidence are needed to give meaning.	Rigid; there is mental representation, but without flexibility.	Mental representation, but without depth or emotional connection.

(Continued)

Table 5.1 (Continued)

	Body mode	Teleological mode	Equivalence mode	Pretend mode
Response to Physical complaint	Direct action based on physical sensation.	Search for evidence or a tangible solution to understand or remedy the physical complaint.	Being absolutely convinced the own interpretation is correct and leave no room for doubt.	Talking about the physical complaint without real mental processing or (emotional) impact.

In the case of someone having a physical symptom such as a belly ache, his response will largely depend on the body-oriented mentalization mode in which his mind is:

- Body mode: The belly pain is experienced without mental representation. The person cannot imagine that stress or emotions are involved. Their thinking remains very physical and concrete. They do not think things through and will react directly and impulsively to the pain, for example by calling the hospital immediately.
- Teleological mode: The person is still thinking in concrete terms, but is looking for an external, observable and provable explanation or action to justify or resolve their experience. The person recognises their complaint as something that could have meaning, but this meaning must be tangible and immediately visible. They may think: 'My stomach hurts. That means something is wrong medically. I need to have a scan to prove that something is wrong, and the doctor needs to give me a diagnosis and medication'.
- Equivalence mode: Here there is a mental representation, but it is experienced as absolute and indisputable. The thought 'My belly hurts, so I have a tumour in my stomach' feels as real as an actual serious abdominal disorder. There is a subjective certainty: 'What I feel is reality'. Doubt or alternative explanations are not possible because the inner experience is experienced as direct truth.
- Pretend mode: There is a mental representation, but it is disconnected from reality. Someone may talk about physical complaints and emotions, but without any real involvement or inner experience. To others it seems distant or superficial. Someone might think: 'Yes, my stomach hurts, maybe because of stress, but hey, everyone has problems sometimes, it's not that bad, I'll just ignore it, etc. etc.' (They recognise it, but feel little about it and do little about it).

For a comprehensive overview of the different signs of non-body mentalizing, see Appendix A.3.

Recognising the patient's mode of (non-)mentalizing is not so much about making a fixed diagnosis such as 'this patient is bad at body mentalizing'. Rather, it is about recognising the moments when patients stop (body-oriented) mentalizing in order to switch to an intervention that will help them to get back on track.

In assessing whether patients are body mentalizing, the therapist pays attention to their response to a question designed to evoke body-oriented mentalizing in the here and now, such as:

- What do you notice in your body now that you are so tired?
- What feelings are you experiencing with this pain in your back?
- What thoughts are going through your mind now that you are feeling dizzy again?

The capacity for body-oriented mentalization is situation-specific. For therapy, the question 'can someone mentalize in a body-oriented way?' is not so relevant and also difficult to answer. It is more important to notice in which situations the patient is better or less able to mentalize in a body-oriented way. Therefore, assessments during and after different situations are necessary, such as:

- During physical activity or just at rest
- With physical discomfort or with little discomfort
- With high or low emotions
- With high or low stress
- In the presence or absence of a trusted person
- With certain therapists and therapies or just outside of them

We prefer to ask the body-mentalization-oriented questions in such specific situations. If a patient was not able to mentalize in a body-oriented way in that situation, the therapist can still assess whether the patient is able to do so afterwards, which also says something about the mentalizing ability in that situation.

5.1.2   Therapist mode

As therapists we check during or immediately after the session what mode we are in or have been in. By monitoring this, we can switch back to body-oriented mentalizing if we have stopped doing so. This is necessary because if the therapist is not in a mentalizing mode, there is little chance that the patient will start mentalizing. A mentalizing therapist is more likely to evoke mentalizing in the patient than a non-mentalizing therapist. For example, in order to check his mode, the therapist examines:

- Do I respond mainly physically? (body mode)
- Am I strongly dominated by my own inner or physical experiences? (equivalence mode)
- Do I experience my own reactions as unimportant? Am I pretending? (pretend mode)

- Am I primarily focused on an immediate solution or immediate change in the patient? (teleological mode)
- Am I aware of my body signals and what is happening within me? (mentalizing mode)

(See also Appendices A.2 and A.3 for signs of body-oriented (non-)mentalizing)

From an awareness of the (non-)mentalizing mode of ourselves and the patient, we apply interventions that promote body-oriented mentalizing. The choice of interventions described in the next section is a matter of timing and taking into account the patient's non-mentalizing mode, attachment style, perceived tension and perceived safety.

5.2   Exploring body signals and inner experiences of the patient

The exploration of body signals and inner perceptions of the patient involves a range of interventions designed to assist patients in a non-judgemental manner to investigate their own and others' body signals, posture, movements and inner experiences. The objective of this exploration is to facilitate the recognition, investigation, appreciation, tolerance and integration of these signals into communication with others. This exploration is conducted in a mindful atmosphere. The focus is deliberately directed towards the here-and-now experience, with a particular emphasis on physical signals, sensations and inner reactions. This approach is characterised by an attitude of acceptance and curiosity, both on the part of the patient and the therapist, and without the desire to alter what is perceived (Wallin, 2010). Maintaining attention can be challenging for patients, particularly in cases of intense physical symptoms or emotions. Exploration can be regarded as a form of 'pressing the pause button'. This process entails the endurance of current physical and mental experiences, thereby facilitating the ability to tolerate unpredictable yet significant physical experiences. This, in turn, creates space for new experiences and change. Exploration does not necessarily entail rational or intellectual activity. Rather, it is an endeavour to become aware and learn to observe, to engage in a sensitive and affective reflection on physical and mental experiences of oneself and others in the present moment. In this manner, patients are also instructed in the observation of intimate experiences as a component of communication with others. In the exploratory interventions that will be described in the rest of this chapter, the therapist will naturally also pay attention to the patient's 'windows of tolerance' and whether they are in a safe zone of arousal, so that exploring makes sense.

5.2.1   Reading the patient's body language

By observing the patient's physical expression from moment to moment, we gain access to the emotional meaning of non-verbal communication. For example, we look at facial expressions, breathing, posture, arm and hand movements, rhythm and tone of voice. We pay particular attention to the physical expression of inner experiences such as facial tremors, tense hands or shoulders, rapid head movements, unusual eye contact, sighing, blushing, sweating, sudden headaches, dizziness, fainting or vomiting. What are the hands, face, posture, movement, voice doing now? Is the patient happy, anxious, sad? Is the patient's calm, deep breathing an expression of contentment? In this way we get to know our patients better and feel the mutual contact better. As an aid to reading body language, we can also use the overview of common physical signals for inner experience in Appendix A.4.

By reading body language we can also see if the patient is in touch with their inner experiences, if their body language matches what they are saying and how strong the emotions are. In interpreting the patient's body language, the therapist keeps in mind the opacity of mental states. He assumes that we can never know someone's physical experience and inner reaction for sure, but can only make well-considered guesses about what other people are thinking and feeling. It is an interpretation, an assumption, a thought, and not 'reality'. When exploring, we should be aware that the body language of our patients is one of the most important sources of awareness of the inner self. Because we are using language during exploration, the patient's words, phrases and stories can almost automatically demand our attention. We should then consciously shift our attention back to the patient's body language.

5.2.2 Teaching patients to listen to body signals

For many therapists the question, 'What are you feeling right now?' is obvious. In B-MBT, the most obvious question is a question about a body signal. This is because we assume that by opening up to and accepting body signals, awareness of inner experience begins. Standing still at body cues is particularly important for patients with a deactivating attachment style, who avoid bodily sensations and are in an pretend mode. For example, the therapist asks: 'What are you experiencing in your body right now?' By focusing attention on the body, we can help the patient to focus attention on different types of body signals, such as:

- Internal body signals: 'What are you feeling in your body right now?'
- Sensations of the skin and surface muscles and joints: 'What do you feel in your muscles right now? What does the outside of your body feel like now? What are you experiencing in your muscles right now?'
- The overall physiological state: 'How does your body feel now?'
- Posture: 'What do you notice about your posture right now?'
- Movement characteristics: 'What do you notice about your movements?'
- Identifying a desire to move: 'What movement does your body want to make right now?'
- Characteristics of a physical symptom: 'How does the pain in your back feel now, sharp, dull or any other feeling? How tired are you now, expressed in a number between 0 and 10?'

- Physical tension or excitement: 'Where do you feel tension in your body now?', 'How intense is this tension now, expressed on a number between 0 and 10?'
- Breathing: 'What do you notice about your breathing right now?'
- Physical signals of inner turmoil: 'Now that you are so sad, what do you notice in your body?'

For a more comprehensive overview of the main areas of focus when exploring body signals, see Table 6.1 and Table 6.2 in Section 6.7.2. We can help patients learn to focus their attention on body signals by first guiding them through a body scan exercise: focus attention mindfully on different parts of the body. After a body scan, the therapist can address the increased awareness of body signals with questions such as 'Where in your body are you feeling tension now?'

During treatment, patients first learn to focus on everyday physical experiences, such as breathing or muscle tension. This helps them to build awareness and tolerance of physical sensations. This is followed by the exploration of previously avoided bodily experiences, as a gradual build-up is necessary to avoid overwhelm and disruption. This process promotes the ability to understand and integrate physical signals, which is essential for self-regulation, body awareness and self-awareness.

5.2.3   Learning to become aware of inner experiences

Next, the therapist can reflect with the patient on the inner experiences he or she is having. Again, we keep in mind the way in which the patient's inner processes can be expressed through the body and read the language of the patient's body. As we focus the patient's attention on their inner experiences, we keep in mind different categories of inner experiences, such as

- Emotions/feelings
- Thoughts
- Beliefs
- Intentions
- Memories
- Wishes
- Needs
- Motives
- Tendencies
- Fantasies
- Images

One of the first points of attention when reflecting on patient's inner experiences is the internal representation of a bodily sensation. We ask our patients to reflect on a physical sensation and to express their experience of it with a shape, material, colour, sound, pitch, movement, etc. For example: 'If you focus on this pain in your back, what shape do you experience with it? And what colour do you think belongs to it?' It can also be very helpful to use symbols and metaphors that represent the inner experience of a body signal (see also Section 5.2.6 and Section 6.6.2).

Examples of asking about other inner experiences:

- 'If you now put your attention upon what is happening inside you, what thoughts are you experiencing?'
- 'If you put your attention on the pain in your leg, what emotion do you feel at the moment?'
- 'Now that you are aware of the restlessness in your legs, what desire are you experiencing?'
- 'What memory do you have when you're paying attention to your trembling hands?'
- 'When you stand still and focus on what is passing through you, what images do you notice?'
- 'What desire goes with that heavy feeling in your head'?
- 'This tiredness in your arms and legs, what or who does it remind you of'?
- 'What images do you have'?
- 'What tendency do you have?'.
- 'How do you feel this in your body?'

The therapist can draw attention to a physical sensation and ask about the patient's inner experience of it. The therapist can also focus attention on an emotion, memory, thought or tendency and then ask about the bodily experience associated with it at that moment. During the course of treatment, patients first learn to reflect on everyday inner experiences, such as thoughts, emotions and memories. This helps them develop awareness and tolerance for their inner world. Then the previously avoided inner experiences are explored, because a gradual build-up is necessary to prevent overwhelm and disruption.

5.2.4   Learning to extend attention

The aim is for patients not only to consciously pay attention to their physical and psychological response, but also to stay with their attention for some time with their experience and tolerate it. This is the realm of mindfulness: to be in the 'here and now', to be aware from moment to moment, with flexible attention to both inner experiences and physical sensations, even when these are accompanied by negative sensations. It is an active process of openness and acceptance. The therapist can introduce mindfulness into a conversation: 'Let's take a moment to notice your anger and how it feels in your body . . . (silence)'. The patient's mindfulness can also be enhanced by the many exercises offered in the mindfulness literature, which are well compatible with B-MBT.

5.2.5   Mirroring the patient

Although in B-MBT we focus on all inner experiences such as thoughts, memories and tendencies, there is a particular emphasis here on emotions. The most basic way to become aware of emotions is through mirroring. After reading the patient's bodily expressions, we always keep in mind which bodily expression we interpret as an expression of an emotion. We then mirror our findings back to the patient: 'I see you clenching your fists' (the therapist emphatically demonstrates this with his own fists) 'and I wonder what emotions you are experiencing. Could it be anger?'

In mirroring emotions, we focus our attention mainly on the physical expression of what are called proto-emotions: the first stirrings of emotions that are expressed mainly physically and that the patient does not yet experience as emotions. These are subtle physical expressions, such as a small change in facial expression or a subtle change in posture or movement. Mirroring physical expression and (pro-) emotions is an essential intervention of B-MBT. It is based on mirroring as the earliest form of emotional learning between caregiver and child. It is also a powerful tool for adults in learning to recognise their own emotional physicality.

The therapist clearly shows that he is not mirroring his own inner experience but that of the patient. In his mirroring he shows that it is his interpretation of what is happening inside the patient. In this 'marked mirroring' we may, for example, magnify the clenching of the fists a little to illustrate what we have noticed. Mirroring is a form of exploration when patients themselves have little awareness of what they are experiencing physically or mentally. Here we assume that emotions can be expressed through the body in many ways, but that they are often expressed through facial expressions, glance, hand and arm movements. In verbal and non-verbal mirroring, for example, we might say: 'When I look at your eyes' (the therapist mimics the patient's eyes, magnifying them a little) 'I get the impression that you are full of sadness'. We can enhance the effect of a marked reflection by asking patients to perceive the reflection clearly. For example, we can ask: 'What emotions do you see in my posture, facial expression, eye gaze and movements?' Or the therapist can ask the patient to repeat the mirrored posture and ask: 'How does that feel?', 'What emotion goes with that?', 'What word comes to mind?'

Although marked mirroring mainly concerns the patient's emotions, we can also direct attention to other internal phenomena such as thoughts, needs, tendencies or images. After a marked mirroring we can also ask: 'What thoughts accompany this posture? What tendency do you feel with this movement? What images do you get with this facial expression?' Once the patients have gained some awareness of their emotions through marked mirroring, the therapist can ask them about their emotions without mirroring.

5.2.6   Increasing emotional self-awareness

Awareness of (symbolic) images

As we saw earlier in this book (Chapter 3), the awareness of emotions proceeds in part through the perception of physical signals. These lead through (symbolic) images such as dreams, fantasies, metaphors and memories, to words and narratives through which we communicate emotions to others. So, to stimulate emotional awareness in patients, we should ask them to focus their attention on bodily signals and sensations and ask for images, memories, symbols or metaphors. For example, a patient might focus on their back pain and get an image of the bars of a prison. Without explaining the metaphor, we ask him to concentrate on it some time. It is only then that they are asked if they can put anything about it into words. With this method, patients may be able to say only a few words at first, or just describe the image: 'It feels like a prison' or 'I get a picture of an angry face and I hear someone screaming'. Slowly the words that express the emotions, such as despair or powerlessness, begin to emerge. By putting an emotion into words in the here and now, the patient can experience what previously had no words or attention, but was contained in their body. This can bring a tremendous sense of relief and awareness. After the tears, a form of peace and inner space can emerge (Nicolai, 2017a).

Awareness of action tendencies

Another aspect of awareness of emotions is the tendency to act on them. For some patients it is important to ask: 'What bodily tendency are you experiencing now?' or 'What does your body want to do now?' For example, a patient who feels the need to lie down on the floor can become aware that he feels helpless.

Awareness of basic emotions

If patients are still having difficulty recognising their own emotions, we can also point out five basic emotions: anxious, sad, happy, angry and ashamed. When asking about their emotions, we can then suggest that they first check which of the basic emotions comes closest to their experience. In the course of treatment, however, we will also need to pay attention to the differentiation of emotions. For example, we might ask patients to focus on the distinction between sad and moved and the physical sensations associated with each.

Shift to cognitive mentalization when emotions are temporarily intolerable

If patients fear that their emotions are irrevocable, that they will never go away, it is important to emphasise the dynamic side of emotions. We can explain to patients that emotions are temporary and will subside when the trigger is gone or the message from the emotional system is understood. Emotions come and go (Nicolai, 2017a). It is therefore important to ask not only about the nature of the emotions, but also about their intensity, and to repeat this regularly: 'On a scale of 0 to 10, how strong is your anxiety right now?' For patients with a hyperactive attachment style and those who are in an equivalence mode, asking directly about emotions may be too overwhelming. Then, when physically expressing emotions, we can focus more on thought patterns, own and others' beliefs, and intentions. Or we can ask for a change of perspective, such as 'If your best friend was here, what would he say about this experience?' In this way we move from the affective component of mentalizing to the cognitive component.

5.2.7   Verbal labelling of inner experiences

People with PPS may have difficulty recognising and acknowledging their own inner experiences. For example, they may not yet be able to distinguish between a thought, an emotion, a memory or a wish. If the patient is still unable to articulate what they are experiencing inside, the therapist can help them to identify the different inner experiences by marking them. For example, if a patient is repeatedly misunderstood by a friend because of his physical condition, he might say, 'I'm fed up with it'. The therapist can mark the inner experience with, 'Inside you are experiencing a desire for his prejudice to stop'. If a patient with chronic fatigue expresses hopelessness and says, 'It will never be all right again', the therapist can respond, 'You are experiencing the feeling of hopelessness and you notice the thought, "It will never be all right again."'

If patients are more used to focusing on their mind, the therapist can also help them to identify different types of thoughts, such as worrying, analysing, thinking of solutions, planning, thinking back or catastrophic thoughts. For example, if a patient with recurrent paralysis symptoms says, 'This is terrible', the therapist can mark: 'You are having a catastrophic thought that says this is terrible'. It is not uncommon for patients to encounter problematic inner experiences precisely by tuning in on their inner life. The therapist can mark these in terms of ambivalence, contradiction, conflict or dilemma, e.g.: 'I see that you are experiencing a contradiction inside: on the one hand, you notice the tendency to stand up for yourself; on the other hand, you experience the thought: "That might hurt him, and I don't want that."'

5.2.8   Attention to 'don't know yet' experiences

In B-MBT, the therapist focuses less on the unconscious and more on the 'almost conscious' experiences of the patient. Furthermore, we assume that the patient's inner self is opaque and therefore difficult to perceive directly, both for the patient and for the therapist. The exploration of physical and mental reactions will therefore, especially in the beginning, involve the patient not knowing for sure and trying to find words. The therapist then gives the patient space to not know yet. For example, when we ask a patient, 'What does the pain in your leg feel like?' the patient may respond, 'I don't know, it's like . . . it's on the tip of my tongue, but I don't know . . .' The therapist tolerates, empathises with and validates the 'not-yet-knowing' by saying, for example, 'You don't quite know what you're feeling. It's hard to find the right words. I can imagine'. The therapist also tries to allow his own 'not-yet-knowing'. For example, a patient may suddenly slump in his chair without the therapist being able to guess what that means. The therapist might say, 'I notice that you are slumped in your chair. I'm not quite sure what that means. What's going on inside you?' Further joint exploration may then bring some more clarity.

5.2.9 Emphasising being perceptive

The therapist addresses the patient as someone who is curious about physical sensations and inner experiences. He emphasises that he sees the patient as someone who can be an observer of his own physical and inner reactions: 'I have been thinking about you and what you are seeing, hearing, noticing', or 'I realise that I am curious about what thoughts you are noticing in yourself this time'. Optionally, the therapist can reinforce the patient's awareness with statements such as, 'I notice how well you can perceive your thoughts, bodily sensations and emotions now'.

5.2.10   Listening, asking open questions, probing, summarising

The therapist listens attentively and respectfully to the patient's story, observing his (physical) expression. He tries to establish an open dialogue, using different interview techniques. Open questions are preferred. These are questions to which more than one answer is possible. So not, 'Are you feeling well?' but 'How do you feel now?' or 'What are you experiencing in your back now?' or 'What is going through your mind?' Open-ended questions invite more elaboration than closed questions. We can ask further questions if the patient does not give a clear answer, is vague or if something is just not clear to us. If the patient responds to the therapist's question 'What do you feel in your back right now?' with 'It just goes its way', the therapist can ask further questions: 'Where exactly in your back do you feel the pain now?' To validate what the patient has said and to emphasise that we have heard what the patient has said, we use summaries. These give an overview and order to what the patient has just told us. If a patient gives a detailed description of different situations with chest pain and all sorts of associated anxieties, the therapist can summarise: 'You often feel pain in your chest, including now, and you are afraid that something is wrong with your heart'.

5.2.11   Giving intrinsic value to bodily and inner experiences

The therapist's way of questioning and commenting acknowledges, accepts, confirms and validates the patient's experiences. The therapist confirms that the personal perception of bodily signals and the inner experience is a valuable reality in itself, which he acknowledges and respects. In order to accept and validate the patient's experience, it is necessary for the therapist to tolerate and make space for both the patient's response and what it evokes in the therapist. Only when the therapist tolerates and acknowledges his own reaction to the patient can he really validate the patient's experience and say, for example, 'I can see that you are really in a lot of pain', or 'You are really very tired and feeling gloomy'. Validating the patient's experience has a supportive aspect as in, 'That seems also difficult to me ' or in 'I can well imagine that'.

5.2.12   Giving an 'I' message

The idea is that we give our feedback (like a verbal reflection) in the form of an 'I' message. We name our observations and experiences with this patient as our personal impression: 'I see . . .' 'I notice . . .' 'I feel . . .' 'I notice that I think . . .'. So not: 'You are angry', but 'I have the impression that you are angry'. The 'I' message thus expresses a personal impression and not 'the only possible truth', because this could lead to a mode of non-mentalization in the patient. For example, if the therapist notices that the patient has a hunched posture and gets the idea that the patient is sad, the therapist could say, non-mentalized without the 'I' message, 'You are sad'. This can lead the patient to believe 'I am sad because the therapist said so', which blocks body-oriented mentalizing.

By using an 'I' message, the therapist shows that he can also be an observer of his own physical and inner experiences: 'When I see you sitting hunched over like that, I notice that "she is sad" runs through my mind. I notice through my breathing that this moves me'. So with an 'I' message we are not only giving feedback, we are also a model for the patient to start giving more 'I' messages themselves.

5.2.13   Putting oneself in the patient's shoes

The therapist imaginatively puts himself in the patient's situation. He applies a per- spective shift by asking himself what physical sensations and inner experiences he would undergo in the patient's own situation. For example: 'If I were to put myself in your shoes at this moment, I can imagine feeling tension in my arms and hands, feeling powerless and thinking, "Does this match what you are experiencing at this moment?"' With such an empathic response, we help patients to ask themselves what they are really experiencing. Is it as the therapist imagines? Or something else? We also distinguish between what we would experience in this situation and what the patient is experiencing, which may not be the same. Empathy is especially evident when we notice and verbalise emotions or thoughts in our patients that we would not have at that moment or in a similar situation.

5.2.14   Noticing and naming incongruences

The therapist addresses inconsistent verbal and nonverbal behaviour. The therapist looks for inconsistencies between what the patient says and what he shows, for example through muscle tone, facial expressions, tone of voice, posture, gestures or movement. We can highlight incongruences by naming them: 'You say you are not angry and at the same time I see you frowning and clenching your fists'. With the aim of mentalizing, incongruities can be noticed, named, mirrored or explored. This could then be the start of a further exploration of a physical sensation: 'What are you experiencing in your fists right now?'

5.2.15 Strengthening the connection between body and mind

Exploration also involves helping the patient to become aware of the connection between a physical sensation and an inner experience. For example, the therapist might note: 'I notice that you feel tension in your arms and that you are angry inside. Could there be a connection between these two things?' One can also help the patient to explore the body-mind connection with questions such as, 'Let's see to what extent the pain in your stomach occurs when you are worried about your mother'. It could also involve a connection in time: 'Could the fact that you are so tired now be a reaction to the intense emotions you experienced yesterday?' We have to be careful that patients do not become overly sensitive to the possible suggestive effect of such questions. Patients may also tell us what they think we want to hear, for example, 'Now that you mention it, I am indeed tired because I was so sad and angry yesterday'. We should also be alert to possible pseudo-mentalizing or hypermentalizing, with excessive rationalising and intellectualising about mind-body connections without actually making the connection.

5.2.16 'Stop and stand still'

When exploring the patient's 'here and now' state, the therapist can use the explicit intervention of 'stop and stand still'. In a respectful way, the therapist stops the conversation or an exercise when the patient is no longer body mentalizing and addresses current body signals and inner experiences: 'Stop, let's see what's happening now. What are you noticing in your body right now?' Or: 'Stop, let's see what's happening inside you right now. What feelings are you experiencing right now?' We can accompany the 'stop and stand still' intervention with a slight lifting of the hand with the palm facing forward towards the patient. This is similar to what a police officer does when asking us to stop in traffic. Allen and colleagues (2008) call this the 'mentalizing hand'. This is not meant to be a punitive gesture, but a suggestion to move on to exploration.

Stop and stand is a particularly powerful tool to use when the patient moves into non-mentalization. For example, when the patient switches to firm opinions or rational statements, starts an emotionless story, or makes unclear or confusing statements. In order to 'stop and stand still', we must have the willingness to interrupt the patient immediately. Otherwise, the moment when non-mentalization occurs in the patient may be long past and difficult to recall.

However, many therapists find it difficult to interrupt the patient. After all, in everyday social situations, it can be perceived as rude to interrupt, and we do not want to hurt the patient by being unkind. However, it is important to interrupt in a friendly, respectful but firm way with a 'stop and stand still'. We can raise our hand and say, 'May I interrupt you?' or 'May I ask you something about this?' If the patient agrees, we can follow up with, 'There is something what is still unclear to me. Can we take a moment to reflect on what you are experiencing in your body right now?'

5.2.17 'Stop and go back'

In 'stop and go back' the therapist and patient explore what happened earlier in the session when the mentalizing stopped. Again the therapist may use the 'mentalizing hand': 'Stop, let's look back at what just happened when you started talking about the argument you had with your partner yesterday. What body signals did you experience and what else was going on inside you at the time?' This is like 'rewinding the film of a recent moment', starting just before the patient stopped mentalizing.

Stopping and going back is also appropriate when emotions or bodily sensations become uncontrollably intense. One can then go back to the moment within the session just before the emotions or bodily sensations became overwhelming. In order to re-explore the process that took place in a mentalizing way, we can say: 'Stop, before your emotions/body sensations get higher, I think it's important to go back to the moment when . . .' Particularly with patients with PPS, we can also use 'stop and go back' to look back to a recent moment outside the session when the patient was bothered by increasing physical symptoms and ask: 'Just before this started, what did you notice about your body? What emotion did you feel then? What was going through your mind?'

5.2.18 Explore the absoluteness of thoughts and change perspective

B-MBT wants to help patients explore the absoluteness of their way of seeing the world in order to open up to different perspectives. One way to do this is with simple questions like, 'Is there also another interpretation possible? Is that so? Are there other possibilities?' These short questions help to soften the absoluteness of thoughts without immediately directing the conversation.

We can also ask more directly for other perspectives. Questions about changing perspective related to persons, time or place can help patients develop more flexibility in their mental representations and gain new insights into their experiences. This can help patients see their symptoms not as fixed or unchangeable, but as dynamic and open to influence. Here are a few examples:

'Suppose you meet yourself in a year's time. How would you feel about how you are dealing with your symptoms now?' This can help develop more hope and realistic goals.

'How do your symptoms feel when you are at your favourite campsite in Italy?' This supports the realisation of how context influences the perception of symptoms.

'Suppose you were the doctor, and you had a patient with exactly your symptoms. What would you think or recommend?' This could help us to look at our symptoms less from a place of fear and more from a place of reason.

Asking for a change in perspective is a very powerful tool against the absoluteness of someone's point of view. For patients with PPS, however, a change of perspective can also have unwanted effects. Asking for a change of perspective can, for example, lead to a weakening of the connection with one's own body. One may begin to put oneself in another person's shoes without reflecting on one's own physical and inner experiences. Patients may also experience excessive feelings of guilt, shame or powerlessness when they switch perspectives with others. For patients with a history of severe trauma, perspective-shifting may also evoke intense resistance or overwhelm them. In patients with a poorly integrated self-image, a dissociative disorder or severe attachment problems, a perspective shift that is too rapid or too far-reaching can lead to confusion or depersonalisation. We must also be aware that with some patients a request for a change in perspective mainly evokes a cognitive response, while they avoid reflecting on their own emotional experience.

To achieve the right effect, it is important that questions about perspective shifts go hand in hand with questions about the patient's own physical and inner experiences in the here and now. For example, patients can be asked to maintain good contact with their own body by briefly feeling their feet on the floor or observing their breathing. It is best to end a change of perspective by returning to one's own perspective, e.g, 'How does it feel to look back on this now? What do you feel in your body now?' This can help to integrate both perspectives without the patient losing himself.

5.2.19 Exploring when physical symptoms or inadequate illness behaviour worsen

When working with people with PPS, the therapist will regularly experience an exacerbation of physical symptoms. The therapist may be tempted to respond with behavioural advice. However, the primary aim of B-MBT is for patients to become more aware of their own and others' bodily signals and inner experiences. When symptoms worsen, we can focus the patient's attention on what physical and mental reactions are triggering the worsening of symptoms in the patient and in ourselves.

When our patients lapse into inappropriate illness behaviours in session or outside, we can ask them to explore its background. Sickness behaviours common in PPS include: excessive doctor visits, avoidance of activities, over-activity, excessive seeking of help or reassurance, excessive seeking and testing of diagnoses, frequent accosting, obsessive monitoring, and active checking of symptoms and of the body.

The idea is not to focus initially on correcting the pathological behaviour, but on the physical sensations and inner experiences involved. A starting point can be to ask about the impact of the behaviour on the patient himself: 'I wonder what feelings you had when you overexerted yourself', or 'What did you notice in your body and inner life when you stayed in bed all day?' The therapist can also explore with the patient what physical sensations and inner symptoms preceded the illness behaviour. For example, with a patient who searches excessively for diagnoses on the Internet, the therapist might say: 'Let's think about what you experienced in your body just before you sat down at the computer . . . and what thoughts went through your mind . . .' The aim here is not to point out to the patient all the possible causes of his or her behaviour. The therapist assumes that inappropriate illness behaviour is a sign of intense emotions, stress, thoughts or physical sensations in a relational context. The therapist tries to increase the patient's awareness of these physical sensations and inner states. In this way, patients can better tolerate intense emotions, stress and physical symptoms without automatically switching to inappropriate illness behaviour. Once patients can leave behind their automatic reflex on experiencing physical symptoms and become aware of the background of their illness behaviour, they can eventually more easily switch to consciously different behaviour.

If a patient has dealt with worsening symptoms in a body mentalizing way, without falling into inappropriate illness behaviour, the therapist may acknowledge or praise the patient for this. For example, a patient with chronic abdominal pain may have been an automatic caller to the family doctor's office when the symptoms worsened. She may now refrain from calling, for example, after a good conversation with a friend, and decide to wait and see how her stomach feels tomorrow. The therapist can compliment her on this: 'How good that you didn't follow your first instinct and call the GP's office, but first talked about your physical and inner experiences'.

5.2.20 Continue to explore in case of change or start of medication

It is obvious that when medication is prescribed, all attention is focused on how it works, both for the patient and for the practitioner. This can block the process of body-oriented mentalizing. The art is to prescribe medication and continue to use B-MBT interventions. Therefore, during the consultation, the doctor will not only prescribe the medication and discuss its effects. He can continue to explore the patient's perceptions of physical and mental experiences when identifying, prescribing, taking and discussing the effects of the medication. For example, the doctor might ask, 'What's going through your mind now that I'm telling you I'm going to prescribe you a different medication? And what do you notice in your body right now?' Or we can mirror: 'I see your eyes getting bigger' (open our eyes wide). 'I wonder what's going through your mind now that we're going to try a different medication'.

If necessary, we can explain to the patient that for the medicine to work properly it must be used with attention to both body and mind. It is not just about the biological effect of the drug, but also about what a person tends to perceive, think and feel in their own body. And it is also about the influence of mutual cooperation when prescribing medication. It is a sum of these three factors we can explain.

5.3 Exploration of the therapist's own body signals and inner experiences, and being transparent about them

During B-MBT, the therapist is reflective about his own bodily signals and inner experiences in the here and now, and in contact with the patient: 'What am I feeling in my body right now? What tendency, thoughts and emotions am I having right now?' As he does this, he reveals this to the patient: 'As I hear you say this, I notice a feeling of tightness in myself and I think, "What is happening to me inside right now?" Then I notice that your story touches me, and I think, "How alone you must have felt at that moment."' Self-disclosure is a core element of B-MBT. According to Wallin (2010), mentalization-based therapy without self-disclosure is like 'playing the piano with one hand'.

Our transparency can consciously and unconsciously encourage patients to practice similar openness. Many patients want to find out how safe it is to acknowledge, know, feel and articulate what they are personally experiencing on a physical and mental level (Wallin, 2010). By being transparent and subjective, the therapist tries to signal that it is safe enough to be open about subjective experiences in the here and now. In doing so, the therapist is probably also signalling that being transparent is safer than the patient had assumed. Self-disclosure also underlines the fact that the therapist himself has physical and mental experiences in relation to the patient. In this way, the patient learns the impact they have on others and can check their assumptions about what the therapist is experiencing.

Transparency has two aspects: openness to ourselves (self-awareness) and openness to the patient (self-disclosure). Both aspects are important. We should not take this willingness lightly. As therapists, we may not be used to paying attention to what our body signals are telling us about our emotions and motivations when in contact with the patient. This may stem from our training, which tends to emphasise paying attention to the patient's experience. Almost automatically, we assume that becoming aware of physical and mental reactions is mainly for the patient anyway. After all, they have the problems. So we forget our own bodies and our unconscious drives behind our therapeutic interventions. If the therapist is unwilling to really reflect on himself in the here and now, the suggestion of openness (pseudo-openness) not only has little effect, but can also hinder the mentalization process.

The therapist acknowledges that he is part of the therapy with his transparency. He experiences emotional excitement, agitation, relaxation, a lump in the throat, fear, or emotion and can reflect on this with the patient at the same time. He is both participant and observer; it is like 'standing with one foot in the water and the other on the land.' (Wallin, 2010) Our transparency is obviously not about working out our own problems. Nor is our openness about our private lives at home. It is about openness about the here-and-now experience with the patient in the session. We simply try to be aware of what we are doing and what personal, physical and mental stimuli are involved. We then communicate about this in an pedagogical way with our patients.

Transparency is also a tool in dealing with transference. The therapist tries to be aware of his bodily sensations, thoughts and feelings during therapy and to put them into words. The better he can do this, the better he can get rid of the constraining influence of the transference and relate to the patient more openly, honestly and clearly (Wallin, 2010). A more detailed description of this can be found in Chapter 7. Before going through the interventions related to transparency, here is an overview of possible goals of transparency in B-MBT:

* To be clear about what is going on in the therapeutic relationship
* To strengthen the therapeutic relationship and establish a bond
* To promote a mutual process of body-oriented mentalizing
* As a therapist remaining in a mentalizing mode
* Transference unravelling
* Patients learn how they influence others (the therapist) in order to understand more about themselves
* Allow patients to test assumptions about what the therapist is experiencing
* Emphasising the reality that the therapist experiences things (physically) in the relation with the patient and that understanding their origin is an aspect of full body-oriented mentalizing

There are several aspects to the therapist reflecting on and revealing his or her own physical and mental experiences in contact with the patient, which we will now discuss.

5.3.1 Explaining transparency

If patients show that they find it strange or even inappropriate that we reveal something about ourselves, it may be necessary to explain that this is part of our method. We can then explain, for example: 'In B-MBT, we assume that how we experience physical symptoms also depends on what we experience in our relationships with significant others, such as loved ones and carers. For example, fatigue may feel different when we are in good company than when we talk about it with a stranger we don't trust. We live with our physical complaints in constant contact with others who influence us and our perception of physical complaints. Learning to mentalize in a body-oriented way therefore means not only noticing what we are experiencing, but also what the therapist is experiencing and how he is responding to us. I will therefore be transparent about what I experience in contact with you'. See also the patient information leaflet in Appendix A.1.

5.3.2 Maintaining a basic pedagogical attitude

Self-disclosure involves a pedagogical and didactic stance. This didactic attitude is physical, mental, affective and relational. It is not about transparency as an end in itself, but about pedagogical transparency.

Openness has also its limits. We always ask ourselves: 'What am I disclosing to this patient in this context, when, why and how?' In such conscious self-disclosure, the therapist tries to be clear, firm but careful (Safran & Muran, 2000). For example, we can formulate a self-disclosure in the form of a question such as: 'I can feel my shoulder muscles tense up as I listen to you and wonder, "What's going on between us? Are you saying something that might make me tense up?"' In this pedagogically coloured transparency, the therapist responds to the patient's possible reaction. Will he or she tolerate the self-disclosure or slip into a mode of non-mentalizing?

Patients who have just started therapy may need more reserve from our side than those who are used to the therapist's self-disclosure. For example, if a female patient tells in a businesslike manner that her boyfriend gave her a bloody nose, the therapist may experience physical disgust and repulsion. The therapist might say, 'As you tell me this, I feel my stomach tighten and I feel strong disgust. I notice that I would even like to turn away and I notice that I feel sorry for what happened to you.\'. If the patient has just started therapy, he can make the self-disclosure smaller and less profound. For example: 'When you say that I feel a reaction in my stomach', the therapist points to his stomach.

5.3.3 Reading your own body and mind

If we are ready for self-disclosure, then during our contact with the patient we will direct our attention to our bodily sensations. For example, we can notice changes in our internal body signals, sensations of the skin and muscles and joints, the general state of the body, posture, movements, physical tension or relaxation or tendency to move. By consciously observing changes in our body, we make contact with what is happening to us mentally in contact with the patient. We become aware of our emotions, intentions, needs, desires, fantasies, thoughts, beliefs, memories, images, motives and tendencies. For example, during a conversation we may notice that we are experiencing a slightly oppressive feeling in our head. We allow it to exist and ask ourselves, 'What is going on in there right now? Is there something pressing on me in the conversation?' This puts us in a body mentalizing mode and helps us to understand not only ourselves but also the patient better. We can feel what contact we are having with the patient, and we can better sense what intervention is appropriate.

5.3.4 Accepting your experiences

It is important that we as therapists accept our current physical and inner reactions. It is not about good or bad, or that things should be different from how they are now. We try to ignore attempts to change the intensity, frequency or form of possible unpleasant (physical) experiences. We open up to what we perceive in ourselves, we allow personal experience without fighting it. This opening or welcoming helps us to mentalize in a body-oriented way. Avoiding what we perceive in ourselves, not opening to it, fighting with it, can be an obstacle in the process of body-oriented mentalizing. Everything we perceive in ourselves is therefore of value and a source for body-oriented mentalizing. We take on the role of an objective, inquiring observer of our own experiences: 'I am experiencing pain in my neck, let me think about it. What exactly does it feel like? And what emotions and thoughts am I experiencing?' It can also be that we are willing to be transparent, but are not yet sufficiently used to being open to our own experiences. Regular practice of mindfulness, acceptance and self-compassion exercises can help.

5.3.5 Reflective naming of one's own body signals and inner experiences

The therapist is transparent by telling the patient about his current body signals. He names his experience with a reflective self-disclosure such as, 'I see you sitting in this position and notice a heavy feeling in my upper body and a sad feeling'. As in mirroring (as part of exploration of the patient's experiences), the therapist gives 'I' messages and reflects on his own experience:

- 'I notice that I have the thought . . .'
- 'I realise I feel tension in my neck'
- 'I am experiencing sadness'

By using the phrases 'I notice', 'I realise', 'I feel', etc. the therapist makes it clear that he is aware of his own perception. This allows him to name the simultaneous occurrence of bodily and inner experiences, implying the connection between the two, e.g.: 'I feel a heavy sensation in my legs and notice that my attention is fading'.

5.3.6 Using one's own physical expression

There is a physical side to being transparent. We are not only open about our physical sensations in words such as 'I feel tension in my shoulders and neck' but we also illustrate this non-verbally. For example, we pull our shoulders up and our neck together. Because it is particularly difficult for people with severe PPS to recognise emotions in body signals, because they do not feel them or do not feel them at the same time, the therapist emphasises emotions non-verbally. For example, when the therapist says, 'I am experiencing sadness right now', he shows a sad face and hangs his head forward. Here the therapist tries to be as congruent as possible: what he expresses physically and verbally is the same. The therapist's bodily expression naturally illustrates his inner state and thus makes the body-mind connection clear. The idea here is not to shoot into pretend mode and start acting.

We should try to follow in our physical expression what our body tends to do when sadness, anger or fear arises.

5.3.7   Recognising and verbalising a tendency to move away or to get closer

Transparency is intended to strengthen the therapeutic relationship into an attachment relationship. This includes mutual physical tendencies to approach and withdraw. Both tendencies are part of relationship building. Reflecting on this is part of the therapeutic process. We therefore try to be aware of whether the patient's behaviour triggers in us a physical and/or mental tendency to approach or withdraw. We then reveal our experience, e.g. 'Now that you are talking about how alone you often feel, I notice that I get a warm feeling and feel the inclination to go and sit next to you'. Or, 'Now that you are showing how angry you are and making kicking movements with your legs, I notice that I am involuntarily inclined to move backwards a little to distance myself'. A little later we can say, 'Now that we are talking together about your anger, I understand it better and feel closer to you'.

The therapist will also ask the patient about his or her physical or mental tendency to approach the therapist or withdraw from him, especially in emotional questions about the relationship between the two. We should be aware of both the physically felt tendency to approach and withdraw as well as the mental reaction. The latter is more about thoughts, emotions and feelings such as feeling distant or aversion or thinking of other things.

5.3.8   Recognising automatic mirroring processes

Because of our empathy, our physical experiences can also (unconsciously) reflect what the patient is (unconsciously) expressing physically. We may feel an increased heart rate, tension and anxiety when we (unconsciously) perceive that our patient is anxious. So our physical and emotional perception can vibrate with the physical and emotional state of the patient. It can be part of the therapy to explore whether our mental and physical reactions are due to empathy and physical co-vibration, or whether they have some other background. For example, do we become anxious in the presence of a patient with intense fears because we are co-vibrating with their fears, or because we are afraid of failing to respond appropriately? If co-vibrating, the therapist might say, for example, 'I notice that my body is vibrating with your fear, I can feel it in my throat'. Otherwise, the therapist might say: 'I can sense that you are anxious, and I can also sense that I would like to help you relax, and that I feel a little insecure and wonder if I can do that now'.

5.3.9   Breathing as a tool for awareness of one's own body

If, in contact with our patients, we are overwhelmed by uncomfortable feelings such as tiredness or restlessness, this can make it difficult to be open to our own experiences and those of the patient. Especially when we are simply not feeling comfortable in our own skin, it can be difficult to focus our attention on our experiences in the here and now. Then a simple, quick tool can help: focusing our attention on our breath. This allows us to reconnect directly with our physical and inner experiences in the here and now. The aim here is not to control the breathing. We simply pay attention to the movements of inhalation and exhalation where they are most clearly felt, and let them go as they go, without directing them.

5.3.10   Establishing a sense of openness and transparency in advance

Paying attention to one's experience in the here and now is a skill. The therapist can practice this skill regularly, for example through mindfulness exercises. The therapist can also get into the mood for body- oriented mentalizing immediately before the session by paying attention to his or her own bodily signals and inner experiences for a few minutes. It is certainly useful to think about the patient (e.g. by visualising or evoking the patient's voice). If the last session ended in a non-mentalizing mood, the therapist could recall this situation before the next session starts and focus on bodily signals and inner experiences. Then, at the beginning of the session, the therapist can be open about what he experienced during this 'stop and go back' regarding the last session. And if we are looking forward to a certain expected situation in the next session, we can also think about it beforehand in order to notice our physical and mental reactions in advance.

5.3.11   Creating space for transparency: 'Stop and stand still'

When we are ready to be transparent, we may find it difficult to focus our attention on our own bodily signals and inner experiences because we naturally keep our mind focused on the patient and their current condition. For example, we may find ourselves puzzling over the right interventions to make. How can therapists create an island of attention to their own present experience in the session?

The therapist can use a 'stop and stand still' intervention. When the patient is talking about how their partner reacts to their fatigue, the therapist can say: 'Stop, I want to take a moment to reflect on what is happening to me right now as you are telling me this'. We can then be quiet for a few moments and focus our attention on ourselves. We may want to close our eyes to consciously internalise the current therapy situation: how does the patient impress us physically and emotionally? When the patient speaks, what facial expressions and gestures attract our attention? What do we experience in our body and inner self? Then we share our experiences: 'When I think about what you're telling, I feel an oppressive feeling in my chest and ask myself, "What emotion am I experiencing right now? Am I experiencing fear?"' So, the therapist, despite any embarrassment, takes the space to really reflect on one's experience in the here and now before making a self-disclosure about it. Again, our experience is that if the therapist uses this intervention with determination for self-reflection, the patient will do the same and thus learn to mentalize in a more body-oriented way.

5.3.12   Creating space for transparency: 'Stop and go back'

Self-disclosure through 'stop and stand still' is most effective when it occurs in the moment, i.e. when it is directly related to an event in the meeting. However, it is not always easy to decide when is the right time for a self-disclosure. Sometimes it is also just unavoidable or more convenient to respond in hindsight and come back to the situation such as, 'I notice that you regularly have trembling attacks in your hands in the session. I notice afterwards that although we just continue our conversation, my attention keeps going to your hands and I then get restless and ask myself, "What's happening right now?"'

The therapist can also reflect immediately after the session on a situation in the session in which he had difficulty with body-oriented mentalizing. We then recall such a situation and reflect on what we feel physically and mentally about it. Reflection after the session is recommended anyway. Where were difficult moments when we could have used body-oriented mentalizing? If necessary, we can ask a colleague to help us look back. We can also choose to bring up situations where we found it difficult to mentalize in a body-centred way in peer intervision or supervision at a later date.

5.3.13   Taking the level of arousal into account

Of course, the therapist continues to monitor the patient's level of arousal. If it is too high, he may make a self-disclosure that has a relaxing or validating effect such as, 'It really touches me to see you so upset'. A self-disclosure that encourages exploration such as, 'I notice that I am now experiencing tension in my whole body', might be better left out at this point; it might be too unsafe for the patient. It is better to first ensure that the patient's level of arousal is brought back into the tolerance zone through structuring interventions such as summarising, giving reality value to the patient's experience and supportive comments. A short relaxation, movement or mindfulness exercise may be helpful.

In B-MBT, it is essential that the therapist also monitors whether he himself remains within his own 'window of tolerance'. When the therapist notices signs of being pushed outside this window—such as emotional overwhelm, intense stress, highly aroused—it is important to pause and regulate. This might involve grounding techniques, bringing attention to one's own breathing or consciously relaxing the muscles. Being open about this with the patient, in a pedagogical way, can model transparency and emotional regulation. For instance, the therapist might say: 'I notice I'm feeling a bit overwhelmed right now—let me take a short moment to relax so I can really stay present with you'. Such openness can enhance trust and model healthy self-awareness in the therapeutic relationship.

5.3.14   Being transparent about one's own background and motives

The therapist is also transparent about the background of his or her inner experiences: 'I feel that I want to help you'. Our physical and mental reactions, such as tension or anger, may come from our desire to help, to support, to advise, to clarify or to break through problems. It promotes transparency to name the motive behind our statements and the background to any negative feelings, such as 'I want to help you' or 'I feel I want to suggest a solution'. This allows our patients to better understand our internal and physical reactions.

5.3.15   Openness about one's own shortcomings in body-related mentalizing

B-MBT also requires the therapist to reflect honestly on his own 'non-mentalizing errors' and how they may have affected the patient. For example, the therapist might say: 'I see now that my reaction was thoughtless and completely ignored what was really going on with you and me at that moment. I can imagine that you were stunned by my sudden reaction'. In this way the therapist provides a transparent example of his own limitations in body-oriented mentalizing. He sends the message that acknowledging mistakes and reporting shortcomings is part of therapy.

5.3.16   Revealing unpleasant feelings

The therapist should also be transparent about less pleasant feelings, such as indifference, irritation, boredom or anger. It is understandable that we may find it difficult to acknowledge, let alone reveal, difficult feelings in contact with the patient. However, hiding unpleasant physical and mental reactions to what is happening in the session can be counterproductive to the therapy. As a result, they can intensify and eventually take on uncontrollable forms. Suppressed anger, for example, can bubble to the surface and echo in our questions and comments without us being aware of it or wanting it to. The reluctance to reveal negative emotions may be related to our image of what a therapist should be like: helpful, unaffected, sympathetic, strong and authoritative. However, when experiencing difficult feelings, we can also remember that, as in a good friendship, sharing them can deepen the relationship. Therefore, when disclosing uncomfortable feelings, the therapist chooses words that express the desire to deepen the contact. For example, when noticing one's own boredom, the therapist might say: 'I notice that I have a lot of trouble paying attention to what you are saying, my mind wanders, I feel sleepy. It could be that this is all down to me. It could also be because of what is going on between us at the moment. Can you tell me how you are experiencing this conversation right now?'

5.3.17 Transparency in case of transference and countertransference

The therapist pays attention to whether what he is experiencing in the contact with the patient is coming from thinking along with the patient and from empathy. It may be that something else is involved, such as a reaction based on powerful experiences from the therapist's own history, and a strong positive or negative countertransference. Section 7.7 describes how we can deal with transference and countertransference by maintaining an open mutual exchange of bodily and inner experiences with patients.

5.4 Triggering mutual exchange

B-MBT is about the interconnectedness between patient and therapist and, in group therapy, also between patients. This is based on the principle of intersubjectivity: our physical and inner reactions are always somehow connected to and influenced by the physical and mental reactions of other people. For example, a leg that is shaking and trembling violently, and over which the patient has no control during the session, may cause the therapist to feel tense shoulders and feelings of insecurity. If the therapist makes this known, the patient may feel that he is a burden to the therapist, which makes him feel oppressed. Patient and therapist are in a process of mutual influence. This reciprocity is a far-reaching process because of people's innate social orientation. The therapist reinforces reciprocity by encouraging open communication about personal, physical and mental reactions, and mutual contact. This creates a series of reciprocal feedback that reinforce the mutual relationship: 'What are you experiencing in your body now that you hear that I have a lump in my throat?' In this mutual communication we strive for equality. During therapy we make ourselves vulnerable, just like our patients. However, as therapist and patient, we are also unequal in the therapeutic relationship, which is characterised by asymmetry. The therapist offers help, and the patient asks for it. Therapy and the therapeutic relationship revolve around the patient's (physical) symptoms, problems and vulnerabilities, not the therapist's. The therapist's transparency serves the patient's learning process. We as therapists, through our capacity for body-oriented mentalizing, should help the patient to do the same in order to cope better with physical and psychological problems. From this division of roles, help-giver and help-requester, therapist and patient, we seek an equal, congruent, symmetrical emotional alignment through attention to our own and others' bodies and minds. In doing so, we offer patients a relationship that is presumably more attuned, inclusive and collaborative than the relationships that originally formed them (Wallin, 2010).

Therapist and patient listen not only to each other's verbal messages, but perhaps even more to the underlying non-verbal communication. If a patient says in a sad tone that everything is going his way, the therapist will respond to the sad tone. This is not only because non-verbal communication can play a crucial role in transmitting a message in human communication. It is also an expression of the unconscious physical and inner experience that is the focus of B-MBT. Experiences that our patients cannot yet articulate are expressed through non-verbal communication to which the therapist responds physically (unconsciously or consciously). The non-verbal underlying message of mutual communication will influence the patient and therapist and determine their attachment relationship. The art for the therapist is to create an atmosphere in which patients can explore the non-verbal underlying tone of communication and learn to put it into words.

In other therapies, the exploration of nonverbal underlying tones is particularly necessary when the interpersonal relationship is not going well or when there are severe physical or emotional reactions. In B-MBT, the mutual exchange of implicit experiences is an integral part, so that the patient becomes familiar with open communication about personal experiences. The patient can use this skill in other circumstances, such as communicating effectively about physical problems with medical specialists or family members. In encouraging the sharing of personal experiences, we should be aware of a common phenomenon. A significant subgroup of patients with severe PPS tends to put themselves intensively in another's shoes. They can empathise intensively with other people's bodily signals and inner experiences. For example, patients may be overly concerned with the condition of the therapist. Are there signs that the therapist is not feeling well? Are there signs that the therapist is dissatisfied or not interested anymore? Can the patient still do body-oriented mentalization in the face of this monitoring of the therapist? Normally not. After all, body-oriented mentalizing involves focusing on the other person while remaining attentive to one's own bodily signals and inner experiences. This can be very difficult for people with severe PPS. They put themselves in the other person's shoes, but lose awareness of their own bodily signals and inner experiences. Therefore therapist and patient seek the right balance between attention to self and attention to others. All the more reason to be alert to modes of non-mentalization when promoting mutual exchange.

The therapist also pays attention to the patient's 'window of tolerance'. What about the patient's emotional arousal level during the mutual exchange of 'here and now' experiences? If it is too high, the therapist can switch to stress-regulating interventions. If it is too low, then we can intensify the sharing of emotional experiences, for example, around PPS.

What follows now in this chapter is a description of different ways of triggering mutual exchange. The process between therapist and patient in individual B-MBT will be described. However, the techniques can also be used in group B-MBT (see Chapter 9), in reflections during non-verbal group therapy (see Chapter 6) and in systemic B-MBT (see Chapter 10).

5.4.1   Reading each other and sharing observations and reactions

Therapist and patient try to notice each other's body signals in order to understand each other's inner experiences during the sessions. As described earlier in this chapter under 'Exploring the patient's body signals and inner experiences' (Section 5.2), the therapist pays attention to the patient's body signals that indicate emotions or other inner experiences, such as worrying or an inclination to move. He observes, for example, facial expressions, breathing, posture, movements of arms and hands, and listens to rhythm and tone of voice. He then shares his impressions with the patient: 'I see your hands shaking and I get the feeling that you are nervous and the idea that you might be afraid of what is to come'. The therapist will ask the patient to do the same in relation to the therapist's body signals and inner experiences. For example: 'What body signals do you notice about me? And how do you interpret them?' Or 'You think I'm angry now. What body expression of mine tells you that?'

The patient mirrors the therapist's state by describing what physical signs, emotions, thoughts or tendencies he notices in the therapist. The therapist can ask for clarification by non-verbally mirroring and even slightly amplifying this. In interpreting each other's physical expressions and inner states, the therapist again illustrates the opacity of mental states: we can never know someone's physical experiences and inner reactions for sure, but only make well-considered guesses. What the therapist and patient perceive as each other's inner experiences is an interpretation, an assumption, a thought, and not a fixed reality.

The therapist also asks the patient to be aware of his physical and mental reactions to what the therapist is communicating such as, 'Now that you hear that I think you are not having an easy time with all the physical complaints, what do you experience in your body? And what tendency do you notice in yourself now? And what images?' Here the therapist can ask what movement the body would like to make in response, and whether the patient feels a tendency to draw closer or further away from the therapist. For a comprehensive overview of body-oriented points of attention that we can be aware of in our interaction with patients, see Table 6.2 in Section 6.7.2.

5.4.2   Both putting themselves in each other's shoes

A powerful way to change perspective and empathise with each other is to put oneself in the shoes of the other (see also Section 5.2.13). The therapist can regularly try to imagine being in the patient's shoes. What physical sensations does he experience, what emotions does he feel, what thoughts go through his mind? The therapist can ask the patient to do the same and put himself in the therapist's 'here and now' situation: 'Now imagine that you are sitting here in my place and that you are me. What is going through your mind, do you think? And what physical sensations are you experiencing?' By changing perspectives, patients not only learn to empathise with others, but also that they can look at their problems in different ways. This can help them to let go of an overly one-sided focus on their own physical and mental experiences.

A further shift in perspective is to look at yourself from someone else's situation. The therapist can then ask: 'If you were me, what would you notice about how you are sitting there?' This shifts in perspective require a cognitive effort on the part of the patient. It is a form of cognitive mentalization. It can teach patients not to merge with their own emotions, perceptions and beliefs as they make an effort to see the other perspective. In this way one can get, for example, out of an equivalence or teleological mode. Switching perspectives also promotes the development of the observing ego (Lapsley & Woodbury, 2016). Patients can become aware of the difference between what they perceive (such as pain or fatigue) and the perspective from which they perceive it: the perspective of themselves as the observer. But to avoid purely cognitive responses, we should also link perspective change questions to the patient's own current bodily and emotional experiences (see also Section 5.2.18).

5.4.3   Encouraging an 'I' message

We can ask patients to give us feedback in the form of an 'I' message. For example, a patient might say to the therapist: 'I see your shoulders slumped and I get the thought, "He's having a hard time", or I notice that you are weighing your feet up and down, which I interpret as impatience'.

At the very beginning of B-MBT treatment, we explain to the patient the difference between a 'You' message, such as 'You are tense', and an 'I' message, such as 'From what I observe, I have the impression that you . . .'. We explain that mutual feedback is clearer with an 'I' message. We also explain that an 'I' message makes feedback specific by saying what you have objectively observed in the other person. What body signals did you see, what posture, what movements, what facial expression, what breathing, what rhythm of speech, what tone of voice? Then we can explain: 'By being as concrete and objective as possible about what you have observed, the other person will be able to see more quickly what kind of physical expression you mean'. You can try to make your observations as concrete and neutral as possible, without value judgements. So not 'You are tense', but 'I see that you are tense in your shoulders and neck and that you are frowning'. It's about what you actually see, as if you were looking through a camera. Then you use an 'I' message to say what you've inferred from what you've observed about someone's emotions, thoughts, tendencies, needs, etc. This is our subjective perception, our interpretation of reality (the other person's body signals). For example: 'I see that you are pulling up the muscles in your shoulders and neck and that you are frowning' (an observation as objective as possible). I get the idea that you are impatient and unhappy' (subjective perception)'. If the patient forgets the 'I' message during therapy and says, for example, 'You are definitely tired today', the therapist can kindly ask the patient for his impressions in the form of an 'I' message.

5.4.4   Responding to patient feedback

After the patient has told what physical and mental reactions he or she notices in the therapist, the therapist will communicate as transparently and thoughtfully as possible what he or she is physically experiencing, feeling or thinking. If a patient reacts with disbelief, 'I can't believe you're moved by my story', the therapist can ask the patient to observe again. What do they see in the therapist's face? What about the therapist's gestures and posture? And the use of the voice? By asking in a non-judgmental way and paying attention to what the patient perceives, they can learn to notice non-verbal cues even more accurately. Patients can learn that their first automatic interpretation of the therapist's body signals does not correspond to a second, more conscious impression. And they learn that what they think the therapist is experiencing is not the same as what the therapist is experiencing (reality checking).

However, we should also be open to the fact that the patient is paying attention to a body signal and emotion of ours that we were not yet aware of. Of course, we are always open to this possibility and can ask the patient to tell us even more about what they noticed about our body expression. After all, becoming aware of previously unrecognised physical and inner reactions is a mutual process. When responding to the patient's feedback about what they have noticed about us, we can also reflect on how this feedback is now affecting us physically and mentally: 'I notice that my muscles are relaxing, and it moves me that you say that you have the impression that I am a busy therapist'.

5.4.5 Encouraging alternating attention to the other with attention to the self

When we ask patients to give feedback on our bodily expressions, we are asking them to mentalize about the other in a predominantly body-centred way within the 'self versus other' dimension. The pitfall here is that many patients with severe PPS are already inclined to do this, but lose sight of the body-oriented mentalization of their own experience in the process. They must therefore alternate attention to the other person with attention to themselves. For example, the patient may tell us that he notices the therapist's frowning eyebrows and that he perceives this as the therapist's displeasure with him. We can now choose to shift the focus back to what the patient is experiencing in the process. For example, we can ask: "What physical reaction do the frowning eyebrows cause in you?' or 'What emotions do you experience at the idea that I am dissatisfied?'

5.4.6 Emphasising the relational context

The therapist always emphasises the relational context of physical and inner experiences. For example, to a patient who suggests that he might consider seeing another expert in the field of PPS to find out exactly what is causing his symptoms, the therapist might say: 'Does your desire to see another expert perhaps also say something about the relationship we have with each other?' The therapist can also strengthen the relational context by emphasising the 'we' aspect of the therapeutic relationship (Hafkenscheid, 2014): 'I notice that we are analysing together' or 'We can take a closer look together at the tension that you are experiencing again and again'. By emphasising the 'we' aspect, we can metacommunicate with patients about the relationship we have with them, and explore what effect the relationship has on the patient and ourselves: 'How does it affect you that we are circling each other?' In particular, the therapist will also emphasise the relational context of emotions. For example, if a patient suddenly experiences more pain and sadness in the session, the therapist might ask: 'Does this sadness perhaps also say something about how we are engaged together in this therapy?'

5.4.7   Identifying relational patterns

In order to emphasise the relational context, the therapist may also note relational patterns such as, 'Every time you have a pain in your stomach, you think you are doing something wrong. You feel fear and the thought that I am unhappy with you and have to do your best. Then when I tell you something about what I notice about you, such as you putting your hand on your tummy, you do your best for me even more. Do you recognise that this is happening between us?' The therapist can also return to the patient's attachment pattern discussed earlier in the session. For example, we might ask the patient, 'Is this perhaps the avoidance pattern coming back?'

5.4.8   Validating differences

The therapist emphasises the differences in the patient's and his own body signals and inner experiences. We show by our attitude and questions that differences are important. We emphasise the subjectivity of bodily sensations and inner experiences. The therapist shows interest in the differences and presents them as a valuable fact. For example, he might say: 'Look what is happening now. This event is causing you to feel tense muscles and you are getting the idea that "he wants to make life difficult for me and he thinks I'm nothing". And what happens to me? I feel sadness and think: "She's having a hard time. How can I help her?"'

5.4.9   A reflective response to a direct question

The trick with direct questions such as, 'How was your holiday?' or 'You look so pale. Are you ill?' is to respond from a self-reflective position. The therapist clarifies his current physical and mental state in relation to the question (Bateman et al., 2020), e.g. 'I didn't expect that question. I'm getting hot and a bit scared and thinking, "What's appropriate for you to tell now?"' If the therapist does not know the answer to a question or feels uncomfortable with it, he or she will examine his or her own state of mind in the presence of the patient: 'I am not sure what the answer to this question is right now, although I am aware that I am expected to know'. Or: 'There is something in this question that makes me feel uncomfortable answering you. I'm not sure what it is. Can we think about it together for a moment?' (Bateman et al., 2020).

If we do not feel uncomfortable with a direct personal question, a direct answer can also have a therapeutic effect. We then follow our answer with a body-oriented mentalizing question. For example: 'As far as I know, I am not sick right now. What is going through your mind when you hear this? And what do you experience in your body?'

5.4.10   Taking responsibility in discussing mutual problems

The therapist has an initiating, active stance. He takes the initiative to clarify and resolve any mutual problems. If the patient regularly feels very tense and insecure, the therapist asks himself: How can I make him feel insecure now? He then discusses this: 'I hear that you regularly feel tense and insecure. I suggest that we look at this together. Are you feeling tense and insecure now? Do you notice anything about what I am doing or saying now that is related to you feeling tense and insecure?'

5.4.11   Complimenting for body-oriented mentalizing

When patients show signs of body-oriented mentalizing in their interaction with the therapist, the therapist can praise the patient in a friendly way. For example, has the patient discussed an emotionally charged issue with the therapist and reflected on the physical and internal reactions this has triggered in the patient and the therapist? Then the therapist can say: 'How good that you didn't run away and ask for more medication, but that you were able to stay with your own body and inner experiences'! This compliment can strengthen the relationship and increase the patient's confidence. Compliments give patients recognition that they have demonstrated a skill that is important in the relationship and for the purpose of therapy.

5.5   Tailor intervention to mode of (non-)mentalizing

5.5.1   Aligning the therapeutic goal with the level of body-oriented mentalization

There is a certain hierarchy in the different non-mentalizing modes when we consider the extent to which a person is able to mentalize in a body-oriented way.

In general, these modes can be seen as a continuum from the least to the most sophisticated, but still deficient, forms of mental representation. Therapists take this hierarchy into account in their goals of interventions:

Body mode: This is the most primitive form of non-mentalization. There is no distinction between bodily sensations and mental states; feelings are experienced purely physically and not understood as mental experiences. For example, 'My chest feels tight. I'm dying', rather than 'I feel anxious'. Important aims of the interventions are: to become more aware of bodily experiences and to perceive them as less threatening. In this phase, the therapist focuses on the physical experience without looking for other meanings.

Teleological mode: Here there are already some traces of awareness of an inner reality. However, the patient still understands mental content only in terms of observable physical actions and consequences. What is not observable is not recognised as 'real'. For example: 'I must have an abnormal blood test and a diagnosis, otherwise my tiredness is not real'. One of the therapist's areas of focus in this mode is experiencing the body as changeable. Exploration involves experimenting with variations of the body and their effect on the experience of bodily signals. In order to trigger inner experience, the therapist encourages the patient to mentally imagine bodily experiences in a concrete way and to explore basic emotions such as joy, fear, anger, sadness or shame through metaphors and symbols.

Equivalence mode: In this mode, the patient already has awareness of an inner self with emotions, tendencies, memories, etc. However, the inner experience is seen as a direct reflection of reality. Emotions, thoughts and tendencies may be experienced as overwhelming. There is little distance between the inner experience and the person. One merges easily with the inner self. There is no room for differences in perspective: what a person feels or thinks is 'the truth' according to the patient. For example, 'I feel ill, therefore I am ill'. An important aim of therapy in this mode is to develop a more flexible, less absolute relationship to physical sensations, symptoms and inner experiences. One learns to perceive these experiences attentively and with some distance, so that one does not coincide with them.

Pretend mode: This is the most sophisticated form of non-mentalization, but where mental states are still too disconnected from bodily experience. Physical experiences, feelings, emotions, memories and thoughts can be apparently talked about, but still without any real emotional meaning or connection. For example, a patient may talk analytically about his car accident, but without any tangible involvement. Therapeutic goals in this mode include strengthening body awareness, deepening emotional experience in order to experience physical and inner experiences as more real and integrated.

Table 5.2 Examples of the focus of exploration in different modes of body-oriented
mentalizing.

Body mode
• Noticing bodily sensations, both neutral and problematic, without directly
  attributing meaning to them.
• Becoming aware of the physical effects of physical changes such as posture,
  movement, muscle tension and temperature.
• Describing the quality of body sensations (e.g. stabbing, pressing, throbbing).
• Notice the size and shape of body sensations.
• Recognising one's own non-verbal behaviour by supportive mirroring by the
  therapist.

Teleological mode
• Noticing differences in perception of body sensations with changes in posture,
  movement or muscle tension
• Noticing how body sensations change due to external factors (e.g. temperature, posture) and internal factors (tension, relaxation, exertion, rest). (For
  example: 'Just some minutes ago you were walking outside. How did your leg
  muscles feel then and how do they feel now that you are sitting in here?')
• Tentatively compare the quality of bodily sensations with colours, materials,
  shapes, movements, density, etc.
• Discover metaphors for bodily sensations (e.g. a heavy helmet or a sharp stone).
• Recognise basic emotions in metaphors for bodily sensations (e.g. notice fear,
  anger or sadness in back pain as barbed wire).

Equivalence mode
• Noticing and labelling inner and physical experiences: e.g. 'this is a thought'
• Recognising basic emotions such as fear, anger, sadness, shame, joy
• Validating patients' experience but also changing perspectives such as, 'Put
  yourself in another person's shoes,' or 'broadening perspectives': 'Do you
  have this every day of the week?
• Exploring the absoluteness of an opinion: 'Is there also another possible
  interpretation?'
• Mindfully observing a physical or inner experience and learning to tolerate it:
  e.g. with a mindfulness exercise.

Pretend mode
• Becoming aware of inconsistencies between verbal and non-verbal behaviour
• Deepening exploration of all kinds of physical and mental experiences
• Exploring and differentiating emotions
• Exploring links between physical and inner experiences
• Focusing attention on avoided experiences, such as an unpleasant physical
  experience, memory or negative emotion

5.5.2 Adjust 'exploring' to the mode

The therapist not only recognises the mode the patient is in, but also accepts it and
tailors interventions accordingly. Each mode requires a specific approach with a

different focus of intervention. Table 5.2 includes some examples of different areas of focus when exploring physical and inner experiences in the different modes.

5.6   Conclusion

In this chapter we have read about basic individual interventions, summarised by the acronym MEET:

M = Mode (of mentalizing) recognising
E = Exploring body signals and inner experiences of the patient
E = Exploring by the therapist of one's own body signals and inner experiences and being transparent about them
T = Triggering mutual exchange of body signals and inner experiences

We have seen that we tailor the application of these interventions to the mode of (non-)body-oriented mentalization that the patient is in. It is very important to realise that these basic individual interventions are verbal methods. There is attention to physical signals and sensations, but the medium is verbal. However, the non-verbal approach is equally important. B-MBT is always about a balance between verbal and non-verbal approaches. If there is too much emphasis on one or the other, we can compare it to 'playing the piano with one hand'. The next chapter deals with non-verbal methods.

Chapter 6

Non-verbal therapies

6.1 Non-verbal therapies

Non-verbal therapy is an essential part of B-MBT because patients with severe PPS may have difficulty understanding the language of their body. Non-verbal therapies have in common the use of physical experience, action, creativity and expression. Non-verbal therapy as part of B-MBT has two elements, which are described in this chapter:

- The expression of the inner experience without words and the reflection on it
- Reflecting on physical signs and sensations and the inner experiences associated with them

Other components of nonverbal therapy may include activity building, learning physical skills and improving physical functioning. They can also be considered part of B-MBT as long as they are based on body-oriented mentalizing. Activity building is discussed in Chapter 8. Learning physical skills and improving physical condition are discussed in Section 6.7.3. Non-verbal forms of therapy that are part of B-MBT may include:

- Physiotherapy
- Exercise therapy
- Occupational therapy
- Expressive therapies, such as:
    - Art therapy
    - Music therapy
    - Dance therapy
    - Drama therapy
    - Psychomotor therapy

Expressive therapies use physical expression such as: movement; body poses; creative expression such as painting, drawing or modelling; musical expression or role play. The emphasis is on experiencing rather than thinking, explaining or rationalising.

DOI: 10.4324/9781003637486-8

There are many advantages to using non-verbal therapies in groups. After all, we assume that giving new meaning to physical and mental experiences takes place in interaction with others. To this end, group therapy offers more opportunities than an individual approach, assuming the atmosphere in the group is safe enough. The quality of learning body-oriented mentalizing is related to the nature of interaction with others. Nonverbal therapy with B-MBT therefore also takes place in the context of exploring the relationship between self and others (Havsteen-Franklin, 2019).

Patients get to know each other through what they can observe in non-verbal communication. For example, if a patient in the group, at the request of the therapist, expresses his feelings about his back pain in a non-verbal way with a hunched posture, this says something about his very personal feelings about his back pain. At the same time it says something about his interaction with the therapist and the group members. The patient communicates his feelings to them and the group members can recognise and validate his message and, if necessary, recognise his feelings in themselves.

Through the therapist's sincere attention, 'not knowing' and validation of non-verbal expression and personal experience, the patient dares to stand still and focus on previously unobserved bodily experiences. Respectful group feedback and safe interaction with other group members play a crucial role here. By sharing thoughts and feelings about what someone has shown, by being curious about each other's opinions and by searching for a common language, the patient can find new meanings for physical and inner experiences.

So a group approach has advantages in non-verbal therapies. It is only when there are issues that are (still) too distressing to work on in a group, such as intense emotional reactions to previously unspoken traumas, that individual sessions may (temporarily) be more appropriate. When conducting non-verbal therapy, the therapist can keep in mind the B-MBT principles and methods described in this book and follow the points of attention we describe in the rest of this chapter.

6.2   Considering the difficulties of patients with non-verbal therapy

Non-verbal therapies can be very confrontational for people with PPS. They are used to shutting themselves off from their own physical signals. They may avoid bodily sensations or scan them obsessively. Either way, they are not comfortable with it. Exercises that involve opening up to one's own and others' body signals can be problematic, painful or even traumatic for patients with (severe) PPS. In addition, many patients are unfamiliar with the non-verbal approach, which adds to their feeling insecure.

Expressing oneself through visual materials such as painting, drawing or modelling can feel like a fish out of water. Especially if a patient has never been asked to express himself in an artistic way. A patient's first thought may be that they are simply unable to express something inner. Even if patients want to express a physical sensation, a memory, a feeling or a thought, they may not be familiar with these forms of expression and the qualities of the materials or techniques. Non-verbal methods also often have something unpredictable and unforeseen about them (Havsteen-Franklin, 2019). All of this can initially make patients anxious and feel the need for more control, which in turn hinders body-oriented mentalizing.

Some patients make their difficulty with non-verbal therapy clear ('It's not for me') or react with clear, intense, overwhelming emotions (equivalence mode) or with pure physical avoidance behaviour (body mode). Patients in the body mode of mentalization may simply shut down and say nothing. Patients in the teleological mode may have difficulty with a non-verbal approach because it does not focus on solutions or explanations but purely on awareness. They will protest with, 'What use is this to me?' or 'What kind of woolly stuff is this?' and may drop out. In all these cases, the patient's response to non-verbal therapy is clearly noticeable to the therapist.

In the pretend mode, patients do not clearly show their difficulty with the exercises, although it is there. They can pretend that non-verbal therapy comes easily to them. They cover up their insecurity with an apparently neutral or even seemingly competent attitude and with apparently appropriate wording, while there is no real body-oriented mentalizing (pseudo-mentalization). We should be aware and understand that these patients may also have difficulties with the non-verbal approach, even if they are not overwhelmed or protesting.

It is our job to be open to the different forms of difficulty that patients may have with non-verbal methods. We can best validate and label uncertainty and anxiety as an understandable reaction to something unfamiliar. We can also agree with our patients that it is initially difficult to be explicit about what the body and mind are trying to say or express. It is, after all, not an everyday activity. It may be difficult at first to take an interest in what is currently unknown and unpredictable. Moreover, the inner self cannot be known so directly; after all, the mind is often opaque. The process of expressing and becoming aware of the physical and inner experience is therefore more a process of searching, more a matter of feeling than of knowing for sure, as we can explain to patients. It is better not to take the patient's initial response to non-verbal therapy as a measure of ultimate success. The first uncertain, anxious or reluctant reactions are best seen as one of the possible precursors of body-oriented mentalizing. We take it as the starting point for eventual openness to one's own and others' non-verbal expressions.

6.3 Balance between bottom-up and top-down learning processes

By focusing on direct experience and action, bottom-up learning processes take place in non-verbal B-MBT more than in verbal B-MBT: from bodily experience to the perception of emotions and then to conscious cognitions. Central to this is becoming aware of the inner self, such as emotions and thoughts, for example through arousal, posture, movement, facial expressions, gestures and bodily sensations (Ogden & Fisher, 2017). Translated into the triple brain model: sensorimotor processes from the brainstem regulate emotional functions at a 'higher level' such as the limbic system (the mammalian brain) and, at an even higher level, cognitive functions in the neocortex (MacLean, 1990). We can think of this automatic process as part of the implicit mentalization of the body. In the reverse process, top-down processing, insights, reflections, beliefs and reasoning, in short, neocortical processes, consciously direct the body and the processing of emotions. This is more the process of explicit body-oriented mentalizing. For example, in music therapy, a patient expresses his feelings by beating a drum (bottom-up process). After a minute, the therapist asks the patient to reflect on the physical sensations and inner experiences. This evaluation and feedback from the therapist and the group ('I heard you beat the drum hard and thought I was angry') is then the entry point for explicit body-oriented mentalizing (top-down process).

In non-verbal therapy it is important to recognise that bottom-up stimulation should always go hand in hand with the more cognitive top-down processes. This is to ensure that patients are not overwhelmed by physical sensations and emotions. The personal experience of bodily sensations and emotions and their expression through movement, painting, singing or dramatic expression always goes hand in hand with a shared cognitive reflection on them. Thus, in body-oriented mentalization we try to find the middle ground between different poles of mentalization, such as automatic versus controlled and affective versus cognitive. In this way we help patients to find a middle way between 'getting lost in feelings' and 'getting lost in thinking'.

6.4   Keeping an eye on the regulation of bodily state and 'arousal'

Working with non-verbal means is a powerful medium that can quickly trigger intense emotions and stress. Patients with (severe) PPS may also experience a rapid increase in physical symptoms such as a sudden conversion attack or a severe pain episode. The therapist must therefore proceed with caution and care, for example when touching, approaching, evoking emotions, images and symbols, and allowing complicated situations to arise in a group (Kalisvaart & Van der Maas, 2017). When patients exceed their tolerance when confronted with painful topics, the therapist should respond understandingly to stress symptoms and physical complaints. The therapist can temporarily switch to arousal-regulating interventions (see Section 4.8.8).

6.5   Relevant themes

Expressing and becoming aware of physical and inner experiences is particularly important in relation to emotionally relevant issues associated with PPS, such as

- Living with physical discomfort and limitations
- Recognising and acknowledging physical and mental boundaries

- Negative body perceptions
- Being able to experience positive and negative feelings in the body
- Building trust in the body
- Expressing emotions physically
- Learning or relearning motor skills
- Dealing with traumatic situations
- Social problems such as: not being respected, experiencing resistance, being ignored, not being understood, lack of or inability to receive or ask for support and help, lack of emotional closeness from others and difficulties with touch

Non-verbal therapy based on B-MBT involves reflecting with patients on how they express themselves non-verbally around the relevant themes and helping them to increase their body awareness in the process. The non-verbal experience of a theme can take many forms. For example, a patient may physically perceive the theme 'experiencing resistance' when group members physically try to stop him from moving in a desired direction. For example, 'experiencing support' may be experienced physically by a patient when someone physically supports him in an action he is involved in. However, such themes can also be addressed in a drawing in art therapy or in a role play in drama therapy.

It is preferable that the themes of non-verbal therapies be aligned with the themes and topics of the more verbal B-MBT components, such as the verbal group therapies (see Chapter 9). It is also advisable to involve patients in determining the theme and to agree with them what the 'living theme' is at the moment. For example, the recent departure of a group member may be on people's minds. Then the theme could be 'How do I experience the departure of a group member?' Placing an empty chair somewhere in the room and walking around it while thinking about the person who has left could be a starting point for reflection on body and mind.

6.6   Non-verbal expression and its reflection

6.6.1   Expression of the inner self

Patients with PPS are often unable to find the right words to describe their physical/internal experience. They remain silent or use short, not yet nuanced sentences such as 'I feel bad' or 'I'm not feeling well'. Patients do not yet know exactly what they are feeling emotionally and express themselves physically through discomfort. Non-verbal therapy then provides an opportunity to give these experiences a personal colour, shape, rhythm, volume, pitch or movement. It is not about mastering a technique such as painting, singing or movement. It is about the process of expressing and discussing physical sensations and inner experiences. For example, a patient may non-verbally illustrate his experience of constant neck pain with a stiff back and neck, wringing hands and a painful facial expression. Patients learn to consciously and unconsciously represent and learn about subtle aspects of their physical sensations, emotions, thoughts and tendencies through non-verbal expression.

We can ask patients to make a body drawing that focuses on their perception of their own body. This gives the patient, therapist and group members an impression of the patient's inner body image (Kalisvaart et al., 2018). During the afterview, they look together at, for example, the connection between different parts of the body, exaggerations, omissions and distortions. An example: a 24-year-old woman with a combination of chronic fatigue, back pain and loss of strength in her legs has a history of sexual abuse and draws a body without legs and a lower abdomen. When we discuss this afterwards, she tearfully tells us that in her experience, her lower abdominal body does not exist in her experience and is not part of her.

The therapist can also ask the patient to focus on how they experience a physical complaint and draw it freely. For example, a patient might express back pain by drawing a piece of barbed wire. In the group reflection afterwards, the meaning of the sharp, stinging pain and the feeling of bondage that the pain causes emerge. In a non-verbal expression of physical or emotional problems, a person places their physical and emotional experiences outside of their own mind in the world (Verfaille, 2018). This 'outward placing' allows patients to step back with the therapist and other patients to review what they have created. According to Bateman and Fonagy (2004), the typical feature of nonverbal therapies is the outward placing of a problematic aspect of the inner self. By transforming feelings and related bodily sensations into movement, gesture, painting, modelling, melody or rhythm, they are externalised. This guarantees a certain distance from which the patient can experience them as less dangerous and more bearable. Inner and physical experiences can then be experienced as safer than asking more directly about physical sensations, emotions, thoughts or memories.

However, other patients, especially those who are predominantly in the psychic body or equivalence mode, may experience an increase in anxiety in their expressive work. The product they are making—now visible to the outside world and to others—makes this aspect of themselves too 'real' and may overwhelm them. Therefore, in non-verbal therapy, we need to match our assignments to the stage of non-mentalization that the patient is in (Bales, 2019).

6.6.2 Use of metaphors and symbolic images

One aim of B-MBT is that patients learn to give meaning to physical sensations and inner experiences for which there are no words yet. Metaphors can help to express meaning symbolically. A metaphor is an imagery in which the image depicted corresponds to how reality is experienced, such as 'my body is like a car that cannot be controlled'. In a metaphor, we always make a comparison between a perceived reality (I have a headache) and another experience (wearing a tight, heavy helmet on my head) in order to create a new perspective. There are many metaphors in the area of coping with physical complaints that can be appropriate, such as 'coping with my illness is like a wrestling match' or 'living with these limitations is like walking a difficult road'. Metaphors often follow the physical experience: having a heavy heart, feeling a hand around my throat. But even 'air out my feelings' in which the word 'air' can be experienced physically as space in the chest (Nicolai, 2017a). Experiencing our inner self through metaphor and imagery is a deeply rooted, original way of representing the inner self. Before we had words for our inner experiences as children, we learned to represent affects in symbolic images.

When using metaphors and symbols in therapy, we aim to teach patients to use their imagination to represent their situation in a comparative image or symbol. For example, we ask the patient to focus on a physical sensation, such as feeling hot or cold, and on images that best match it in the imagination. For example, drawing a fire as a symbol of warmth, or a tree without roots as a metaphor for the feeling uprooted. An open-ended task such as 'draw a picture of your back pain' gives patients the opportunity to express the emotional dimension of their pain experience without words.

However, we can also ask the patient to fill in a fixed metaphor or symbol on a personal basis, for example: 'Describe your life with this fatigue in a drawing of a road that you are walking on'. Or they may be asked to make a monster out of clay to represent their leg pain. Through the personal interpretation of the metaphor, the patient's physical and inner experience comes forward.

Art therapy in particular makes creative use of metaphors (Havsteen-Franklin, 2019). However, metaphors can also be part of physical exercises such as: 'Together with a number of other group members, symbolically represent in a tableau vivant (silent static arrangement) what you find most important in your life'. For example, a patient asks the others in the group to form a circle and join hands. This circle and the contact with each other's hands reflect something valuable in the patient's life. In the following discussion, the therapist and group members can exchange possible meanings: making contact, being included, having a connection, feeling protected.

The therapist must be careful not to present too obvious metaphors as some kind of new knowledge to the patient. For example, telling a patient with paralysis of the legs that the paralysis is like 'not being able to stand on your own two feet' can also disrupt the process of body-oriented mentalizing. However correct such a metaphor may be, it may disrupt the patient's own process of searching for an appropriate metaphor. We can, however, facilitate this process by presenting the patient with a number of metaphors and asking him which one is most appropriate.

Patients who still have limited body-oriented mentalization abilities can turn to common, obvious (non-creative) symbols such as a heart (love), a V-sign (peace), a smiley face (joy) or a clenched fist (strength and power). The therapist can go along with such a 'borrowed symbol' while encouraging the patient to add a more personal touch to their expression (Verfaille, 2018).

When symbolising, the patient may also remain in the teleological or equivalence mode. Having drawn a dead end street as a metaphor for current life, the patient may conclude that it is now proven that his life is also a dead end. So we do well to always emphasise the difference between the symbol and the reality, to avoid the equivalence and teleological modes. For example, we emphasise the difference between 'this pain feels like a block tied to my leg' and 'this pain is a block tied to my leg', or 'this contact feels like my safe haven' and 'this contact is my safe haven'.

We should also be wary of over-analysing metaphors. This quickly leads to the pretend mode. For example, if chronic fatigue is described as a car with a stiff gas pedal, some patients may respond with a technical view of car engines. This distances them from the very feeling they were expressing with the metaphor.

6.6.3   Exploring and reflecting

Standstill

Exploring each other's nonverbal expressions is a basic element of nonverbal B-MBT. The focus is not on the patient, but on their artistic or physical expression. By exploring together what someone has expressed, patients learn how something as abstract as bodily sensations or an emotion can be derived from something like posture, a drawing or a melody. Important techniques for exploring non-verbal expression are 'stop and stand still' and 'stop and go back' (see Section 5.2.16 and Section 5.2.17). 'Stop and stand still' means that the therapist asks the patient to stop, e.g. moving, painting, modelling, etc., and asks him to reflect on current physical and inner experience. He gives space for interaction with the therapist or with group members. In 'stop and go back' the patient, therapist and group members look back at what someone has expressed in order to reflect on it together.

Attention to the 'how'

When exploring a movement, posture, painting, drawing, modelling or music, the focus is on how one expresses oneself, the 'how', rather than what one expresses. The patient's inner self is best known through the way they express themselves non-verbally in the here and now. The therapist will therefore first focus the attention of the group members on the elements of form. How does someone sit, stand, move, make music, paint or model? Does someone move stiffly, smoothly, hurriedly, controlled? Does someone play music with a high or low rhythm? Does someone use bright, light colours or dark shades when painting?

Giving each other feedback on the 'how' of non-verbal expression is one of the first steps in body-oriented mentalizing. When one patient says to another, 'I notice that your modelling is big and angular', this is the first sign of noticing and acknowledging each other's inner selves. It is advisable not to end this phase of exploration too quickly. It can be rich in the exchange of details of expressions that the patients were not yet aware of. For example, hearing from group members about a stooped posture, a shuffling gait or a lot of yellow in a painting is a non-threatening way for patients to learn about their own minds.

Interpreting what is observed

After reflecting on the way someone expresses themselves, the therapist will ask what this expresses. For example, the fact that someone is using a lot of yellow when drawing may give a group member the impression that this person is in a good mood. By asking about the meaning of how someone expresses themselves, what emotions or thoughts are being expressed, the therapist appeals to the patient's imagination and empathy. The therapist needs to make sure that the group members take into account the meaning that each person already gives to his or her expression. At the same time, the therapist can help patients to see that others may see their work in a different way to them, allowing alternative perspectives to emerge. The therapist always makes clear that a person's inner world is opaque and not directly observable.

To make deeper meaning, exploration requires sincere attention from the group and therapist. To facilitate this, the therapist adopts a particularly curious attitude and will encourage group members to do the same: 'I wonder, what is the background of all those red colours in your painting?' or 'I suddenly saw you accelerating in your movement and wondered, "Is he in a hurry?"'

We make it clear to patients that the interpretation of a non-verbal expression involves a complex range of possibilities. Someone walking around the room with a hunched posture could be despondent, or tired, or sad, or having back pain or something else entirely. The therapist is not supposed to give 'the one right answer' of what, for example, a body posture expresses. The patient and the group members themselves have to start an inner process of searching for the meanings embedded in their own minds. This search process is the actual body-oriented mentalizing. The therapist tries to navigate sensitively between the meanings given by the group members, always labelling them as reactions of the body and mind to seeing the drawing, movement, posture or hearing the rhythm or melody. For example, the patients listen to one of them beating a drum. The therapist validates the impressions of the group members (including the one who showed the non-verbal expression) as a possibility. He summarises these in a common language for the group members, e.g. 'it seems that his way of beating the drum is perceived as loud and rhythmic by several of you'.

The next step is to identify and name emotional states (Havsteen-Franklin, 2019). What emotions might be conveyed by this non-verbal expression? What impression does the loud and rhythmic beating of the drum give? For example, anger and frustration might emerge from the group. We could also ask about the story behind the hard, rhythmic drumming: 'If you think about how he is beating the drum, what emotional story could be behind it, do you think? Then someone might say, for example, 'I think he has frustration at work because of the heavy workload'.

The therapist always makes sure that the group members place this interpretation in the context of a subjective exchange of impressions and not of 'finding the truth'. The therapist emphasises that his own reflections are also subjective. He makes this particularly clear when patients make comments such as 'he (the therapist) can see through people' or 'he can see things that others cannot', thus taking the therapist's subjective perception as unquestionable reality. We make it clear that we are not experts in reading people's minds. Rather, we are experts in guiding the process of mindful joint exploration of each other's non-verbal expressions. To encourage a subjective exchange, the therapist also encourages putting oneself in the other's shoes, non-verbal mirroring and giving feedback through an 'I' message (see Section 5.12).

As well as cognitively interpreting what a group member's expression says about their inner experience, their expression can also evoke all kinds of feelings, thoughts and memories among group members originating from their own life history. Someone may say, 'Her posture gives me a strange feeling. I knew someone who I liked very much. She turned out to be very shy'. The therapist can now ask, 'What do you think that says about her?' (the other patient). If, for example, the patient says: 'That she is indeed people-shy', the therapist will first state this as a hypothesis: 'It could perhaps be that she is expressing a fear of people'. Or he might call it a subjective experience: 'You think her attitude expresses a shyness'.

Mirroring

Non-verbal therapists, more than verbal therapists, will observe patients' posture and movement expressions to get an idea of what is going on inside them. We can mirror their posture and movement in a marked way (see also Section 5.2.5) to give patients an insight into what is going on inside them. The therapist will especially try to mirror what the patient is expressing emotionally. We will be more able to mirror movement or posture if they are part of our physical abilities. To increase their skills, non-verbal therapists can practice unfamiliar or awkward physical postures and movements. This increases their ability to express physical empathy with the patient.

Too hasty mirroring without empathy for the patient carries the danger that our mirroring does not emphasise the patient's inner self, but expresses our own inner self. Genuine, marked mirroring of posture and movement shows empathy, compassion and connection. If the therapist regularly mirrors marked postures and movements in group sessions, patients are more likely to do the same with each other. We should guard against an atmosphere of imitation without empathy. If necessary, we explain the difference between the two. The therapist can also combine non-verbal mirroring of posture and movement with verbal mirroring. He can mirror a patient walking on tiptoe during a movement exercise by walking on tiptoe in the same way and saying, 'I see you are walking on tiptoe. I then find myself thinking, "She's trying very hard."'

6.6.4 Therapeutic stance and demonstration of exercises

In non-verbal B-MBT, the therapist uses the mentalizing therapeutic stance as described in Section 4.6. He is engaged, transparent, attentive, accepting and empathic. He is clearly in charge, but at the same time maintains an open 'not knowing' attitude to what the patient expresses. The therapist openly shows his personal reaction to what the patient expresses with an 'I' message such as, 'Looking at your drawing, I notice that I am shocked'. Because we ask patients to be vulnerable, we ask the same of ourselves. That is why we demonstrate exercises ourselves as much as possible and then be transparent about what we experience. For example, if we are doing a movement expression exercise, we can say: 'When I do this, I feel muscles in my back that I don't normally feel. They feel very tense, and I also notice that I think: "Oh dear, I hope I do this right."'

6.6.5   Recognising modes of non-mentalizing

Encouraging non-verbal expression may initially lead to a non-mentalizing mode. For example, we are likely to encourage our patients into a body, teleological, equivalence or pretend mode because we are asking them to transform the unobservable inner self into an observable form. However, we can also unintentionally encourage them 'to deliver a performance' and to a pretend mode. If a patient draws, for example, a picture of a child who is alone and wrapped in a blanket, the question is in which mode of mentalization the patient is while drawing. We can investigate this by, for example, asking ourselves:

- Is he driven mainly by his physical impulses? (body mode)
- Does he want to convey a message or evoke a feeling in someone? (teleological mode)
- Is he completely absorbed in his work and forgot about himself and all that he is? (equivalence mode)
- Does he perhaps want to perform or imitate? (pretend mode)

For a more comprehensive overview of more examples of traces of non-mentalizing in various forms of non-verbal therapies such as art, movement, posture and musical expressions, see tables in Appendix A.5.

Then comes the retrospective reflection on the patient's expressive effort. In non-verbal therapy, group interaction aimed at reflecting nonverbal expression is one of the most important elements. How do the patient and the group members look back? What particular elements have they noticed and what inner experiences are they expressing? Again, the therapist pays attention to any non-mentalizing states in the group members (see Section 5.1 and Appendix A.3). One phenomenon that can occur in patients with severe PPS after using a certain form of expression is being caught in the literal content of one's expression. For example, after making and discussing a drawing about their feeling, patients may argue that it is now conclusively proven that they are really suffering. After all, others have confirmed that this is evident from the drawing (equivalence mode). They may also believe that they have found the explanation and thus the solution to their problems (teleological mode). Moving from non-mentalizing evaluations back to body-oriented mentalizing can be achieved in a number of ways, as described in Chapter 5.

In this section, we have focused on learning body-oriented mentalizing through reflection on non-verbal expression. Non-verbal B-MBT also focuses on increasing body awareness by attending to the different bodily sensations and related inner experiences.

6.7   Paying attention to body sensations and related inner experiences

6.7.1   Strengthening body awareness

Non-verbal exercises and advice fit into a B-MBT context when they focus on consciously noticing, recognising and opening up to bodily sensations and related inner experiences. In addition to the expressive function (see previous section), physical exercises aim to strengthen body awareness. This is mainly the field of (psychosomatic) physiotherapy, psychomotor therapy, (psychosomatic) exercise therapy and occupational therapy. The exercises or instructions aimed at body awareness can be carried out with the therapist, in the group as a whole or in the group in pairs or triples. Kalisvaart and Van der Maas (2017) describe how both individual and group therapies aimed at body awareness go through different phases. First, we work on creating a safe therapeutic climate. Then we choose a theme such as 'setting boundaries'. Around this theme, we offer movement exercises and interactions with therapeutic groups with the aim of becoming aware of bodily sensations and inner experiences.

6.7.2   Body-centred points of focus

To help patients become aware of their bodily experiences in the here and now, the therapist can explore them with the patient and with group members. To this end, the therapist can draw the patient's attention to particular bodily experiences in the here and now, such as, 'What physical signals are you feeling in your stomach right now? And in your arms?' Or, 'How does your whole body feel right now?' An overview of examples of commonly used body-oriented areas of focus in B-MBT is given in Table 6.1.

There are several ways of using these attention points. Firstly, before a non-verbal exercise, such as a drawing or a posture or movement exercise, we can ask the patient to keep an attention point in mind during the exercise. For example, he might suggest 'walk around the room in a moment without bumping into people and be aware of how you are moving'. The therapist can also ask the patient(s) to stop during a non-verbal exercise and ask them to be aware of a current physical or internal experience (from Table 6.1). We can also use the focal points by looking back immediately after an exercise and asking about one of the focal points, e.g.: 'What body position did you just take?' To explore using the focal points, we can use the basic interventions described in Section 5.2, such as 'stop and stand still', 'stop and go back', mirroring, validating, etc.

The focal points in Table 6.1 can relate to experiences in general, as well as to complaints, physical sensations and inner experiences in particular. For example, in the case of back pain, one might focus on posture, the location, shape and intensity of the back pain, and the emotions and thoughts associated with it. The focal points in Table 6.1 can also be used by the therapist to reflect on one's own bodily experiences in the here and now. Finally, B-MBT always involves interaction with others, such as the therapist. We are therefore always aware of our own bodily and inner experiences, which we can reveal in a pedagogical way (see also Section 5.3).

Table 6.1 Examples of commonly used individual body-oriented points of attention.

Physical experiences

Body signals such as heart rate, tightness, dizziness, localised pain, sensations in the skin and muscles, sweating, tension in the facial muscles, but also less problematic physical signals such as a light feeling in the legs.

Characteristics of the experience of a physical sensation, such as location, sharpness or dullness, size and shape of the sensation, and intensity (possibly expressed as a number between 0 and 10).

Fluctuations in physical sensations when changing, for example changing posture, movement or muscle tension, or environmental changes such as a change in temperature, walking indoors or outdoors.

The overall physiological state, such as tired or energetic, hungry or full, calm or restless.

Body posture, such as hunched over, open or closed posture.

Skin discolouration and changes, such as turning pale or flushed.

Movement characteristics, such as the way you walk and use your hands and legs.

Restrictions in movement or muscle use, such as not being able to fully extend an arm or sit up straight.

Orientation in space, such as where you are in relation to others in the room.

Sensory stimuli to physical sensations, such as listening to music or taking a hot shower to stimulate physical relaxation, or bumping one's head that causes a headache.

Biological rhythms, such as recognising the rhythms of hunger, sleep, tiredness, vitality, relaxation and tension.

Arousal, such as high and low arousal or stress, or estimating levels of stress using a tension meter.

Stress response, such as fight, flight, freeze/faint, including a tendency to the previously suppressed physical fight or flight when exploring an old trauma.

Breathing, such as inhaling and exhaling, the up and down movement of the abdomen or chest, and other movements caused by breathing throughout the body.

Use of the voice, such as pitch, volume, speed of speech.

The physical response to events, such as experiencing a stomachache or chest tightness when quarrelling.

Physical signals for inner experiences, such as feeling tight when afraid, sweating when thinking about an embarrassing experience, feeling warm when feeling ashamed. See also Appendix A.4.

Body-related inner experiences

The internal representation of a bodily sensation as a shape, material, colour, sound, pitch, movement, etc.

Internal reactions to physical signals, such as the thought 'I have to pay attention' with tense muscles, or the physical tendency to run away when scared. Particularly important are emotions associated with physical signals, such as anger with clenched jaws.

Symbolic (dream) images associated with physical sensations: e.g. the image of a room without doors for a stomach ache (an image that later turns out to symbolise the feeling of being imprisoned).

Core beliefs associated with physical sensations, such as 'I am nothing' in the case of physical exhaustion.

(Continued)

Table 6.1 (Continued)

Memory triggered by physical activity, such as the memory of falling off the bike when doing a fitness exercise on a stationary bike.
Body image (and related self-image), such as beautiful or ugly, sick or healthy, attractive or disgusting, fat or thin, friend or enemy.

Patterns and mechanisms
Patterns of body posture and movement, such as always bending the head forward in the same way, hunching the shoulders and holding the breath when feeling insecure.
Survival mechanisms, especially sensory and motor mechanisms, such as overexerting oneself physically or not paying attention to one's feelings.

Physical experiences

Interacting with others while experiencing bodily sensations and inner reactions is essential in B-MBT. People learn the language of the body in interaction with others when there is space for body awareness. In non-verbal B-MBT, attending to each other's bodily expression and noticing what one experiences physically and emotionally in contact with others, a new awareness of physicality emerges. Table 6.2 lists common body awareness points of attention used in contact with others.

The therapist can explore body-oriented interactional points of attention with the patient. To do this, he can again give instructions before the exercise, such as, 'In the following movement exercise, be aware of how the way others move affects you'. We can also stop a non-verbal exercise and ask, for example, 'What emotion do you think the posture of the person standing next to you is expressing?' Or we use the interactional points of attention after an exercise, such as, 'Look back on this exercise. What did you feel in your body when someone came close to you?' We encourage patients to share their insights about their interactions as directly as possible with an 'I' message. For example, a patient might say, 'Now that you have put your arm around me, I feel warm, I feel emotion, but also a little fear'. We can use the instructions in Section 5.4 to encourage a two-way exchange. The therapist also uses the interactional body-centred focal points for himself to remain aware of how contact with the patient works through physically and mentally.

6.7.3 Body awareness in exercises to improve physical skills and condition

Part of the treatment for PPS involves exercises to improve physical conditions. For example, patients may be given exercises and advice to improve their mobility and posture, to use their muscles differently or to improve their fitness. This may be part of (psychosomatic) physiotherapy, (psychosomatic) exercise therapy or occupational therapy. These physical change-oriented exercises are compatible with B-MBT if they sufficiently integrate the treatment principles and methods of B-MBT. This is the case when there is a balance between instructions for physical

Table 6.2 Examples of commonly used interactional, body-oriented points of attention.

Physical expression of the other person, such as posture, movement, facial expression (see points of attention in Table 6.1).

Physical and mental reactions to the other, such as getting teary-eyed and feeling sad when someone is having a difficult time.

Physical and emotional resonance with others, such as noticing that one feels anxious when others feel anxious, or experiencing sadness when others show sadness.

Assumption of another person's inner experience in relation to a physical expression, such as assuming that someone is happy when they smile and lean back in a comfortable chair.

The impact on others, e.g. others showing signs of restlessness when you are pacing around the room.

Orientation in space in relation to others, such as standing far away or close to another person.

Physical and mental responses to feedback and mirroring from others, such as noticing that you feel relaxed but also sad when the other person says you look tired.

Eye contact, such as looking at each other a little longer and noticing the effect on your own body, emotions, thoughts and other inner reactions.

Physical and internal responses to touch, such as feeling warm when someone puts their arm around you.

Reactions to physical distance and closeness, such as feeling smothered when someone sits less than half a metre away.

Physical and emotional responses to emotional closeness, such as feeling warm and happy when you are in contact with someone you care about.

Movements or postures that seek emotional closeness, such as bending over (seeking closeness) or turning away (promoting distance).

Motor and sensory patterns when interacting with others, such as always bending over and tending not to notice one's own discomfort when interacting with a dominant person. This includes the motor and sensory side of interaction patterns with attachment figures.

Mutual playfulness or rigidity, such as movements, postures and emotions associated with playfulness or rigidity.

change on the one hand, and attention to personal body expression and increased body awareness on the other. For example, the therapist may use 'stop and stand' to interrupt a movement exercise for the back muscles so that the patient remains aware of their bodily sensations and related inner experiences.

6.8 Dealing with trauma and transference

Because traumatic events and painful relationships can be translated into implicit (non-verbal) processes, they are likely to come up in non-verbal therapies. In terms of the impact of trauma, non-verbal therapists should be aware of intrusions, re-experiencing, sudden violent behaviour and movements, problems expressing emotions and memory disturbances. For example, a patient who has been emotionally neglected for years may suddenly become speechless when touched by a physiotherapist. When the physiotherapist asks her what is wrong with her, she can only say 'I don't know' and start crying loudly. Once we have the impression that the patient is expressing an unconscious trauma, we can explore this further in non-verbal ways, as long as we are within the patient's tolerance zone. We can ask the patient to draw, paint or sculpt.

Art therapy can be very helpful in accessing, becoming aware of, exploring and giving new meaning to the traumatic experience. A patient with a conversion walking disorder and childhood sexual abuse drew herself without a lower body but with a large red spot in that place. At first she could not talk about what she was drawing, but she was able to show it to others in the group. She later realised that she had lost all kinds of memories of the abuse and preferred not to focus on her lower body.

It is advisable for the nonverbal therapist to report the patient's traumatic experiences in the multidisciplinary team consultation and discuss how to respond. It should be recognised that the impact of early trauma is powerful and that collaboration with other disciplines around trauma is almost always necessary. Non-verbal therapists, such as physiotherapists and psychomotor therapists, can have a particular role to play in recognising and helping to express subconscious physical fight, flight or freeze/collapse responses (see Section 7.9). For more information on responding to trauma, see also Section 7.8.

Past painful relationships are likely to be translated into transference and 'enactment' (the joint staging of older, implicit, relational patterns (Nicolai, 2017b). An example is the patient who used to be oppressed by her father and now feels that she is not allowed to speak in the art group. We consider transference and enactment to be common phenomena in non-verbal B-MBT. We should discuss these phenomena in the multidisciplinary team meeting. Here, the team members can find out who recognises such a transference or enactment. They may then decide who will elaborate on the transference with the patient. For example, a colleague with a more psychotherapeutic orientation may decide to work through the problem with the patient in more detail if there is also an enactment. For more information on working with transference, countertransference and enactment, see Section 7.7.

6.9   Conclusion

Non-verbal therapies are an indispensable part of B-MBT, because PPS patients often express inner processes implicitly, without words, through the body. For many patients with severe PPS, true body-oriented mentalizing will begin with non-verbal therapy. It is here that the first unvarnished physical expression takes place in a context where another person notices the inner self. Here comes the first recognition that the mind does not only manifest itself in words. B-MBT is a powerful tool because it integrates verbal and non-verbal approaches. This interplay combines top-down and bottom-up learning processes. This combined approach is based on the idea that body and mind are inseparable. Psychological and physiological processes are two sides of the same coin.

With a one-sided, verbal approach and too much attention to the patient's verbal language alone, we can easily make the mistake of ignoring the patient's bodily mentalizing capacity. A large group of patients can talk at length about their inner states without making real contact with their bodily signals in the moment. Reflecting on inner states and bodily sensations when the patient is not ready can lead to pseudo-mentalization. Patients may separate bodily sensations from their consciousness. They then appear to be mentalizing but do not report certain physical and mental experiences, such as pain in the arms or anger. Or they may report these experiences to one therapist but not to another. Non-verbal therapists can inform colleagues in the multidisciplinary team about what shapes, gestures, movements and sounds can be recognised as signs of the patient's inner experiences. Other therapists can build on this in their therapeutic work with the patient.

The power of B-MBT's integrated mind/body approach extends as far as the quality of multidisciplinary collaboration will allow. Are team members team players and able to see the relativity of their own rightness? Are they prepared for mutual coordination and peer review? Are they able to apply B-MBT principles to themselves and the team? As we can consider the quality of multidisciplinary collaboration as a driver of treatment, we will discuss this in more detail in Chapter 11.

Using the individual basic techniques (Chapter 5) and the non-verbal approach from this chapter, patients can achieve a basic level of body-oriented mentalizing. Within the context of a safe, transparent relationship with the therapist, it is through body-oriented mentalizing that patients can then acquire memories of unpleasant past traumas and painful intimate relationships. One becomes aware of previously hidden old hurts that have given rise to physical sensations and inner reactions that still affect daily life. How to deal with old mental injuries is described in the next chapter.

Chapter 7

Responding to what is evoked

7.1 Old pain that becomes perceivable

With the basic techniques and non-verbal methods described in the previous chapters, patients can achieve a basic level of body-oriented mentalizing. In a safe relationship with a therapist, patients learn to become more aware of their physical sensations, their inner experiences and the interplay between the two. Old pain that has remained physically and mentally unconscious can be (re)experienced. This old emotional pain that emerges is usually related to painful relational and traumatic events, which are usually in line with each other. Past painful and distressing relationships, which still have a strong negative impact on the patient's health today, often have traumatic aspects. At the same time, physical and emotional traumatic events usually have a relational context that strongly influences the impact of the trauma.

When addressing patients' old pain, it is important to recognise that long-term memories can be stored and recalled in different ways: explicit and implicit. Explicit memories are coherent, verbal descriptions of events that we can consciously recall. Implicit memories about events that we do not consciously remember are non-verbal and unconscious. They take the form of recurring emotions, repetitive patterns of relationships, habits, images, physical patterns, sensations and beliefs (Ogden & Fisher, 2017; Wallin, 2010).

If we intuitively find someone unsympathetic in a given situation, our implicit memory may be triggered. For example, the other person may unconsciously resemble someone with whom we had a bad experience in the past. Ogden and Fisher describe implicit memories as somatic and emotional states of remembrance that are not accompanied by an inner awareness of remembering something from the past. Circumstances in the present can unexpectedly trigger implicit memories. This is why they are called state-dependent memories. Implicit memories of painful events can occur without us being aware that they have a strong influence on our present life. Because implicit memories do not remind patients of anything in particular, they may feel that there is nothing they can do about their condition, no matter how much they would like to. We assume that memories of old pain can have both implicit and explicit elements. This means that we have to take

DOI: 10.4324/9781003637486-9

into account that our patients may remember painful events from the past but only partially.

In exploring old pain, we can start with what people explicitly remember about an event, and discover the more implicit emotional and physical aspects in the process. This is not so much about the content of the memory, but about the emotions and physical experiences that are involved. We can also start by exploring the implicit part of a memory. We then focus on current, intense affects and physical reactions where the patient does not yet know exactly what past experience is behind them. We then have to help the patient to perceive, tolerate and regulate these current affective and somatic experiences. In this way they can learn that their emotional and physical state is similar to the state they were in during the painful trauma or problematic attachment.

Our intention is that, in safe contact with a therapist, patients can express old pain verbally and non-verbally, explicitly and implicitly, while at the same time realising that they are in the here and now. The present safe contact with the therapist and the focus on the here and now prevents people from involuntarily going into body or equivalence mode and confusing painful memories with present reality.

Ogden et al. (2006) described experiencing both the explicit and implicit aspects of a memory while remaining in contact with the here and now as dual awareness. This is experiencing a memory with full awareness of the here and now by consciously focusing attention on one's own current internal and physical reactions and the environment. Patients can use dual consciousness to re-experience the state they were in at the time of the event while being aware of the here and now. This allows them to let go of old hurts. After all, they have become aware that these are memories and not present reality, and that they are now also connected to other experiences in the here and now.

As we noted earlier in this book, the essence of B-MBT is the open exchange between patient and therapist. It is always a two-way street. The patient's old pain that emerges also affects the therapist. First, our mirror neurons do their work, and we will vibrate physically and emotionally with our patients' subjective experiences. Secondly, the mutual influence will depend not only on the characteristics and history of the patient, but also on that of the therapist. As therapists we are not a blank screen. What a patient evokes in us is also partly related to our own 'inevitable subjectivity' (Renik, 1993). In this way, on the basis of the patient's old pain, patient and therapist inevitably arrive at 'enactment': the joint staging of older, implicit, relational patterns (Nicolai, 2017b).

For example, a severely traumatised patient may ask for extra therapy sessions if her therapist appears to have a sniffly cold. The therapist might respond with quiet anger (Davies, 2004). However, it is better to ask oneself: 'How do I deal with what my cold has triggered in this patient? How do I deal with what has now been triggered in me in my relationship with this patient?' This requires a willingness on the part of the therapist to open up to the patient's intense physical reactions, emotions and memories and their impact on him. This willingness cannot happen without sufficient self-reflection and support through training, supervision, intervision, learning therapy or deliberate practice in being open to one's own physical and inner experiences. We hypothesise that implicit memories of old traumas and painful relationships with attachment figures largely trigger non-verbal, implicit, automatic, sensorimotor impulses and responses (Ogden et al., 2006). For example, at a deeper level, the implicit psychological pain triggered the body's unconscious long-lasting stress response (fight, flight, freeze or paralysis). For instance, a patient who was regularly beaten and locked in a cupboard as a child will have repetitive physical twitching in situations similar to when being locked up or beaten. So we see the body as a carrier of the implicit, (until now) unconscious, old hurt but also as a place where awareness can take place. Exploring non-verbal traces of old pain and implicit non-verbal communication is therefore part of B-MBT. As long as the patient's attention is focused only on the explicit verbal description of an (attachment) trauma, no physical change can take place and physical complaints persist. Physical change also requires conscious experience of the implicit elements and non-verbal residues of the memory.

Of course, because of its anchoring in the body, the uncovering of old pain is not limited to the work of psychological disciplines such as psychologists, psychotherapists and psychiatrists. On the contrary, it can also be observed in the practices of more physically oriented disciplines such as physicians, (psychosomatic) physiotherapists, (psychosomatic), exercise, occupational and psychomotor therapists. The results of unconsciously remaining traumatic relationships and events show up, for example, in medical examinations and in the doctor's discussions with the patient about diagnoses, examination results, medication, etc. Physical symptoms, reason to seek treatment, then mix with the physical outputs of unconscious interaction patterns and painful memories. The patient experiences physical symptoms, but also, for example, the pain of the earlier 'feeling unheard'.

This is what often makes the purely medical-biological treatment of severe PPS so difficult. For many patients with this severe complaints, seeking help from a doctor or physiotherapist, for example, is an emotional affair that quickly triggers old painful interaction patterns. For example, patients who have been emotionally neglected in the past can quickly become suspicious, tense and defensive when the physiotherapist or doctor shows interest in the background to the physical symptoms.

If, after a period of time, there is no conclusive diagnosis or therapy outcome, a person with a preoccupied attachment pattern will soon develop a tendency to make demands and react in an angry way. This tends to focus on people on whom one is dependent for care. In someone with a deactivating (avoidant) attachment style, the tendency to avoid contact will occur sooner. If the patient's old pain has a strong impact on our relationship with the patient, this is a reason not only for further exploration with the patient, but also for multidisciplinary consultation. We can inform other disciplines of our interactional findings and share any similar experiences. Physically oriented disciplines may choose to have more psychologically oriented colleagues work through the problem with the patient or, vice versa, a non-verbal therapist may choose to work through the problem first.

In choosing which team member will focus primarily on working with old pain, we should be aware that extensive training with supervision in working with old mental pain is a prerequisite. We can assume that someone who has completed a recognised training as a psychotherapist, supplemented with supervision and further training, has sufficient knowledge and skills to work with old mental pain. Post-master's training plus supervision in sensorimotor psychotherapy (Ogden & Fisher, 2017) also provides such a tool. Some elements of this method have also been adopted in the methodological focus of this chapter.

In this chapter, we draw on insights from attachment, mentalization, 'enactment' and trauma within the MBT tradition as described by Allen et al. (2008), Fonagy and Target (2008) and Luyten and Fonagy (2019). In MBT we look at trauma and transference mainly from the perspective of patients with personality problems. To broaden our perspective to include patients with PPS, we have also drawn on the work of Wallin (2010) and Pat Ogden and Janina Fisher (2017). Ogden and Fisher describe sensorimotor psychotherapy for patients with trauma and attachment issues, and always discuss the connection to how these issues manifest in the body. The work of traumatologist Bessel van der Kolk (2014) on attachment, trauma and the body has also been helpful to us. In our opinion, the theoretical and clinical approaches of Wallin, Ogden, Fisher and van der Kolk are well compatible with MBT and B-MBT. For further reading we refer to the inspiring works of these authors in addition to the (B-)MBT articles and books.

In the rest of this chapter we first discuss the therapist's willingness and readiness to deal with the old hurt of their patient. We then discuss education, taking into account the tolerance zone, the importance of supportive relationships and the recognition of (somatoform) dissociation. These are important both in dealing with transference/counter-transference and in dealing with trauma, which is then discussed in detail. Finally, the chapter ends with a description of how old mental pain can lead to rigidity in the body and how to respond to this.

7.2   The therapist's willingness and readiness to deal with the patient's old mental pain

Working with patients with severe PPS almost inherently involves confrontation with stories of repeated disappointments with counsellors, years of misunderstanding from relatives, trauma and helplessness at not having control over one's own body. These stories may include traumatic separations (such as death or abandonment by parental figures, siblings or partners), affective neglect, threats, blackmail, (sexual) abuse, major surgery, road accidents, physical injuries or failed medical treatments. Exposure to these emotionally charged stories leads some therapists to conclude that they need to be fit to work with patients with severe PPS. This reflects the reality that professional specialisation and affinity with the issues are required to help this target group. Stories of old mental pain can place a considerable emotional burden on the therapist.

The question is whether or not the therapist is prepared to open up to these stories and their implicit non-verbal expressions. Are we ready for these uncomfortable, painful patient experiences? Can we go against our natural tendency to turn away from so much painful material? This also raises the question of how many emotional and physical resources we ourselves have at our disposal. Do we have the ability to calm ourselves down easily and to be mindful in a body-oriented way in the face of trauma and other painful experiences? Do we have enough colleagues with whom we can talk about our therapeutic work?

In addition, the patient's transference and traumatic memories can trigger our own memories in this area. This recognition can be threatening, especially if we were not inclined to recognise our own old pain. How have painful patient experiences that we recognise affected our body and mind, and how do they still affect us? Do we still reflect on it enough? Do we do enough with it in our daily lives?

Some awareness of one's own insecure attachment style, if any, is also important in order to go deeper into a patient's old inner pain. For example, if we have an avoidant style and the patient has an extremely preoccupied attachment style with a lot of clinging, it is good to be aware of this difference. We may be particularly sensitive to clinging in such a case because it takes us out of our familiar position of emotional avoidance. It is important to be aware of this because otherwise it can have a negative effect on our willingness to help a patient. The Experiences in Close Relationships-Revised (ECR-R) questionnaire can be helpful in considering one's own attachment style (Kooiman et al., 2013).

Our willingness to deal with the patient's old pain also requires us to recognise that we 'want to be a good parent'. We want to offer the patient a corrective emotional experience, but we also know that we can't undo what happened in the past. In the eyes of our patients, we are falling short, just in terms of the time available. We must be prepared to endure this if we are to address old psychic pain. Our willingness to deal with old hurts is at the same time a question to ourselves about our professional readiness. Do we already have sufficient knowledge, skills and experience in dealing with enactment and trauma?

In the next section we continue with the points to be aware of when dealing with incriminating past events. They are essential, but also general and limited in nature. Only the most important issues are mentioned. So, as well as taking the advice in this book to heart, you should also take a look at yourself: am I already adequately equipped? Have I had sufficient education, training, supervision or intervision in this area? Do I have plenty of colleagues to fall back on and collaborate with? This awareness shows the extent of our possibilities. Seeking advice from more experienced colleagues or asking them to take over part of the treatment or contribute in another way to the therapy can always be kept open as an option.

7.3 Education

When educating about PPS and body-oriented mentalizing (see Section 4.7), we can also add education about the consequences of past trauma and painful relationships in the past. Topics that could be covered include:

- Types of trauma
- The symptoms of post-traumatic stress disorder and how to deal with them
- The impact of trauma and painful relationships on current emotional life, body and relationships
- The tendency to 're-enact'
- Dissociation as a survival strategy
- Long-term stress after trauma and painful relationships
- The window of tolerance
- The trauma of losing control of severe physical symptoms
- Difficulties with ('body-oriented') mentalizing after trauma and in an insecure attachment relationships

Because implicit memories of trauma or a painful relationship are common in people with PPS and have far-reaching consequences, education about how implicit memories work is important. We explain that people can store intensely painful events (in part) implicitly. They manifest themselves in current life through confusing emotions, uncomfortable physical symptoms and incomprehensible reaction patterns, without us knowing that it has to do with a memory of something painful. We can explain to our patients that implicit memories are 'situationally accessible'. We can explain that they are evoked in the present moment by both internal and external stimuli that trigger a feeling that there is more to it than what the here and now gives rise to: 'Every time someone touches you, can become stressed, and remember, without realizing it, that in the past you were hit. You can brace yourself by tensing all your muscles'.

Understanding the influences of implicit memories can be reassuring for patients. Making a connection between their daily distress and implicit memories can not only reassure patients, but also motivate them to explore their physical sensations and emotional responses further. We should also explain that emotions related to a trauma or long-term painful relationship may be completely out of consciousness due to years of unconscious dissociation. We can give the example of a once trembling hand as a sign of fear. Patients may have taken a lot of distance from their emotions due to painful events. Then we have to teach them, almost scholastically, that 'if your shoulders are tense, your breathing is shallow and you are sweating, you are probably afraid'. Through this explanation, bodily sensations and associated emotions can become part of the therapeutic conversation and body-oriented mentalizing. It is also preferable to talk about old wounds such as trauma and painful relationships in groups, as this allows patients to share experiences and knowledge and to support each other.

7.4   Considering the tolerance zone

Addressing an 'enactment' or a traumatic memory can cause unexpected stress and 'arousal' in patients. It is only therapeutic if the patient's level of arousal remains within acceptable limits, i.e., if we take into account the tolerance zone ('window of tolerance', see also Section 4.8.8). Only then can the patient eventually tolerate increasingly higher levels of arousal when focussing on a past painful experience. One can then maintain the ability to think, feel and act self-consciously at higher levels of arousal. Therefore, when turning mindful attention to the implicit old mental pain, we should be aware of an attack of intense stress, arousal or physical discomfort in which the central nervous system may become over-excited.

7.4.1   Overstimulation of the nervous system

When the sympathetic part of the nervous system becomes overstimulated, the most common physical symptoms are rapid breathing or hyperventilation, paleness, sweating, restlessness and widening of the pupils. In this state, the patient may feel overwhelmed and disorganised. There may also be overstimulation of the parasympathetic nervous system, which may be evidenced by a decrease in respiration, blood pressure and heart rate, constricted or fixed pupils, slackening and immobility.

The dorsovagal system is part of the parasympathetic nervous system. It is triggered by great danger, when fighting or fleeing is no longer possible. This leads to immobility and physical rigidity, weakness and paralysis. In this state of 'surrender', there is no longer any perception of the outside world (Nicolai, 2017a). In mammals, this collapse is known as the Totstell reflex. It is a protective mechanism during periods of extreme stress or arousal, when fighting or fleeing in the face of an attacker appears not to be an option. As many predators are sensitive to movement, the Totstell reflex prevents them from noticing a living creature.

According to Porges (2011), the dorsal parasympathetic system, which controls the Totstell reflex, is evolutionarily the oldest part of the autonomic nervous system. Under a very severe threat, this system dominates socialisation (the ventral vagal system) and fight or flight (the sympathetic system). When faced with danger, the first thing people usually do is seek contact with others. However, the ventral vagal system, which drives this response, is evolutionarily the most recently developed. When there is a very strong stimulation of the autonomic nervous system, the socialisation response is the first to be put out of action. Then, in case of great danger, fight/flight can also be postponed, and immobility occurs first.

7.4.2   Regulating arousal and stress

In all forms of overstimulation of the autonomic nervous system, the patient's body and mind enter the fight/flight/freeze or paralysis mode and the body, teleological, equivalence or pretend mode of non-mentalization (see Section 5.1.1). At these signs of overstimulation, it is time to slow down the physical and inner exploration and move to interventions to regulate stress and arousal and the associated bodily response (see also Section 4.8.8). The therapist structures the session, provides advice, behavioural guidance and validates the client's experiences and feelings. We may then use stabilising techniques, for example asking the patient to focus attention on non-threatening bodily sensations such as breathing or the feel of the feet on the floor. We may use a guided body scan exercise, a breathing exercise or a relaxation exercise to help reduce arousal. The well-known traumatologist Bessel van der Kolk recommends 'tapping' in case of signs of trauma. This involves tapping on acupuncture points with the fingers (van der Kolk, 2014). Physical activity, such as a short walk, can also help.

If focusing on the body is stressful, we can also ask the patient to focus on something outside himself, such as the clock on the wall or an object on the table. All of these interventions aim to consciously bring the patient's attention back to the present, allowing them to release the connection with the unpleasant past or enactment. This allows the autonomic nervous system to return to rest. In patients with severe PPS, hyperarousal is strongly associated with worsening physical symptoms. Patients often do not relate these physical complaints to their arousal, stress or intense emotions. It is therefore necessary for the therapist to focus on the patient's level of arousal during acute exacerbations of pain, fatigue or loss of a physical function, and then help them to reduce their arousal. We can then focus on reducing physical discomfort, for example, by changing sitting or lying positions, moving or resting, or other physical discomfort-reducing activities.

Later, when the patient has emerged from the extreme 'storm' of arousal/affect/ stress/physical complaints, the therapist and patient can look back on the intense situation via a 'stop and go back' (see Section 5.2.17). Here the therapist and patient can explore what preceded the occurrence of the intense feelings or complaints. For example, did they occur in the presence of a particular object, the physical or emotional closeness or distance of the therapist, a statement made by the therapist? The therapist then can try to refocus the body-oriented mentalizing on the here and now. For example, with a patient who has had an attack of abdominal pain, after the patient has calmed down, the therapist might ask: 'What did you experience just before the first pain shot?' After the patient says that he became very tense when a new group member stood too close to him, the therapist might ask: 'What physical cues do you experience now when you look at your neighbour?'

Apart from the therapist's help in staying within the tolerance zone, patients themselves can learn to expand and use their coping repertoire. These resources can be diverse, ranging from social skills to yoga, religious practice or social support. To increase self-efficacy in staying within the tolerance zone, it is necessary for patients to be able to apply stress and emotion regulation themselves. This could include self-application of mindful self-monitoring; breathing, relaxation or movement exercises; yoga; mindfulness; 'grounding'; practising switching between past and present; practising dual awareness; tapping (acupressure points) or visualising a safe place. They can also use resources such as building a social network so that you can talk to a close friend (see Section 7.5).

It is recommended that traumatic memories, transference and counter-transference should not be addressed until the patient has some experience of adequate self-regulation of stress and emotions. We can ask our patients to practise these skills regularly, possibly with the help of another counsellor. Reference can also be made to group training in self-regulation. The patient can then use these self-regulating skills when exploring transference and trauma (see Section 7.7 to Section 7.9). If the patient's self-regulation fails repeatedly when discussing painful events, there is a risk of re-traumatisation. Treatment for intrusive trauma symptoms such as Eye Movement Desensitisation and Reprocessing (EMDR) may then be indicated. If, as a result of such an approach, the patient suffers less from uncontrollable arousal, they can continue training their self-regulation skills and continue B-MBT if regulatory skills are at a sufficient level.

7.5   Using supportive relationships

To ensure that patients have people to turn to for emotional support when exploring old mental hurts, they can take stock of their network of relationships. Is there a network of secure relationships in which conflicts and disturbances in one relationship can be buffered by another? If not, we should work with our patient to inventory and strengthen their social network. When inventorying the network, it can be helpful to draw up an ecogram (Vlaeminck, 2005). This is an overview of the size and quality of the patient's informal social network. When taking stock, the therapist can help reflect on which people are important in the patient's life. Who does he consider to be a good friend? Who can they count on and turn to when they are having a hard time? Does this person make them feel safe? The therapist can encourage the patient to think back to a positive experience with one of these people. Then we can ask the patient to think about who it was, where it was, what he heard, saw, smelled, tasted or felt. And what bodily signals does he notice when he recalls the positive experience? What thoughts, feelings, desires and inclinations? In this way, the patient can draw on his or her own experience in constructing the ecogram. We can consider the role of direct relatives and any supportive role of neighbours, acquaintances, colleagues, (informal) caregivers and spiritual guides. Using the ecogram as a starting point, we can guide patients towards closer contacts. Making an ecogram can also be a reason to involve members of the social network in treatment. This may include work on body-oriented mentalizing within the system (see also Chapter 10).

7.6   Keep an eye on (somatoform) dissociation

Discussing old mental pains can be accompanied by severe (somatoform) dissociation, such as loss of consciousness, numbness and paralysis. Dissociation is the placing of certain thoughts, emotions, physical sensations, perceptions or memories out of consciousness. Dissociation can be seen as a helpful process in the case of drastic events. It is a protective mechanism against the overwhelming influence that unpleasant experiences and their memories can have. Dissociation can be problematic if it persists when the reason for it (a distressing event) has long since passed. In B-MBT, the therapist is alert to the occurrence of both psychological and somatic forms of dissociation. For example, in the psychological aspects of dissociation, we look for

- Loss of memory for (aspects of) the trauma and in the present
- An altered experience of time
- The absence or flattening of emotions
- An unrealistic perception of the environment (derealisation)
- An altered sense of identity
- Perceiving oneself as alien (depersonalisation)

In patients with severe PPS, we should pay particular attention to the physical aspects of dissociation, known as somatoform dissociation (Nijenhuis, 2000). Here, bodily experiences, reactions and functions are not well integrated into perception. Perceptions such as touch, smell, sight, hearing and taste are disturbed. A person may lose control of motor skills, such as in an arm or leg, or have difficulty speaking or swallowing. One may lose sensation in a part of your body or be unable to feel pain. One may show physical reactions related to inner images and emotions in the area of the trauma without noticing it: for example, a constantly clenched fist. A person may also perceive a body part as distorted, or experience a body part as foreign, as if it does not belong to oneself.

Through somatoform dissociation, consciousness can distance itself from the physical aspect of a traumatic event. For example, someone who has been punched repeatedly in the face may have no feeling in the face for a long time. One distances oneself from the event and the physical experience: 'It's not my body this is happening to. It's not me going through this. It's someone else'. Fragments of the event thus become unconscious, but then return unasked, for example in the form of physical pain such as headaches, physical numbness, intrusive bodily sensations and a dysregulated autonomic nervous system.

When patients behave in extremely contradictory ways, this can also be a sign of dissociation. For example, one moment a person may report that an incident in the past was painful to them, only to report moments later that it was nothing important. Patients may express themselves inconsistently because they suffer from gaps in their memory of traumatic experiences. For example, a patient with severe PPS, once the victim of a serious road accident, becomes very upset during art therapy because of a memory of the accident. In a subsequent therapy session, however, she reports that the art therapy did not cause her much distress this time.

Dissociation can also occur because people are unaware of the meaning of their behaviour or physical expression. A person's left leg may shake for an hour during therapy without them noticing or being aware of what's going on. When we notice (somatoform) dissociations in the patient, we take this as a sign that the patient is no longer capable of body-oriented mentalizing and that strong emotions are involved. If we feel that there is an increased level of stress in the patient, we can offer stress regulation as described in Section 7.8. When regulating dissociation, exercises and instructions aimed at conscious attention to the present moment are particularly valuable. We can think of many simple stabilising exercises, such as paying attention to an object in the room, breathing, feet on the floor, etc.

If we observe dissociation in a patient, we should be aware of previous trauma and counsel the patient as described later in Section 7.8. If there is evidence of structural and severe dissociation, we may decide to investigate its nature and extent, for example using the SCID-D, the structured clinical interview for DSM-V dissociative disorders and the SDQ-20, specifically designed for somatoform dissociation (Nijenhuis et al., 1996). In the case of persistent dissociation, we may consider teaching the patient to develop skills in dealing with dissociation (Boon et al., 2012). If necessary, we can make a temporary referral to a colleague who is a specialist in this field.

7.7   Addressing transference and counter-transference

7.7.1   What is (somatic) transference, counter-transference and enactment?

Through the exchange of bodily signals and inner experiences between patient and therapist, a personal relationship soon develops between the two. This personal relationship naturally reflects the implicit traces of previous relationships. Impressive bonding experiences are usually mainly physical and emotional in nature. Memories of the emotional atmosphere of early painful relationships with significant others may be largely implicit in nature. We cannot consciously retrieve these memories from our memory, so we relive them in our current relationships. This is especially true if the past relationship was insecure in nature. Many patients with severe PPS have multiple negative interpersonal experiences in their past. These are usually related to emotional neglect, abuse or violence. Even relationships that were pleasurable in many ways may have been painful at the same time, for example because they were oppressive, involuntary or belittling. Intense negative experiences with the primary caregiver(s) in childhood can implicitly make a deep impression and can have far-reaching consequences for later socio-emotional development.

The literature on attachment therefore refers to attachment trauma. This can include obvious abuse or neglect, but also a prolonged lack of affection or response from the caregiver. Attachment trauma can also occur, for example, in the case of repeated intense domestic tensions, a long-term seriously ill sibling, the absence of the primary caregiver due to divorce, or serious illness or death. In addition to negative interpersonal experiences in early childhood, many patients with severe PPS have multiple disappointing therapy experiences, such as not feeling understood or recognised in relation to physical problems. In addition, PPS also leads to current problems in coping with loved ones. On the one hand, symptoms such as severe pain, prolonged severe fatigue or paralysis of arms or legs may cause concern among loved ones, while on the other hand, family members may become suspicious and overburdened in the long term.

Experiencing strong alternations between compassion, care and closeness on the one hand, and suspicion, distance and hostility on the other, causes patients stress and impairs their well-being. The negative interpersonal experiences of early and recent life eventually lead to epistemic distrust, the inability to be open to learning from others in new situations (Fonagy & Allison, 2014). Relationships become narrowed into repetitive patterns, where one cannot be open to the other, but mainly experiences (implicitly) the repetition of what took place before. Transference symptoms are therefore a natural part of a deepening therapeutic relationship with patients with severe PPS.

Therapeutic contact evokes experiences and feelings towards significant others from the past, which patients transfer to the therapist. For example, the patient may soon perceive the therapist as a perpetrator or neglecter. However, transference can also be seen as broader than the therapeutic relationship. If, based on past relationship experiences, a person assumes that all sorts of other people around them will perceive and treat them in a harmful way, we can also see this as transference. Counter-transference is our own unconscious response to the other's transference. In counter-transference, the therapist unconsciously goes along with the patient's transference, which strongly determines his or her physical and mental reaction. This may be due to the therapist's own sensitivities combined with a strong appeal emanating from the patient. For example, if the patient reacts to the therapist as he did to his cold-hearted father, the therapist may unconsciously take on the role of the cold-hearted therapist. In this way the therapist reinforces the patient's transference.

Counter-transference only occurs when we are not sufficiently aware of the patient's approach and our ideas, feelings and physical sensations in response to it. Without being aware of it, we approach patients on the basis of transference. We become caught up in an automatic pattern of response, a mode of non-mentalizing, and are not fully aware of our possible implicit biases about the patient.

The transference-counter-transference situation can be referred to as enactment, the staging of older implicit relational patterns that enter the therapeutic interaction (Nicolai, 2017a). Both patient and therapist respond on the basis of implicit memories of past (painful) relational situations. This is an unconscious pattern of interaction into which they both enter. Enactment occurs at the moment when transference and counter-transference interlock. It is at the intersection of the unconscious needs and vulnerabilities of the therapist and the patient that enactment occurs, in which both can get stuck. For example, a patient who repeatedly feels inadequate and a therapist who tends to feel inadequate can get stuck in an enactment. In this situation, for example, they can only see their relationship through the lens of being neglected and being the neglecter.

In patients with severe PPS, we should always consider the physical dimension of the enactment. Patients with PPS can have great difficulty being aware of the language of their body. They are not yet able to express in words what their inner being is expressing through the body. Strong transference feelings are then translated into non-verbal 'somatic transference'. The patient is then mainly in the body mode of (non-)mentalizing. The intense thoughts, affects, tendencies, fantasies, memories, which are still unknown to the patient, are expressed mainly through bodily sensations or through inner images of bodily activities and movements (Dosamantes-Beaudry, 2007). These bodily experiences are expressed through subtle bodily cues, such as a certain look in the eyes or small waving movements with the arms as an implicit anger towards the therapist (Dosamantes-Beaudry, 2007).

The somatic manifestations of the patient can easily get under our skin. For example, we may not notice at first that our shoulders and neck muscles are cramping, and only later, after the session, do we notice that we have shoulder and neck pain. Our own (as yet) unawareness of what we are experiencing in the relationship with the patient also determines the somatic counter-transference. We react physically and feel, for example, fatigue, pain, restlessness, drowsiness or physical tension. In this way, we and our patients embody what we cannot yet communicate through words. A 'somatic enactment' takes place: a mutual physical response without words in which both are in a body mode of non-mentalizing.

Many therapies emphasise the transference phenomenon in the patient. In B-MBT, however, we assume that the therapist can also evoke an enactment because, like patients, we have our implicit memories and unconscious response patterns and express feelings through our bodies. Enactments make it clear that what takes place in the therapeutic relationship, as in other attachment relationships, is always the result of a two-way traffic. The unconscious physical and inner experiences of the patient and the therapist are, on the one hand, determined by who they are, independent of the therapeutic relationship, but at the same time always in response to the therapeutic relationship. We assume that the therapist can never completely transcend himself in therapy. So we are always subjective in our contact with the patient. No matter how well thought out our interventions are, they always contain subjective elements that contribute to transference, counter-transference and enactment. Our therapeutic interventions, no matter how well thought out, are always also related to associations that the patient evokes in us based on our personal learning history. In B-MBT, enactment is not an unusual and annoying obstacle; it is a logical and necessary building block of therapy. Through open mutual communication, the therapist consciously moves towards transference and enactment.

By continuing to mentalize in a body-oriented way, the patient and therapist reflect together on the hitherto unconscious communication pattern, in order to be able to let it go, if desired, after becoming aware of it. The more the therapist is aware of his contribution to the enactment and the associated bodily sensations, thoughts and emotions, and can put them into words, the better he or she can release the coercive influence of the transference (Wallin, 2010).

Addressing transference patterns should not be forgotten. After all, in patients they lead to ongoing relationship problems with parties who need to be dealt with in order to recover from PPS, such as caregivers and loved ones. Failure to address enactment perpetuates the inability to mentalize, continue relationship problems and the limited way in which patients experience themselves. This prevents them from fully recovering from PPS or learning to deal with their physical symptoms with sufficient flexibility.

The methodological points described in the next part of this chapter are important for all disciplines working with people with PPS. If working with transference, counter-transference and enactment gets stuck, unproductive or confusing, it is better to leave it to a therapist with recognised psychotherapy training who has also completed supervision in the field of enactment.

7.7.2 Methodological aspects of dealing with transference, counter-transference and enactment

Recognising counter-transference and enactment in ourselves

First of all, the therapist needs to become aware of his or her own (somatic) counter-transference. It is part of our work as therapists to find out if and how we are involved in enactment with the patient. Which of our bodily sensations, emotions and thoughts are involved? The first step is to ask if we experience strong physical sensations in contact with the patient, such as: tiredness, drowsiness, tension, pain symptoms. Next, we ask if we have strong emotions or absolute thoughts related to the patient. We check whether we fall into a repetitive pattern of behaviour towards the patient, such as being overly helpful or, on the contrary, repeatedly correcting the patient. Once we are in an enactment with the patient, we can quickly fall into a non-mentalizing mode. In order to recognise enactment it is therefore very important to be aware of our non-mentalizing modes (see Appendix A.3). Here are some examples of what we might experience physically and mentally in the different non-mentalizing modes when we are in an enactment.

- *Body mode:* In contact with the patient, we react strongly physically. For example, we become restless and want to move. We can also easily become physically stiff. We solve physical discomfort physically, for example: change position, stand up for a moment, have a drink. We do not think much about our physical reactions, we just react. We are easily stressed without being aware of it. We can also be very relaxed. The pleasant feeling of relaxed muscles is so prominent that we make no connection with the context of the therapeutic relationship at that moment.
- *Teleological mode:* When patients have physical symptoms, we look only for a somatic solution, we are alert because there must be an immediate solution now. We tend to refer the patient to a colleague (doctor) for a quick medical solution. We make all sorts of lists of advice and behavioural strategies for both the patient and ourselves from a strong solution-oriented mindset. We act out of fear because 'if we don't intervene now, things will go wrong'. Meanwhile, we are hardly free of our fear. We think we are forced by the patient's condition to find solutions, without realising what our own emotions are behind this.
- *Equivalence mode:* We may experience strong physical signals associated with strong emotions and thoughts about the patient that bother us a lot, such as severe pain in the shoulders or severe tension. We feel insecure, irritated, very

sad or angry and want the situation we are in with this patient to end as soon as possible. Outside the session, we often think about the patient and experience a strong negative physical or emotional reaction. In the case of positive counter-transference, we feel a strong need for more contact with the patient. We tend to have strong and absolute views about the patient that we hold, such as 'he is just very special' or 'he is just a very nasty man'.

- *Pretend mode:* We may feel very tired. We feel flat, bored or sleepy and disconnected from the patient. Our attention is elsewhere, and we tend to react routinely, dismissing the patient's comments as unimportant or uninteresting. We rationalise a lot and want to analyse and explain, using many words.

Particularly characteristic of the teleological mode and the equivalence mode is the lack of freedom we feel to respond spontaneously. We can also feel this lack of freedom physically when we are in the body mode: we do not feel free to move or make gestures or adopt a physical posture as we would like. We are physically trapped, as if we are frozen. In all modes of (non-)mentalizing we can't feel free enough to stand still and reflect on our own bodily sensations, to think about them, to feel about them and about ourselves. Do we notice strong physical and mental reactions in contact with the patient? Do we notice that we are no longer mentalizing? Then we ask: 'Is there perhaps enactment here? What exactly does this look like? What precisely am I reacting to? What is my contribution to the enactment?' The therapist can also use a self-report questionnaire to identify counter-transference. The Impact Message Inventory-Circumplex (IMI-C) is a widely used measurement tool that helps therapists to become aware of counter-transference they experience in therapeutic contact with patients (Hafkenscheid & Rouckhout, 2009).

Recognising non-verbal traces of transference in the patient

The body expresses in posture, gesture and movement how a person relates to another, such as the therapist. We suggest that current body expression may also reflect body expression in previous attachment relationships (Ogden & Fisher, 2017) and the associated transference. The repetitive judgmental tone in the voice or the constant frowning and sighing may be a repetition of the original attitude towards the parents. In his patients, the therapist pays particular attention to repetitive non-verbal signals such as a subtle look of contempt, a sad tone of voice or a dejected, limp posture. Are these signals part of repetitive communicative messages towards the therapist, the therapy as a whole or the multidisciplinary team? Does the patient get stuck in this attitude, just as they get stuck in this pattern in everyday life? Are the relational stagnations accompanied by a (non-) mentalizing mode? If so, there is reason to explore the likely transference further. Identifying transference patterns can also take place during non-verbal therapies where attention is paid to the physical aspects of making contact with others.

Recognising transference scenarios

Common transference patterns of patients with severe PPS include:

- You are not really interested in me and my physical complaints.
- You are not really available to me.
- What I feel and want does not matter to you.
- Others are much more important to you than I am.
- You don't think I'm worth anything.
- You think I am a nag or a poser.
- You think my physical complaints are exaggerated.
- In the end, I have to do it all by myself again.
- You know everything and I am stupid.
- You think I have failed.
- I have nothing to contribute.
- You are no good and deserve to be punished.
- You hurt me and I am the victim.
- You are no good. I must be careful of what you do to me.

Recognising these patterns of communication in therapy or in the past outside of therapy is part of the therapy. These patterns can be part of the attachment style of the patient. We may refer to earlier meetings in which the patient's attachment style was discussed. In recognising the patient's communicative patterns and attachment styles, it is explicitly not the intention to give explanations and analyses of these patterns from the position of an expert. Nor is it appropriate to over-explain how unconscious relational patterns can cause or maintain physical complaints. This is likely to lead to intellectualisation, which would stop body-oriented mentalizing.

Distinguishing patterns of transference and enactment aims at patients learning to recognise them as phenomena, and then to mentalize them in a body-oriented way. For example, the therapist might say: 'Are we perhaps back in our pattern where you think I find you a nag and I think I am very inadequate in relieving you of your physical symptoms?' In time, the recognition of the enactment may be enough for the patient and therapist to get out of the un-mentalized relationship trap. Having recognised the pattern, they move on to further body-oriented mentalizing.

Validating transference

In B-MBT we don't avoid transference; we try to consciously notice it. If we are genuinely willing to experience transference and counter-transference and to be open to eventual enactment, we are more likely to achieve patients breaking free from their old relational response patterns. By being open to mutual enactment we also communicate to patients that it is not about who is 'to blame'. It is about becoming aware of almost inescapable enactments. The therapist validates the patient's transference experience as an inner experience that is as important as any other. These bodily experiences, thoughts and feelings are not less worthy or wrong. We want to make it clear to our patients that this is really how they are experiencing the repetitive pattern and that this experience has a right to exist. If a young woman with chronic fatigue is constantly convinced that others, including the therapist, think she is a whiner, the therapist may say: 'Obviously, I have done something to convince you that I think you are a whiner, just as you think your partner and your friends think you are'. He can continue with: 'Let's see when this belief comes back to you and what happens between the two of us then or what I say or do then'. See also Box 7.1.

Box 7.1　Therapy fragment: 'You think I'm a whiner'

If the young woman with chronic fatigue mentioned earlier remains convinced that the therapist thinks she is a whiner, the therapist can continue the conversation by saying something like, 'Stop. Let's think about what's happening now. How does my behaviour or posture contribute to you thinking that I think you are a whiner?'

Patient: Sometimes you look bored and sit slumped.
Therapist: Ah, that doesn't sound very encouraging. How exactly do I sit and look?
Patient leans back and stares into space.
Therapist: I see, you see me sitting there staring into space and you think, 'He thinks I'm a whiner'.
Patient: Exactly.
Therapist: Ah, yes. I would like to try to understand a bit more. What else do I have to imagine is going through your mind in this situation?
Patient: That you are tired and would like to go home. Why would you want to be with someone who is tired and nags?
Therapist: Yes, yes, you have the impression that I would rather do something else than talk to you because I am tired, and I would rather not have to deal with your whinging about being tired.
The patient is silent and begins to shake and cry.
Therapist: I can see that you are shaking, and I can see that this is affecting you. What are you feeling?
Patient: Afraid. I'm afraid, afraid that you might just stop the therapy like that.

This seems to have opened up a new emotional scenario: the assumption that the therapist might unexpectedly leave the patient alone. A reason for further exploration.

Collaborative enactment exploration

Enactment exploration takes place as a collaborative project. Bateman and Fonagy (2006) describe this collaboration with the patient as 'sitting side by side and looking together at the patient's feelings and thoughts from an attitude of curiosity'. Feelings such as anger and a thought such as 'you're not really interested in me' become the focus of joint attention and inquiry: 'Let's see together what is happening between us now'. Because of the enactment during this exploration, the patient may soon fall back into the thought already noted ('You are not really interested in me'). It is now the therapist's job to continue the joint exploration using techniques such as those described in Section 5.2, such as: focusing attention, asking open questions, asking follow-up questions, summarising, putting oneself in the other person's shoes, stopping and standing still, stopping and going back, etc. We consider in detail which of our actions are linked to which of the patient's emotions and thoughts, and vice versa. This is not about looking for a cause or an explanation, or blaming anything or anyone. It is about looking for subjective physical and inner experiences and patterns in both the patient and the therapist.

If we have the impression that a patient is stuck in a repetitive pattern of communication outside of therapy, the therapist may suggest that this pattern be explored within the therapeutic relationship. In the case of a patient with chronic facial pain who is sure that neither her partner nor her social workers or friends understand her pain symptoms, he might ask: 'Could it be that you feel that this therapy and I as your therapist do not really understand your pain either?'

Transparency

The therapist is open about his own contribution to the enactment and reports his physical sensations and inner experiences in the enactment. For example, with the patient in therapy fragment in Box 7.1, the therapist might be open about feeling a heavy sensation in his body. 'It is as if something heavy is pressing on me now', when the patient tells him that she thinks he thinks she is whiner.

In order to become aware of his emotions involved, the therapist may, for example, focus for a moment on memories associated with the physical sensation of feeling heavy. In fact, images and memories help to make people aware of the emotions behind physical sensations. In the example, the therapist may be reminded of a difficult period in his life when he was caring for a seriously ill family member. He becomes aware of how worried he was and how heavy the responsibility of caring for him was. With this, the therapist makes a connection to the transference: how his own images and memories are connected to the inner world of the client. In the following therapy fragment (Box 7.2), the therapist shares his bodily experiences, thoughts and memories with the patient.

The therapist's frank attitude gives the patient the opportunity to learn that the therapist's body and mind work differently from what he expects from the transference. This seems to make room for new emotional insights in the patient.

Box 7.2 Therapy extract: Therapist shares body signals, feelings and a memory

Therapist: When you say that, it's as if something heavy is pressing down on me now. . . (silence)

Therapist: When I think about it, I get images of when I was caring for a seriously ill relative and thinking 'I can't make mistakes. It's my job to make her feel well'. That felt heavy and oppressive, just like now. Obviously, I feel it is my job to relieve you of your tiredness and the idea that you are a whiner as soon as possible . . . (silence).

Therapist: How do you feel about what I am telling you now? What do you feel in your body? What emotions or thoughts do you have?

Patient: Strange, I suddenly remember that when my mother used to have headaches, I always thought: 'I shouldn't complain about my fatigue now, otherwise she will get even worse headaches'.

Validating differences

In the transparent exchange of mutual experiences of enactment, the difference between what the patient thinks and feels towards the therapist and vice versa will become clear. The therapist can validate this difference, for example, by saying, 'Look at what happens to you and what happens to me. You think I am tired and that you are a whiner to me. And what happens to me? I have an oppressive feeling. I find myself thinking: "How can I still make her stop thinking that I think that I think she's a nag and make it clear that I want to help her?"'

Our job as therapists is to mark and, above all, to validate the mutual differences in feeling and thinking. We can show through our stance and questions that differences are important, as in, 'What other differences have you noticed between us?'

Offering a different perspective

The therapist may be able to offer a different perspective to what the patient thinks they are perceiving from the transference. This is especially effective when the patient is in equivalence mode. The therapist can say to a patient who thinks the therapist is angry with him: 'Could it be that my furrowed brow indicates that I'm deeply thinking?' We can only use this offering of an alternative viewpoint, also called 'interpretive mentalization', if we have first gone through the basic techniques of body-oriented mentalizing and the steps described earlier in this chapter. The alternative perspective should be offered with caution, as in 'Could it be that . . .' or 'Perhaps you could also see it as . . .'. Many patients with severe PPS have difficulty recognising emotions such as fear and anger in themselves. This colours many times an enactment. For example, the patient who says he is angry with the therapist because he keeps yawning may also be showing signs of anxiety. The therapist might then interpret this by mentalizing: 'Could it be that you are also afraid that my attention is not really with you in the best possible way?' Or, in the case of someone who does not recognise his own anger: 'You are anxious because I am going on holiday. Could it be that you are also angry that I am going away for a fortnight without consulting you?' However, too sudden interpretations can also disrupt body-oriented mentalizing. It requires first a thorough joint exploration of the enactment before an alternative view is offered.

Continuing the exchange

The intention is to continue the sharing of the enactment for some time. It is likely that in working through an enactment, the therapist will tap into a new level of transference. For example, if the therapist and patient have worked through the transference response 'I am not interesting to you', the patient may respond with, 'I am obviously too difficult and too heavy a case for you'. This is what Asen and Fonagy (2012) call the use of the mentalizing loop. This is working through an enactment to then engage in joint bodily and mind exploration on a subsequent enactment evoked by it. However, if the patient remains stuck in the same transference, we continue with body-oriented mentalizing. It is important to notice that the patient is always interpreting interpersonal situations in the same way. Our task here is to recognise our counter-transference and learn to change it. For example, by no longer arguing with a patient who wants to have a lot of control over conversations, the patient may feel more space for other thoughts and emotions.

Our lesson is that in ongoing or new transferences and enactments, we relentlessly return to the exploration and mutual exchange of physical and mental experience. This is not about achieving a particular end goal, such as solving a problem or enactment. Above all, it is about continuing to stimulate the process of reflection. We try to get patients to continue with body-oriented mentalizing despite setbacks, such as complicated relational and emotional problems combined with physical complaints.

Addressing memories of past relationships

Enactment, transference and counter-transference originate from past relationships where certain themes played out over time, such as experiencing a lack of emotional warmth, being dominated or being treated too harshly. The therapist can focus on explicit memories of these relationship experiences being repeated in the current relationship with the therapist. He then asks the patient to tune in on the physical sensations and inner experiences of this memory. If the memory is still mainly implicit, we first ask the patient to be aware of the repetitive physical and inner experiences within the therapeutic relationship, such as pain, fatigue, disappointment, regret and fear. Exploring these in the way that is characteristic of B-MBT (see Chapter 5) can make space for any images or memories. Of course, we pay attention to the patient's tolerance zone and switch to stress or emotion regulation if arousal is too high. When exploring an (implicit) memory, we can ask patients about the relational aspects of a memory, such as, 'With whom did you have this experience? Who was with you?' If the memories that emerge are traumatic in nature, such as a situation of physical or sexual abuse, we can respond with the approach described in the next section.

7.8   Dealing with trauma

7.8.1   Trauma

Many patients with severe PPS have experienced one or more types of trauma. For example, early attachment trauma, a car accident, unsuccessful medical treatment, sexual abuse or physical abuse (Roelofs & Spinhoven, 2007). Traumatic memories can also be about radical but not life-threatening events, such as unpleasant experiences with the diagnosis and treatment of a physical illness, the reactions of others to the illness (treatment), or unpleasant experiences with the illness itself. Examples of the latter are: a severe attack of chest pain, waking up with tinnitus, or chest tightness so severe that the patient feels extremely powerless, thinks they are going crazy or is intensely afraid of suffocating (van Rood & de Roos, 2017).

Based on theoretical and empirical literature, we can assume that repeated involuntary intrusive (implicit) memories and bad dreams associated with trauma contribute to physical stress and PPS. Long-lasting implicit memories of trauma cause prolonged stress reactions and physical symptoms, presenting a reason for the therapist to address these memories. Patients may tend to block intrusive memories persistently in their consciousness. This is accompanied by their being pushed back into consciousness all the time, the so-called 'thinking-not-about-white-bears effect'. For example, the patient who persistently tries not to think about a car accident will experience more and more flashbacks and will think that he is being run over all the time. The flashbacks can become dissociative and take on a life of their own, separate from reality. The experience of the trauma can sometimes seem to return without the patient being aware of it. This also happens during B-MBT. For example, a patient who has experienced physical abuse a long time ago may suddenly, overcome by a flashback, put her hands over her head and chest and moan, 'No, not again'.

We believe that traumatic memories that still have a serious impact on patients' lives years later may be (partly) implicit. The somatic and emotional aspects of the trauma are then stored in the implicit memory and patients cannot consciously recall them. The intense fear and the instinctive tendency to fight or flee are implicitly present without us being aware of it. The implicit emotional and somatic responses accumulate. Psychosomatic outbursts, attacks of physical symptoms, are then often the only way to channel intense emotions in cases of unprocessed trauma. Ogden and Fisher (2017) suggest that the original survival responses to trauma, such as socialising, fighting or fleeing, are still present somewhere in the body and mind. However, they have long since been dominated by the immobility response (rigidity, numbness and paralysis), which brings with it many physical symptoms. The urge to socialise, fight or flee is still present in the form of unfinished, fixed movements.

Trauma can be divided into: non-personal trauma, such as a natural disaster; interpersonal traumas, such as abuse by a stranger; and attachment traumas, such as abuse by an attachment figure (Luyten & Fonagy, 2019). In a trauma that initially appears as a physical trauma, the reactions of others have often also played a role in determining the outcome and processing of the trauma. Therefore, even when treating the consequences of a physical trauma, we should always consider the interpersonal aspects of the trauma as well as the attachment trauma.

The starting point of B-MBT for trauma is that secure attachment relationships are one of the strongest working factors in recovery from trauma. It is a natural response of children and adults in time of emergency to seek the safe closeness of others, such as partners, family and friends, who are outside of the trauma. When loved ones create attachment in a loving way and provide opportunities to communicate physically and verbally about the trauma, a person can come to rest. Through the implicit ('body-oriented') mentalizing of this care, the victim can become aware of and release his or her own physical and inner reaction to the trauma. If this has not been possible, our task in therapy is to provide this opportunity. We continue to work with the physical reactions, images and feelings in a safe, confidential therapeutic atmosphere.

In B-MBT we take care that the patient can reflect on the trauma and at the same time realise that he or she is in the here and now, in the safe proximity of the therapist. With this dual awareness (Ogden, 2006), one realises that one is in the here and now and that one can also let go of the intrusive memory. By bringing awareness to the implicit aspects of remembering traumatic events, we provide 'containment'. According to Allen et al. (2008), this consists of providing information about the trauma and its treatment, ensuring a safe working environment, activating sufficient supportive relationships, and increasing capacities for emotion and stress regulation. Containment can also include 'attending to the tolerance zone' and 'attending to (somatoform) dissociation' as described earlier in this chapter (see Section 7.4 and Section 7.6). The ultimate goal of standing still and focussing on the trauma, with all its painful physical and emotional sensations, is not to eliminate the painful memories altogether. The goal is to move towards tolerable pain when remembering the trauma (Allen et al., 2008).

7.8.2   Methodological aspects of working with trauma memories

Recognising traces of trauma

We should be alert to intrusive re-experiences, nightmares and strong emotional and physical reactions to trauma-related situations in our patients. We look for any kind of avoidance of trauma-related situations. We also look for excessive alertness, skittishness, tense reactions and irritability. If there is a sudden increase in physical symptoms, such as increased pain, increased fatigue, or increased conversion reactions, in the absence of current triggers, we should be alert to implicit trauma memories. An example: a patient with a history of sexual abuse passes out when sexuality is discussed. Another example: a young man with a history of physical abuse by his father, who used to hit him on the back with a belt, experiences severe back pain when the therapist asks about his relationship with his father. If a patient shows dissociation, this may be a trace of trauma.

Dissociation is often an extension of the (implicit) traumatic memories that many patients with severe PPS carry with them. We should therefore be alert to a variety of dissociation signals (see Section 7.6) as signs of (implicit) trauma experience. As trauma is accompanied by bodily processes, there is a good chance that traces of trauma will emerge in non-verbal therapies (see Chapter 6).

Carefully exploring bodily sensations

Care should be taken when helping patients to become aware of traumatic memories. Too much direct attention to emotions can be disruptive. We better start by patiently exploring physical sensations such as chest pressure, a feeling of collapsing, a feeling of melting, sinking away or getting cold. These are the essential signs of primitive parasympathetic survival mechanisms (Nicolai, 2017a). By taking these bodily sensations seriously and responding to them with empathy, associated implicit memories can become explicit at a pace appropriate to the patient. For example, with a patient with a history of multiple traumatic hospital admissions, the therapist asks her to be present with the experience of the pain in her arm. After some time, she tells how she received images of her stay in hospital when she was five years old. She was alone and the infusion needle was hurting her, but there was no one to respond to her crying.

Addressing trauma

If we have the impression that the patient has experienced trauma and is not yet able to deal with the explicit memories of it, how do we address this? How can we avoid unintentionally influencing a memory? Sometimes it is enough to ask, 'What happened? What was going on?' It can also be important not to go round in circles but to ask directly, for example, 'Did he hit you then?' Further questions are often required, such as, 'Can you tell me more about this?' We should be aware that the patient's first answer, such as 'Yes, he hit me', is the starting point for further exploration. It is the current perception and not (yet) the 'final truth' that is revealed. It is the starting point for body-oriented mentalizing, which may later clarify what was happening at the time.

We begin by attentively addressing and validating the physical sensations and emotions that are now emerging. Using the principles and techniques described in Chapter 4 and Chapter 5, we explore in a safe atmosphere what the patient is now feeling, noticing, thinking and possibly remembering. Without going into detail about memories, we can ask some exploratory questions such as where it was, what, when, how, by whom, through what, etc. When exploring the trauma, the patient may react with unpleasant physical symptoms such as chest pressure or intense muscle tension. We should always be aware that verbalising the trauma can be difficult because the memory is not only very painful but also implicit and opaque.

In the exploratory phase, we must also be careful to give the patient enough time to respond. Just as important as verbalising that a trauma has occurred is giving space to the difficulty of doing so. Patients have been silent for years in order to avoid the inner pain, the physical pain, the fear, the shame or the guilt. Paradoxically, for the sake of their health, we ask them to do exactly what they have been fighting against: to become aware of the trauma memory. We should always be aware of this paradox (Allen et al., 2008). Starting to talk therefore requires a lot of trust in the therapist. Patients sometimes respond to our questions non-verbally, for example with a nod or shake of the head, a deep sigh or a shrug of the shoulders. Then it may be necessary to ask how to interpret this non-verbal signal from the patient: 'I see the movement of your shoulders. Does that mean "I don't know?"' Or, 'I hear a deep sigh, does that perhaps mean "yes?"'

Some patients with severe PPS and a history of trauma may find it easier to start with a questionnaire asking if they have had a traumatic experience. The Life Events Checklist for DSM-5 (LEC-5) is a suitable instrument for this purpose. It is recommended to administer this or a similar questionnaire right at the beginning of treatment. However, this takes into account that some patients may not be aware of past traumatic experiences at that time.

Approaching trauma memories

The automatic response of the patient to push away emotional memories of the trauma and to continue to fight, flee, freeze or paralyse in trauma-related events is gradually broken down in therapy. If the patient still remembers the trauma mainly implicitly, we first deal with the physical sensations and possibly the emotions and stress response experienced, as we saw in earlier examples. Here we keep a close eye on the patient's tolerance zone. Exploring physical sensations and emotions (see also Section 5.2 and Section 6.7) can create space for images or memories. It is precisely by following the patient at his or her own pace of discovering his or her own current physical and inner reaction that space is created to become aware of multiple aspects of a memory. In this way, the process of making the memory of the trauma increasingly explicit can unfold. As we work with both the implicit and explicit aspects of the trauma, we agree with the patient that he or she is responsible for stopping the exposure to the memory. If the patient already has some explicit memory of the trauma, we can ask him to consciously stand still and focus on this explicit memory and the accompanying physical and inner experiences with attention. Our task is to address the patient's perceptual capacity (the observing ego) in the here and now, as in, 'If you go here now with your attention to the memory, what do you see now, what do you hear now, what do you feel now and how strong is it?' We always emphasise that the perception takes place from the here and now:

- What are you experiencing right now in your body?
- What emotion are you experiencing here and now?
- What thought is going through your mind right now?
- What tendency does this bring about in you here and now?

The therapist can even further emphasise the here and now with phrases such as, 'As we sit here in this room today and focus on this memory, what are you experiencing in your body right now?'" In this way, the patient realises that his physical and inner reaction is linked to a memory that he is experiencing in the present (dual consciousness). This prevents re-traumatisation. By shifting attention from the here and now to the memory, the context shifts. First there was an unconscious experience that the past was still the present. Now there is an awareness that the past is a memory in the here and now. The memory is no longer a fearful reality, but a painful memory that does not need to be acted upon automatically. This allows the patient to be aware of trauma-related physical sensations, thoughts and emotions, while at the same time acting on what is important for good physical and mental health in the present moment.

Reflecting on the relational context of trauma

Most traumas have a relational context. Severe neglect, maltreatment or abuse are related to unequal relationships. Patients have been victims of power mechanisms that have strong relational consequences. Even with more physical traumas, such as a car accident or a painful operation, there is usually a traumatic relational context that can lead to enactment, as in the case study in Box 7.3.

Box 7.3 Case study: 'They think I am a cruel perpetrator'

A young truck driver was involved in a head-on collision with a passenger car through no fault of his own, seriously injuring two passengers. He sustained minor injuries but suffered from unexplained pain for years afterwards. He was constantly reminded of the way he had been treated very coolly in the emergency room of the hospital: as if he had been a vicious criminal. He repeatedly dropped out of subsequent counselling: he always felt misunderstood and treated as the guilty one. During B-MBT he and the therapist went through the physical and inner experiences linked to the memory of the traumatic visit to the emergency room. He increasingly realised that deep down he himself had the thought, 'I am the cruel perpetrator'. Only when he realised that could he believe that the current therapist did not see him as a cruel perpetrator. He then was able to gradually release this negative image and have much less muscle tension and pain.

Once it is clear that a patient has experienced severe physical trauma, we always ask what the relational context was, because that can also be an essential aspect of the trauma. So we always ask whether there was someone who was supportive or not, how others reacted to the trauma, whether there were others or whether the patient was all alone. It is particularly important to ask which safe figures the patient could turn to.

We are always alert to whether the relational traces of the trauma are reappearing in rigid positions in our relationship with the patient, such as victim-perpetrator, victim-passive bystander, victim-rescuer or victim-accuser. Among other things, our own posture can be very revealing here. If there appears to be a rigid relationship pattern with our patient, we can investigate whether we have entered into an enactment with the patient and respond to it as in this chapter in Section 7.7.

Cautiously offering deeper interpretations

When exploring the traumatic memory, the therapist may offer cautious supportive interpretations of the trauma situation, such as 'Maybe you were very afraid of what was going to happen? Maybe you wanted to call for help, but that would also put you in danger?' With a mentalizing interpretation, we can also gently draw the patient's attention to the fact that, at the time of the trauma, they were very unlikely to be able to mentalize ('body-oriented'): 'Perhaps it was so overwhelming for you that you could not be aware of your body signals and emotions'. We might also gently try to clarify a possible projection, e.g.: 'You think that others blame you for how you acted then and that they still haven't forgiven you. But could it be that something in you still feels guilty about how things went?'

With a careful interpretation, the therapist can relate the patient's past traumatic experiences to multiple perspectives in order to strengthen body-oriented mentalizing. But we should always combine our interpretation with the basic techniques described in this book (Chapter 5) and other points of interest in dealing with traumatic memories and enactments just described. Otherwise, a mentalizing interpretation can come across as intrusive and it may seem that we are not taking the patient's experience seriously and trying to adjust it. Instead, our intention is to make space for multiple points of view.

7.9 Recognising and completing inhibited (physical) reactions

7.9.1 Immobility reaction

One of the most basic ways of responding to great imminent danger is to seek help. One looks to others who are perceived as safe, strong or wise for help. If this is not possible, we try to fight or flee. If this is also not possible, for example because it is too dangerous to get out, the only option is to become immobile in the form of freezing or collapsing ('shutdown response' or 'playing dead'). These immobility reactions are primary and automatic. They can occur in the face of a perceived life-threatening event, such as a physical accident, major surgery or sexual abuse, but also in the face of parental criticism, anger, rigid rules and confrontation with punishment (Ogden & Fisher, 2017). In automatic immobility responses of collapsing, becoming slack, or freezing, the parasympathetic nervous system is activated and we become paralysed: our muscles relax, and our heart rate slows. We may lose consciousness and actually faint. An immobility response to imminent danger can become fixed in the body and then persist for many years. The response remains 'frozen'. Every time something reminds one of the original danger, one freezes or becomes slack. This reaction can become generalised, so that one exhibits the immobility reaction in all kinds of circumstances.

During our therapy, as patients become aware of what they have experienced physically and emotionally in relation to the traumatic event or threatening relationship situation, they can come 'out of their frozen state'. The original freezing response ceases or one emerges from shutdown. Released from this state, patients can recognise their original tendency to fight, flee or seek help. They may feel fear and want to crawl away, experience anger and want to hit, or feel the urge to scream for help. The aim is for patients to become aware of these tendencies so that they can self-consciously express the response to fight, flee or seek help. This allows the body to heal and the patient to experience safety again (Levine & Frederick, 1997; Ogden & Fisher, 2017; Porges, 2011).

7.9.2   Recognising reactions that were inhibited at the time

The therapist asks the patient to focus on a memory fragment just before he or she froze or fainted. The therapist asks the patient to focus on any physical reactions that can be observed, such as muscle tensing, shivering, trembling, small jerks, muscle twitches, small movements, e.g. in the legs or arms. We can point out to the patient that these physical reactions can be incentives to move: 'What movement does your hand want to make now?' This allows the patient to become aware of the inhibited movement. A trembling foot may indicate a tendency to run away (flee). A tremor in the hand and arm may indicate a tendency to push something away (fight). For example, a young man with chronic neck and shoulder pain and a gait disorder was once attacked by a group of aggressive boys. He froze in fear and could not move. The therapist asks him to recall the situation and to become aware of the moment when the attackers came towards him, just before he froze. As he does this, he feels his leg muscles tighten and become anxious, and his arm muscles tighten. He becomes aware of the urge to run away and push the attackers away.

In addition to focusing on movement, we can also direct the patient's attention to the tendency to make sounds. For example, a sigh can be a tendency for an exclamation. For example, a forty-year-old woman with chronic fatigue was found to have been sexually abused as a child. She recognised both her freezing reaction and her tendency to get up and do something, fight back or run away when she thought of the abuse. At the same time, she noticed her tendency to want to shout 'No, go away'! and to call for help from others. Recognising past inhibited responses is a technique derived from sensorimotor psychotherapy (Ogden & Fisher, 2017). As is the technique of 'finishing off inhibited responses' described in the next section (7.9.3). These techniques require knowledge and skills that can be acquired through, for example, a post-master's course in sensorimotor psychotherapy.

7.9.3   Finishing the inhibited response

If the patient recognises an inhibited fight, flight or cry for help response, the therapist may ask the patient to perform such a response in the therapy room. The focus is on the impulse that the body is indicating. The aim is to allow a bottom-up process to emerge: behaviour driven by bodily impulse and affect. The role of non-verbal therapists, such as psychomotor therapists or psychosomatic physiotherapists, is certainly also important here. For example, the therapist may suggest that the initial fight response be expressed by pushing against a pillow as if the patient were pushing someone away. Or we can ask the patient to do the flight response, for example by standing up and taking a few steps away. When doing this, the patient may voice suppressed words such as 'I don't want this' or 'Go away'. Alternatively, the patient may only be able to make a scream or a wordless sound. The therapist can help the patient find words to match the movement. The suppressed movement may also be towards the therapist, for example a hand reaching out to the therapist with an exclamation such as 'Help me'!

If the patient is severely paralysed because of the inhibited response, Ogden recommends that they first do a movement that is still possible, for example stretching the back, pushing against something or jumping. This can replace attention to immobility for the perception of movement. Next, the therapist and patient reflect on which movement the body wants to make in response to the traumatic memory: fight or flight? The aim is for the patient to make this movement or call for help not as a reflex, but consciously, contrary to what was obvious at the time. Self-aware means to be bodily mentalizing: to be aware of one's own bodily sensations, emotions and thoughts. Self-aware also means that the patient is aware of which response is now self-reliant and would work best in a given situation. The therapist can ask, 'Which do you think works better, running away or fighting back?' We can ask the patient to try both responses and choose the most appropriate one. With regard to verbal cries for help, the therapist not only asks which words best describe the patient's feelings. He also asks which expression is most appropriate in the given situation, such as 'Leave me alone' or 'Help me'. The therapist may then ask the patient to shout the cry for help out loud, which can be done literally by the patient in the treatment room, but can also be imagined internally. Visualising the unfinished fight, flight or cry for help can be a powerful tool.

Our patients have often learnt to respond with immobility in current everyday situations that are similar to the original dangerous situation. We can discuss with them, after they have made the unfinished movement or call for help in the session, what they can do in everyday life instead of freezing, slacking or collapsing. We will do this especially in relation to situations that call for action. What do you feel in your body in such a situation, what emotions do you have, what thoughts do you experience? What movement does the body want to make or what outcry do you feel coming? In this way we first ask the patient to mentalize in a body-oriented way. Next comes the question of what is appropriate. For example, what is an appropriate way to ask for help from someone you trust? When we learn to ask for help, we always consider carefully the difference between an instinctive, fearful way of asking for help indirectly, by accosting or manipulating, and an active, confident way of asking for help. By also teaching patients to empathise with others, they can give the other person space to give help in a way that suits them.

7.10   Conclusion

In this chapter we have looked at how to work with past trauma and with relationship patterns arising from past painful relationships. Old painful relationship patterns are repeated in the session through enactment and old traumas can leave their mark in the session through intrusive memories and all kinds of physical stress reactions and dissociations. The message in this chapter is: bring the old pain into the therapeutic relationship. This is difficult because the patient tends to keep their old pain out of consciousness. We need all sorts of treatment principles and basic interventions (already described earlier in this book in Chapter 4, Chapter 5 and Chapter 6) to first get the right mental contact with the patient. Next, we do not avoid enactment and recognise the mutual reaction patterns between the patient and ourselves. We try to recognise our own part in this and reflect with the patient on what our current reactions are during the enactment. Part of it is recognising our own not mentalizing. Our own strong physical reactions to the patients can be a sign of our body mode of non-mentalizing and counter-transference, which we will try to discuss with the patient.

In the case of old traumas, we sit side by side with the patient to look at the memories together in the here and now. We tune in to the patient's present physical and mental reactions. In this way the patient can become aware that the (implicit) trauma memory is a memory and not the present reality. This allows one to let go of memories of profound events. Finally, we have seen that addressing the immobility reactions and holding back from fighting, fleeing and calling for help are part of the therapy. Recognising the immobility response and helping the patient to arrive at a self-conscious fight, flight or cry for help response is also likely to be addressed in non-verbal therapies. Especially when it comes to remobilising the physical fight or flight response, it is clear that non-verbal therapists have a role to play.

This chapter has been very limited in scope given the complexity of the issues faced by patients with PPS and old mental pains. We should be aware that many patients with severe PPS carry multiple traumas and have a long history of disappointing relationships within family and partner relationships, and in therapy situations. The effects of old traumas and painful interpersonal experiences are often intertwined. This creates complex issues and requires the necessary expertise of the therapist.

Simply following the instructions in this chapter is not enough. We believe that targeted training in dealing with enactment and trauma is often necessary. In addition, the trick is to be patient and to recognise that therapy processes for patients with very painful events and relationships in the past require time and attention. It may also be unavoidable that therapy takes longer than a standard protocol approach would suggest.

Chapter 8

Building up activities

8.1 The importance of building up activities

Activity building is an essential part of the treatment of PPS. In recent literature effective treatment of (severe) PPS involves gradual progress towards an active, balanced lifestyle. The aim is to achieve a balance between exertion and relaxation and to (re)establish a social life and work (Akwa GGZ, 2018). However, patients with PPS are often anxious about increasing activity and uncertain about what constitutes a reasonable level of activity. An active lifestyle is not easy, especially if people have to cope with physical discomfort when moving. People were automatically used to avoiding activity as much as possible (passive avoidance) or being overly active (active avoidance), in both cases to reduce physical discomfort.

However, passive avoidance, such as excessive resting, can lead to fear of movement and activity, loss of fitness and social isolation. Forms of active avoidance, besides overactivity, include: excessive seeking of help or reassurance, excessive seeking and checking of diagnoses, frequent accosting, obsessive monitoring and active checking of the body. Both avoidance mechanisms eventually lead to increased stress and physical symptoms, with a decreased ability to body-oriented mentalizing. B-MBT aims to help patients learn to become aware of their own bodily sensations and inner experiences. This increased awareness enables patients to consciously choose a balanced pattern of activities in areas that they find meaningful.

This chapter briefly describes becoming more active on the basis of the B-MBT approach. The question is whether a method such as B-MBT, which focuses on awareness of physical and inner experience, can be reconciled with targeted behavioural change without losing sight of its principles. Is a behavioural approach actually compatible with B-MBT? We believe, as do Fonagy and Adshead (2012), that it is, especially when using third generation behaviour therapy such as acceptance and commitment therapy (ACT), mindfulness-based stress reduction (MBSR) or mindfulness-based cognitive therapy (MBCT). These methods focus on similar processes to B-MBT, such as mindfulness, an emphasis on attitudes towards one's own and others' thoughts and feelings rather than on their content, and reflectivity (metacognitive processes).

DOI: 10.4324/9781003637486-10

Of the third generation behavioural therapies, ACT seems to be the most explicit in building activities from a self-conscious stance (a body-oriented mentalizing stance). Our clinical experience shows that the dosing of activities from an ACT perspective can be a valuable element of B-MBT. ACT has also been scientifically proven to be effective in the treatment of PPS (A-Tjak et al., 2015). According to ACT, committed actions involve setting goals and taking actions based on personal values. These purposeful actions are not aimed at reducing physical symptoms, but at taking valuable steps towards a meaningful life, with acceptance and awareness of physical symptoms and associated physical and mental experiences. In B-MBT, patients first learn to mentalize in a body-oriented way and then to build up their valuable actions with this ability. When building valuable activities, the patient and therapist remain attuned to the patient's bodily signals and inner experiences. The therapist tries to avoid a school-like form of instruction that does not take into account the patient's personal experiences and perceptions. He is careful that the patient will not perform the (new) actions impulsively and in an overly active manner without awareness of body and mind from a body mode of mentalization. Or that he takes action from the teleological mode (entirely instrumental and seeking only immediate effect). Or that he performs the actions from an equivalence mode (without awareness of private thought and overwhelmed by inner experiences) or from a pretend mode (out of touch with his own and others' physical and inner experiences). The therapist therefore combines behavioural instruction with the interventions described earlier in this book.

The aim is for patients to learn to self-consciously perform new patterns of flexibly dosed activities based on body-oriented mentalization, which can be consistently maintained over time and are consistent with life values. The following steps are important (Pielage & Spaans, 2019):

- Inventorying values
- The gradual build-up of valuable activities (committed actions)
- Dealing with fear of movement
- Finding a balance between effort and rest
- Setting limits and boundaries
- Creating a signalling plan

These components do not only belong to the field of psychological workers. They also belong to the field of (psychosomatic) physiotherapists, (psychosomatic) exercise therapists, occupational therapists, nurses or social workers.

8.2   Inventorying values

Taking stock of personal values can be confronting and painful. It exposes the patient's psychological pain of a lack of meaning. Patients with severe PPS can lose sight of their personal values as the disease progresses. Often, a long-term struggle with physical symptoms and limitations completely fills their lives. For example, they may spend more and more time at home, to the detriment of social contacts that could be important to them. As a result, vitality disappears from life.

Values are self-chosen life guidelines (Hayes & Smith, 2005) such as love, honesty, determination or friendship. They are reflected in the actions you take and the way you carry them out. However, many patients assume that they cannot act on these values until their physical symptoms are fully under control. This means that patients will find it difficult to start inventorying values and building up activities while they still have symptoms. But this is meant to be the intention! As in ACT, the aim of B-MBT is not so much a life without physical complaints. It is all about a valuable life with and in spite of physical complaints, through increased awareness of one's own physical and mental reactions and values. It is very important for the therapist to deal, in a body-oriented mentalizing way, with the difficulty patients have in making an inventory of their values.

We can explain that values can be compared to lighthouses in the sea, allowing the captain to steer his ship in the desired direction in stormy weather. A classic exercise for taking inventory of values is 'the speech' (Harris, 2010). Here, patients imagine how others will speak to them on their eightieth birthday: in an ideal situation, what will loved ones say about the role the patient has played in their lives? And what values emerge? Such an exercise also involves body-oriented mentalizing: we teach patients to focus on their bodily sensations and inner experiences during the performance exercise. If it is an essential value in the patient's life, this can also be experienced physically, for example through a warm feeling, feeling moved or a sense of space.

The therapist and patient can also create an exploration of personal values by listening to meaningful music, reading a meaningful story or poem together, or looking at a valuable object. What touches the patient? What physical sensations do they experience? What thoughts and feelings do they have? What makes this valuable? The therapist can then place the perceived values in an interpersonal context and focus the patient's attention on inspiring people and events from the past or present, from a film or a novel, where this value was expressed.

Because many people with severe PPS find it difficult to put their values into words, non-verbal expressions of values can help to clarify them. For example, the therapist may ask the patient to express what gives meaning to life by drawing, modelling a sculpture, adopting a certain posture, or doing a 'tâbleau vivant' with other group members. When exploring personal values, we can also present patients with overviews of different values. Again, it is important not to approach such an exploration verbally with a series of words, just picking out words. Again, attention to physical sensations and inner experiences is essential. When making an inventory of personal values, we can distinguish the following areas of life:

• Partnership/marriage/relationship
• Parenthood
• Family (other than partnership or parenthood)
• Friendship/social relationships

- Work
- Recreation
- Social engagement
- Personal development (including education and training)
- Meaning giving, religion or spirituality

Once patients have more clarity about their values, we take a look at the extent to which these values are reflected in their actions in their current lives (taking committed actions). Is being with friends a value? Are they doing feasible activities that show this? If not, they can make a plan with the therapist, and possibly together with loved ones, to gradually start doing this again.

8.3   Committed actions

8.3.1   Explain and prepare committed actions

Setting goals from personal values and acting on them can be called committed action (Hayes et al., 2006). Committed actions are not about getting rid of physical symptoms, but about taking valuable steps towards a meaningful life with acceptance and awareness of physical symptoms and inner experiences. Exposure is part of committed action, because committed action also exposes one to previously avoided physical sensations and emotions. However, this is not about reducing physical symptoms (as is usually the case with exposure therapy), but to experience (again) freedom of movement with physical symptoms. We can explain to patients that if they are struggling with PPS, it is important to continue to do valuable activities despite the symptoms. Not doing enough activities can eventually lead to anxiety, boredom, loneliness, depression and social isolation. This can reduce well-being and increase physical symptoms. Possibly, we can also explain that fulfilling activities can have beneficial effects on physical well-being, the immune system and the parasympathetic nervous system, as evidenced by increased de-stressing (Pielage & Spaans, 2019). The therapist explains that in committed action, the trick is to become aware of bodily sensations, obstructive thoughts and feelings by continuing body-oriented mentalizing. By being aware of automatic physical and internal reactions to a committed action, one can make a conscious choice: do I want to act according to my life values with my bodily sensations and uncertainties? We can find out with patients in which areas of life they can begin to translate which life values into actions, e.g. in the area of friendships, seeking *mutual support.*

8.3.2   Build up gradually

The next step is to take the committed actions. Starting with small activities, such as a 20-minute visit to a friend, can already be difficult. Patients may still be inclined to adopt an 'all or nothing' approach: 'I'll do it again like before or I won't do it at all'. The therapist can explain that working slowly but surely leads to good results, and emphasise, for example, that a long journey begins with one step. The therapist encourages the patient to take small actions towards self-chosen values in the presence of physical symptoms and disturbing inner experiences such as anxiety or insecurity. Examples are a five-minute walk, picking up the phone once, a one-minute body scan. He then encourages a gradual build-up of these activities.

In the gradual build-up of committed actions, it is best to adopt a time-contingent build-up (gradual build-up regardless of complaints) rather than a complaints-contingent approach (doing the activity 'when the physical complaints allow it or have disappeared'). We can explain here to our patients that the possible experience of worsening physical complaints and increased tension is a normal, temporary part of this approach. A pitfall of a time-contingent structure, however, is that the focus can become too much on reaching the targets and limits. This can be at the expense of focusing on the underlying values, physical sensations and inner experiences of the patient. Therefore, in addition to focusing on the execution of the committed actions, it is important to give sufficient attention to the patient's experience: What are his physical sensations and inner experiences during the committed actions? And did he feel that he was doing something worthwhile?

We should also bear in mind that many patients have had a time-contingent activity-building-up programme in previous treatment and have (repeatedly) got stuck in it because of exercise intolerance. We can then validate the patient's fears of movement and symptom accumulation and consciously join in with body-oriented mentalization. We then focus on the physical aspects of their fear by asking, for example, 'What do you notice in your body when this happens?' and we focus on the inner side of the fear by asking, for example, "What thoughts are going through your mind?' We can also use the other B-MBT techniques described in this book. This allows patients to remain more aware of what they are experiencing, as opposed to a 'normal' time-contingent activity set-up. It also allows the patient to experience a more self-conscious choice between 'Do I let my fears lead me?' or 'Do I self-consciously take a deliberate step in well-considered, dosed building up of activities?' It is precisely in the case of fear of activity build-up that we use body-oriented mentalizing, in which immersion in fear makes way for awareness of one's own experience of a valued action.

8.4 Dealing with fear of movement

In the building up of committed actions, it becomes clear that there can be a lot of fear of movement. One may fear negative consequences of movement, such as tissue damage or extreme pain or fatigue. As a result, one becomes afraid of movement and avoids activities or performs them differently than intended. In the long run, one may not dare to move at all. In these cases, committed action can be combined with a targeted exposure approach to this fear. Patients are then taught to observe the fear mindfully during a movement (exposure to fear).

We use exposure in a different context from cognitive behavioural therapy (CBT), which aims to extinguish anxiety. In B-MBT, exposure is not intended for extinction. It is designed to teach patients to perform committed actions with acceptance and awareness of fear and the associated bodily sensations and thoughts. In the process, one learns that one can move in spite of fear, without being harmed or unable to do anything because of pain or exhaustion. This exposure approach always relates to situations that involve the chance of fear of movement in situations that have a personal value. Examples include 'going for a short walk with a good friend' or 'walking independently to the supermarket and do some shopping there'. First, we explain to the patient how fear and avoidance reinforce each other. Then we emphasise that after a long period of avoidance or adjusting activity, an initial increase in anxiety, pain or fatigue is a logical consequence of exercise/training. Then we ask about the expectations/cognitions that the patient has about the consequences of exercise, such as 'I'll be so tired that my legs will collapse afterwards'.

Because exercise can be aversive, the therapist also looks at the patient's willingness to experience unwanted fear, pain or fatigue. For example, the therapist might say: 'Can you open up to the fear as you walk, as if you were opening up to an uninvited guest?' Then the therapist himself does a small movement, such as three knee bends or walking 50 metres, and reports his own sensations, emotions and cognitions as a body-oriented mentalizing model. The therapist then asks the patient to repeat the same activity. The therapist asks the patient to open up to the fear and to indicate the degree of fear with a number between 0 and 10. After the exercise, the therapist and patient evaluate the level of anxiety, as well as the physical sensations and internal experiences.

Expectations of negative consequences of the exercise, such as 'I probably won't be able to do anything all day', are also discussed. The therapist marks this as an 'anxiety thought' and discusses what the patient still wants/needs to do that day. In the next session they discuss what was possible and what was not. After guided exposure exercises, the patient is encouraged to practice at home. The aim is to gradually increase the number of appropriate actions while maintaining attention to one's own and others' physical sensations, emotions and thoughts.

8.5   Finding a balance between effort and rest

When gradually building up activities from body-oriented mentalizing, the aim is to achieve an active lifestyle with a good balance between effort and rest. Building up strenuous activities while maintaining a body-oriented mentalizing attitude should go hand in hand with sufficient relaxing activities and vice versa. Does one distribute his energy evenly? This is known as energy management. Patients learn to make choices and prioritise daily activities in the context of the valuable social roles they play. As they make these choices and engage in these activities, they also train their ability to listen to the voice of the body: 'what physical sensations, emotions, memories and thoughts am I experiencing?' Many people with PPS are traditionally used to taking external factors into account when planning activities. They plan activities according to what they think others, such as an employer, partner, family members or friends, will expect. The starting point for their activity choices is not with themselves. Choosing activities based on body-oriented mentalizing adds an important element: choosing from one's own experiences, perceptions, possibilities and values. In the past, people would have attended all the birthdays of family and friends, but now they set priorities. In the past, without thinking about it, people would give up 'an evening out with a friend' in favour of taking care of family-members. Now they can consciously make room for this kind of relaxation. The therapist asks the patient to look at his or her own pattern of activity over the course of the week. Which activities are restful, valuable, urgent, inspiring, frightening, stressful or even very stressful? First patient and therapist determine a baseline level of activity after examining the patient's activity pattern. Then they can prioritise and plan activities according to the baseline, and then gradually build up the base level of activities, keeping in mind the time-contingent building up of activities (see Section 8.3.2).

8.6   Setting boundaries

People with severe PPS may find it difficult to set boundaries in social situations. This needs our attention in the context of building up committed actions. For example, they have a constant difficulty saying 'no'. They agree to others' requests even when they don't really want to, and it is too burdensome and damaging to their own health. Or the opposite phenomenon: excessive refusal. Out of fear of physical symptoms or social insecurity, people refuse all requests from others. Patients with PPS may therefore be inclined to set no limits or excessive limits almost automatically, without body-oriented mentalizing.

The therapist may therefore ask the patient to reflect on a recent situation in which he received a request from someone to do an activity such as a going out for a meal, a walk or a visit to a museum. Who made the request? What exactly was requested? Then we can ask the patient what he noticed in his body and what his inner reaction was when he looks back. And how did the patient react to the request? Then the therapist and patient can reflect on the background of the given reaction to the request. What physical and inner signals played a role? The therapist and patient then discuss that, in the future, it might be useful to first do body-oriented mentalizing before responding to a request. Possibly the patient can make room for this by agreeing at the time of the request that there will be a response in the foreseeable future. However, some patients still lack the ability to say no or to ask for time to think about it. In this case, they can practise this with other patients and the therapist in a role play.

8.7   Signalling plan for future difficult situations

A B-MBT signalling plan is a plan for difficult future situations where difficulties with body-oriented mentalizing are expected. It is not a relapse prevention plan about the best things to do to prevent an increase in physical symptoms. It is more in line with the mentalization model to encourage patients to think about future situations where body-oriented mentalizing might decrease and what one needs to resume it. And what does one need to get back into their tolerance zone?

Together with the therapist and possibly other group members, the patients draw up a signalling plan (see an example in Table 8.1). First, they think about difficult situations they can expect to encounter. Then they learn to recognise the different stages before body-oriented mentalizing stops. Using imaginary traffic light colours, they assume the following phases: Green: feeling of control, still within the tolerance zone (see also Section 4.8.8) (stress level between 0 and 3), still capable of body-oriented mentalizing; Orange: tension is increasing (stress level between 3 and 7) and body-oriented mentalizing is becoming more difficult; Red: too much tension (stress level between 8 and 10), outside the tolerance zone, no longer able to mentalize properly in a body-oriented manner.

With the help of the therapist, patients try to identify their physical and mental state and behaviour in each of the phases. The therapist may ask the patient to go back in his mind to different situations that belonged to one of the phases, to recognise the corresponding physical and mental experiences and behaviours. We also reflect on what others notice about the patient when he or she is no longer mentalizing in a sufficiently body-oriented way. Then you can think about strategies to help: what helps to start mentalizing in a body-oriented way again? What strategies have helped in the past? For example, talking about the situation with a partner, talking to a good friend on the phone, doing a body scan exercise or, if you are very stressed, doing something to distract yourself, such as cooking. When developing a signalling plan, we may want to encourage patients to think about how others would experience each stage and what others would (not) do. For an example of a signalling plan, see Table 8.1.

Body-oriented mentalizing is a skill in an interactional context. It is therefore important to ask some persons directly involved, such as a partner, a close friend, a parent, a brother or sister, to help with the development of the signalling plan. We can agree with them that there will be regular contact in the future. In the presence of those directly involved, the signalling plan can be reviewed to see if they have any suggestions. To help the patient choose who to involve in the future in the signalling plan, the therapist can also suggest an inventory of the patient's social network.

Patients who have difficulty with body-oriented mentalizing may also find it difficult to think about the role that close relatives play in their lives. We can then ask patients to think about the people they know. Who really matters? Who would they call a friend? Who can they count on and turn to in a difficult situation? Who do you feel secure with? (Pielage & Spaans, 2019) Then we can ask them to bring awareness to a positive experience with one of these people: 'Find out what situation it was in. Try to make the memory as clear as possible with your senses. Who was with you, what did you hear, smell, taste, feel? Then look at what body signals you notice when you think back to this positive experience, what thoughts, feelings, needs and desires come to you?' This zooming in on the details of an interaction can help the patient make a choice about who to include in the signalling plan as the one who will help make the plan succeed.

Table 8.1 Signalling plan.

1. *Difficult circumstances:*
In what circumstances do I have difficulty mentalizing in a body-oriented way?
For example: In case of a strong relapse of physical symptoms. A long period of
  arguing with my partner. Disappointing results in my studies.

---

2. *Signals:*
a) Which signals belong to the green, orange and red phases?
For example:
In green: few physical complaints, generally feel good and relaxed
In orange: sleep badly, get angry easily, close myself off to my partner, reasonable muscle pain
In red: lots of aches and pains everywhere; sleeping badly; all sorts of worries
  about my body; don't want to see anyone; and don't answer the phone.

---

b) What might others notice about me if I am not body-oriented mentalizing enough?
For example: I avoid social contact. I don't answer the phone or call myself. I go to
  the doctor often and ask for tests. I don't talk about my feelings or thoughts.

---

3. *Helping strategies:*
a) What can I do myself to continue with body-oriented mentalizing?
Example: I do a mindfulness exercise like the body scan once a day or twice
  a day; I sit for 3 minutes and try to be aware of my body signals and inner
  experiences. I will discuss this with my partner. I also will ask for a conversation
  with . . . and I definitely will go to the weekly meeting with my friends.

---

b) What can others do to help me to continue body-oriented mentalizing?
For example: Visit me once a week and talk to me respectfully, taking my opinion seriously. Ask what is going on and what my stress level is at significant
  moments. Ask me about noticeable body signals and inner experiences of
  today. Go through the signalling plan with me.

8.8   The aftercare period

Starting a new life, with or without physical complaints, from a heightened aware-ness of one's own and others' physical and inner reactions, is the challenge that mainly follows the intensive treatment phase. A thorough aftercare programme with weekly or fortnightly sessions is important. This is where patients can share their experiences of putting the signalling plan into practice. In consultation with the therapist and other members of the group, patients can review what signals or situations have not yet been described, what has helped and what has not, and why it has not helped. We also constantly remind patients of their own responsibility to continue body-oriented mentalizing when they take committed action.

Aftercare sessions can also be used to discuss many difficult situations, such as work, doctors' appointments or family gatherings. In the aftercare phase, many patients find that the outside world reacts differently to their new way of dealing with physical symptoms than their fellow patients did during treatment. Patients often feel that it was already difficult to think in a body-oriented mentalizing way within the context of treatment, but that this is really impossible 'outside', in today's social world. After all, they believe, there is no real attention paid to other people's physical and mental experiences. It's best not to discuss these gen-eralisations, but to respond with understanding for someone's experience. We can ask for an example of such a recent difficult social situation and mentalize it in a body-oriented way with 'stop and go back'. In this way, we can bring in the idea that the main issue now is how you can continue to mentalize in a body-oriented way despite what others do or don't do. 'What helps? And which people can help you? Are there people whose company encourages you to respect your bodily and inner experiences?' The therapist will also strongly ask for examples of successful application of mentalizing in daily life, and what the reactions of others around the patient have been in this regard. At the same time, of course, the therapist will continue to encourage body-oriented mentalizing in the here and now of the session.

8.9   Conclusion

This chapter has focused on committed actions from a body-oriented mentaliz-ing attitude. A gradual build-up of activities has proved to be effective. This usu-ally includes dealing with fear of movement, finding a balance between effort and relaxation, and learning to set boundaries. When preparing for difficult future situ-ations in which it may be difficult to perform a valuable body-oriented mentalizing activity, patients can create a signalling plan. They can use this to gain experience with the plan in the aftercare phase. Building and maintaining committed activi-ties in a body-oriented mentalizing way is part of a set of therapeutic principles and methods described from Chapter 4 onwards and which we collectively call B-MBT. In the remainder of this book, we will discuss applications of B-MBT through group therapy and systemic therapy, and describe various aspects of mul-tidisciplinary B-MBT treatment.

Part III

Applications

Chapter 9

Group therapy

9.1 Group therapy

Group therapy provides a powerful context for learning body-oriented mentalizing. Patients with severe PPS receive support, involvement and recognition from other group members. This can contribute to a familiar group atmosphere in which it feels safe to share personal emotional and physical experiences. Group therapists take a didactic stance in this respect, structuring sessions and ensuring that tensions do not rise too high so that a 'holding environment' is maintained. Group members can learn together about physical and mental processes. They can engage in emotional interactions with each other in which they learn to understand and manage their own and others' physical sensations. In group therapy grounded in B-MBT, we can distinguish between three types of group:

- An education and skill group with knowledge transfer, skills training and homework
- A psychotherapy group with spontaneous interactions around a theme
- A group with non-verbal, body-oriented exercises

In a complete B-MBT treatment, patients are supposed to attend all three types of groups side by side on a weekly basis. The groups complement each other and respond to each other, for example with similar themes. In addition to group sessions, patients attend individual B-MBT sessions. Prior to group therapy based on B-MBT, an individual session with the patient can be used to discuss treatment goals, motivation, pitfalls and attachment style, among other things. Understanding one's attachment style can help both the therapist and the patient to better understand interpersonal relationships when emotions are heightened. For example, does someone tend to be overly anxious, withdrawn or, on the contrary, clinging to others? Administering an attachment style questionnaire, such as the Experiences in Close Relationships-Revised (ECR-R) questionnaire, can help reach a consensus with the patient about their attachment style. The rest of this chapter describes the education and skills group and the psychotherapeutic group. Methods in a nonverbal therapy group were described in Chapter 6.

DOI: 10.4324/9781003637486-12

9.2   Education and skills group

The education and skills group aims to provide patients with education and skills related to body-oriented mentalizing in case of PPS. The aim of this group is two-fold. Through education, patients gain a better understanding of the relationship between body and mind. By practising with our patients to recognise, acknowledge and verbalise body signals and inner experiences, we break through patients' experiential avoidance of their physical symptoms and related inner experiences (Pielage & Spaans, 2019). A number of fixed parts run through each session, such as:

- Review of the previous session and discussion of the homework given
- Knowledge transfer on the topic of the week with space for questions, interaction and sharing of experiences
- Exercises related to the theme of the week with follow-up discussion
- Discussion of homework for the following week

Education is not a one-way street. The therapist educates, interacts and discusses the topic. He clearly takes the lead and structures the sessions. During the discussions, he adopts a body-oriented mentalizing stance and is proportionately transparent about his own physical and inner experiences in the here and now. At the same time, he is clearly the expert on body-oriented mentalizing and PPS. As therapists we try to make it clear that the contributions of the group members complement, clarify and enrich our expertise. Our message is that our inner self can adapt through the influence of the inner selves of the group members.

We need to ensure that there is a balance between providing information and being open to participants' perspectives. We try to avoid teaching in one direction for too long at a time, as this can make the group passive. The therapist asks group members to respond to explanations on the topic with personal experiences to see if they have understood the information correctly. On the other hand, if participants respond with theoretical arguments, we will ask for more personal examples to support the theory. The therapist in an education and skills group will emphasise that homework is part of therapy. Therefore, at the beginning of each session, he will ask the participants about their personal experiences with homework.

To increase the involvement of the 'home front', we can invite members of the support system to attend a group education meeting halfway through treatment. We can also invite them several times for an individual interview (e.g. once at the beginning and once at the end of treatment). Pielage and Spaans (2019) designed a B-MBT education and skills group with 24 weekly group meetings. Appendix A.6 provides a brief overview of the content of the 24 sessions. In each session, we always distinguish between educational transfer, experiential exercises and homework.

The programme facilitates familiarity with body signals and inner experiences in a relational context through a step-by-step build-up of themes. Some themes lend themselves to two sessions. In the beginning, the theme focuses on exploring and recognising body signals, followed by the inner experiences associated with the body sensations. As the group progresses, more attention is paid to the relational side of experiencing body signals and emotions, desires and tendencies. Towards the end of treatment, patients practice body-oriented mentalizing in relationships with each other and with loved ones at home.

9.3   B-MBT psychotherapy group

9.3.1   Main features

The B-MBT psychotherapy group provides a safe interpersonal context for promoting body-oriented mentalizing. The assumption here is that a change process is mainly brought about by promoting body-oriented mentalizing in a complex interpersonal situation such as group psychotherapy (Karterud & Bateman, 2012). Group members learn to know and understand subjectively the physical and mental reactions of others. The mutual exploration and clarification of bodily sensations and related inner experiences can be seen as the basic process. Patients with severe PPS find it difficult to keep themselves in mind in a group while trying to understand the minds of others. The therapist will therefore always try to maintain a balance between attention to individual physical and mental reactions and the interactions in the group.

While the education and skills group focused on explicit body-oriented mentalizing through educational transfer and experiential exercises, in the psychotherapy group we also try to stimulate the implicit automatic process of mutual body-oriented mentalizing. Our experience shows that it works well when two therapists conduct the psychotherapy group. One of the therapists is a psychologist, psychotherapist, clinical psychologist or psychiatrist who has successfully completed at least a basic B-MBT course. He/she has further had training in theory, literature and research on severe PPS.

It goes without saying that both therapists have sufficient body-oriented mentalizing skills themselves. They are able to keep in mind the treatment principles and methods of B-MBT (see Chapter 4 and Chapter 5) and to adopt a therapeutic attitude (see Section 4.6), including setting clear rules and making clear agreements. Therapists are able to sense what patients are trying to communicate with each other (non-verbally), and what possible physical and mental reactions are taking place among patients in the group.

For anyone who wants to use B-MBT in a group, we also recommend reading the book by the Norwegian professor of psychiatry Sigmund Karterud, *Mentalisation-Based Group Therapy (MBT-G): A theoretical, clinical, and research manual* (2015). This book is about MBT group treatment for patients with borderline personality disorder and for difficult-to-treat conditions such as addiction and eating disorders. The principles and interventions of group MBT in this book also apply to group B-MBT. The difference is that B-MBT involves patients with severe PPS and focuses more on physical experiences. In B-MBT group psychotherapy, the therapist applies, among other things, the basic interventions described in Chapter 5 to the individuals in the group. So it is best to keep the acronym MEET in mind even in group psychotherapy:

M = Mode (of mentalizing) recognising
E = Exploring body signals and inner experiences of the patient
E = Exploring by the therapist of one's own body signals and inner experiences and being transparent about them
T = Triggering mutual exchange of body signals and inner experiences

In addition to basic techniques aimed at the individual patient in the group, the therapist uses group interventions, which we will briefly describe next.

9.3.2   Explanation of the purpose of the therapy

We explain to patients that group members will discuss issues in a personal way. The focus will be on mutual communication in the here and now. Group members and therapists will explore each other's physical and mental reactions in the here and now. We also explain that topics will be linked to what is happening in the group at that moment. For example, if the topic is 'dealing with tension', the therapists might ask the group members to quietly stand still at the level of physical tension they are experiencing at the time. Therapists can also address group rules for interpersonal interaction:

- Active participation
- Show willingness to share personal experiences such as physical and mental reactions
- Showing mutual respect: listening to each other and supporting each other in learning to mentalize in a body-oriented way
- Giving 'I' messages
- Taking responsibility for your own therapy process (being your own chairman)
- Confidentiality of other participants' personal information
- Reporting any obstacles to participation in the group process

9.3.3   The topic

It is preferable that we wait and see what topic the group members themselves bring up. Although this can be difficult for group members, our experience is that they will learn this in time. If necessary, we can suggest topics for the group to choose from. We will do this especially if we feel that the importance of the topic outweighs the principle of group members suggesting topics themselves. To make the topic as lively as possible, we formulate it as much as possible in the 'I' form, e.g., 'How can I deal with my pain differently?' Or if the topic is 'coping with family members', the therapist might suggest rephrasing it as, 'How can I cope with my family members?' and ask the group members if this formulation captures the essence. If necessary, the formulation can be changed, for example, to 'How can I deal with my parents when they don't show any understanding for my physical complaints?' Group members can also suggest a topic that has been discussed in the education and skills group in the same week. Other topics that can be covered, as in individual B-MBT, include:

- Dealing with physical limitations and boundaries
- Feeling misunderstood or ignored
- Lack of support
- Asking for help
- Conflicts with others
- Experiencing opposition
- Assertiveness
- (Lack of) emotional closeness with others
- Experiencing loss
- Daring to express emotions

It is important to keep an eye on current problems in the group, such as tensions, a demotivating atmosphere, mutual misunderstandings, conflicts or irritations. Especially if these phenomena make mutual interaction difficult, we should address them and make them a topic. If the group members do not come up with such a topic themselves, the therapist can say, for example: 'I understand that some of you find the atmosphere in the group demotivating. I suggest the topic today to be, "How do I experience the atmosphere in the group"? Who can say something about this?'

9.3.4   Asking about recent and current experiences with the topic

We always personalise the discussion by asking about the most recent personal experience of the topic, e.g.: 'What is your most recent personal experience with setting boundaries?' The therapist will then ask about physical sensations and inner experiences: 'Your boss asked you to work longer than usual and you didn't dare say no. What happened in your body then? And when you think about it now, what are you experiencing in your body now? And what emotion do you feel now?'

If the patients indicate that they are struggling with a particular issue, the therapist can bring this into the interaction within the group. For example, on the topic of, 'What problems do I have with assertiveness?' the therapist might ask, 'Can you tell if standing up for yourself in this group is also difficult for you now? When and to whom is this happening now?' Or, on the topic of, 'How can I cope with shame about my physical symptoms?', he might ask a patient who has just had an involuntary convulsion attack in the group: 'Can you talk about your feelings of shame about this?' Or he might ask: 'Who do you feel most ashamed of right now?' Of course, when we bring up the topic in the group, we also consider the patient's past vulnerabilities. What experiences, for example, have contributed to feeling ashamed or not daring to speak up? If necessary, patients can explain these experiences. They can then explore whether the meanings they tend to give to current interactions with other group members are still appropriate.

9.3.5   Tension regulation

Patients with severe PPS often have a history of traumatic relationships, such as emotional neglect or negative group experiences, such as being bullied at school. On this basis, patients can quickly become emotionally over-stimulated in complex group interactions. Rigid attachment representations can then be triggered, and one ends up in a non-mentalizing mode. It is then difficult to recognise the subjectivity of one's own experiences. For example, people do not recognise that the feeling of being bullied comes from the past and does not apply to the current group situation. Patients are then unable to verbalise what they are experiencing physically and emotionally. In addition to complex interactions, prolonged silence can also build up tension to the point where people become tense and physically uncomfortable and do not know what to do.

It is the therapist's job to monitor the tolerance zone of tension ('window of tolerance', see Section 4.8.8) of both the group as a whole and the individuals in the group. Is the level of tension not too high? Or is the tension level too low? Are group members expressing too little emotion, or does an intellectual discussion hinder true body-oriented mentalizing? Both situations should be avoided. The art and challenge for us as group therapists is to find an acceptable level of discomfort where patients are able to use the opportunity for self-examination (Kaufman, 2013). Emotionally charged interactions, as important as they are, will therefore be offered in a measured and structured way.

If the tension is too high, we should first validate, support and reassure until patients are able to mentalize again. We can also include a joint mindfulness exercise, such as focusing on breathing or 'feet on the floor', or a joint body scan exercise. As for too little tension, we look out for the characteristic 'alexithymic' way of communicating that PPS patients use: using few words for emotions. This can cause the tension level to drop too much. In this case, we should instead initiate a more personal exchange and, as role models, explore with the group to find words for the body signals and emotions present (Skaderud & Fonagy, 2012). We can then simply stop the interaction with, 'I suggest that everyone now reflects on their own experience and ask themselves, "What is going on in me right now?"'. This automatically raises the tension, and the patient can then continue with body-oriented mentalizing. If the tension is too low, the therapist can also introduce some emotional material to the patient. For example, the therapist might say, 'I wonder if the irritations we discussed last week are still alive with someone in the group. Who can say something about this?'

Table 9.1 Examples of interactional indicators of a decline in body-oriented mentalizing in the group.

- No mutual reflection on physical and inner experiences.
- Many group members show physical restlessness, such as repeated struggling to sit still, restless limbs, shifting in their seat, fiddling with hands, all without reflective interaction.
- Several group members showing remarkably high arousal expression like muscle tension, possibly with physical stiffening, a hyperalert or restless attitude, or on the contrary, remarkably low arousal.
- Focusing mainly on the physical circumstances of the meeting, such as temperature, lighting and noise level, without engaging in reflective interaction about these issues.
- Active or passive avoidance of personal sharing of emotional experiences, for example by talking about superficial, everyday topics such as the weather.
- Long (theoretical) analyses of physical and mental problems.
- Exchanges with a strong emphasis on practical solutions to physical and emotional problems.
- Overt or covert mutual hostility, irritation, aggression or surliness.
- Running away from the group.
- Holding onto (negative) assumptions and fixed patterns of response towards the therapist(s) or group members.
- Communication problems such as taking each other's words literally, ignoring each other's statements, not feeling emotions behind statements, wanting to be right.
- Rigidly following the therapist's suggestions with little initiative.
- Focusing too much on each other without reflecting on one's own experience of the interaction.
- Prolonged arguments about group rules.

9.3.6 Recognising a decline in body-oriented mentalizing

Too high or too low levels of arousal are related to the patient's non-mentalizing mode. The therapist is alert to whether individual group members are still body-mentalizing. We can keep in mind the individual characteristics of non-mentalizing modes (body, teleological, equivalence and pretend modes) (see Appendix A.3). Some common group phenomena that may be indicators of declining body-mentalization are described in Table 9.1.

9.3.7 'Stop and stand still' and 'stop and go back'

In the group, the therapist often uses the techniques 'stop and stand still' and 'stop and go back' (see also Section 5.2.16 and Section 5.2.17) to activate body-oriented mentalizing. With a 'stop and stand still', we encourage participants to pay attention to their own bodily signals and inner experiences in the here and now. Stop and stand still is important, for example, when group members are rationalising an emotion-focused topic such as, 'How do I deal with my anger?' We can also use it when emotions are actually running high because rigid representations of others are suddenly activated in group members.

'Stopping and standing still' is also helpful when the group gets into substantive theoretical discussions with each other. Such discussions can quickly flare up when it comes to topics such as 'body and mind'. Theoretical discussions in a psychologising atmosphere can be a collective escape from personal and body-oriented mentalizing. The group shoots into a state of pseudo-mentalization. As therapists, we may be tempted to join in such conversations, especially when group members call on our content expertise.

During the B-MBT psychotherapy group, there is certainly room for exchanging information, e.g. about PPS. However, conversations can also dwell too long on rational psychologising, where the level of body-oriented mentalizing drops. We then need to use 'stop and stand still' to refocus attention on everyone's current, bodily experiences and explore what personal mental reactions are playing now among group members around the issue. We can use 'stop and stand still' in case of sudden striking group moments. For example, during a discussion on, 'How do I deal with my parents' worries?' a patient suffering from conversion seizure symptoms may suddenly slacken and fall from his chair to the floor. It only takes a moment for him to get back up. The group can then choose to continue the conversation as if nothing had happened. We should stop the conversation at such a moment: 'I think we should take some time to reflect on what has just happened'. First, the therapist will ask the patient who had conversion symptoms how he feels now, what is he experiencing physically, and what inner experiences he is noticing now. But the therapist will also ask him to go back in his mind to the moment just before he fell (stop and go back). What physical and inner experiences did he notice then? We can help the other members of the group to look back on this event by asking them, for example, 'When you noticed him falling off the chair, what did you notice about yourself? What did you notice in your body? And what feelings or thoughts did you have?'

'Stop and stand still' and 'stop and go back' can also be used by ourselves in our role as group therapists. We can do so if we notice that our ability to understand and feel through what is going on in the group is diminishing. Or we can notice that we are barely aware of what we are physically experiencing or what goes through our minds. In these cases, we should at least stop the interaction between group members. It is time to listen to ourselves and say, for example, 'Stop. I want to focus on what I am experiencing right now', or 'Stop. I want to focus on what I have just experienced'.

9.3.8   Encouraging recognition

At the beginning of group therapy, the focus is still on individual experiences in terms of physical sensations, emotions and thoughts. As therapy progresses, the focus is increasingly on exploring and articulating experiences in a relational way. We increasingly encourage interpersonal recognition and sharing. For example, if a patient talks about feeling misunderstood during a recent visit to the doctor, the therapist might ask: 'Who has had a similar experience?' When underlining similar experiences, the therapist will also repeatedly ask about the corresponding physical and mental experiences, e.g., 'You say that your doctor was also grumpy and abrupt the other day. What do you notice in your body when you're thinking about this?' If the patient answers, for example, 'I'm starting to shake just like I did then', the therapist may ask again, 'Who recognises this?'

9.3.9   'Reading' the other

To stimulate empathy for the other, we can ask patients what they notice about a group member's physical expression and what inner experience they think it expresses, as in the therapy fragment in Box 9.1.

Box 9.1   Therapy fragment: 'Reading' body expressions

Therapist to Patient A: When you see her (Patient B) sitting like that, what do you notice about her posture?
Patient A: That her shoulders are very tense.
Therapist: What do you think is going on inside her?
Patient A to Patient B: Your tense shoulders give me the impression that you are on your guard.
Patient B: Exactly. I keep thinking, 'How can I escape from this room?'

The aim of 'reading the other' is also to achieve a reality check. Through conversation, patients can assess whether their assumptions about the other's experience align with that person's own experiences. It is also crucial that, when 'reading the other', patients stay in touch with their own bodily signals and inner experiences and do not get completely lost in the (supposed) experience of the other person. It is therefore best to alternate 'reading the other' with a focus on one's own experiences, such as, 'What do you notice about her body posture?' and then, 'What are you experiencing in your own body right now and what is happening to you inside?'

9.3.10   Changing perspective

A further step in developing empathy for the other person is to put oneself in the other person's shoes (see also Section 5.2.13 and Section 5.4.2). The therapist asks a patient to switch perspectives with a group member by asking: 'What would I experience in terms of physical sensations and inner experiences in my group member's situation?' For example, we might ask: 'If you put yourself in the place of A and her back pain right now, what would you feel? Is there a thought, an emotion or an inclination that comes to you?' The therapist might also ask: 'She feels her back pain is unfair. If you put yourself in her place, can you imagine her reaction?'

An even further shift in perspective than 'putting yourself in someone else's shoes' is 'looking at yourself from someone else's situation' (see also Section 5.4.2). For example, we can ask: 'If you were B, what would you notice about how you are sitting?' This change of perspective can be a cognitive effort on the part of the patient and can take some of the attention away from the emotions. Exploring or hearing the perspective of another group member not only helps patients to develop empathy for others, but also to see their own problems in a different way.

9.3.11 Encouraging feedback sequences

B-MBT involves the process of giving and receiving feedback back and forth about bodily sensations and inner experiences. The therapist encourages reciprocal feedback between patients so that a sequence of reciprocal feedback is created: 'What is going through your mind now that you hear that she (the other patient) feels the shivers run down her back when she hears your story?' Then, for example, if the patient says: 'I get the thought "What am I doing to her?"' the therapist can again ask for a response: 'What are you experiencing now when you hear that she has the thought, "What am I doing to her?"' In order to prevent feedback from getting stuck at the level of verbal exchange, the therapist will also encourage feedback on non-verbal cues, as in the therapy fragment in Box 9.2.

Box 9.2 Therapy fragment: Giving feedback in response to non-verbal cues

A: She is breathing fast and she is holding the chair with her hands.
Therapist: What do you think she is feeling?
A: She is afraid of what is coming.
Therapist: Well, tell her that.
A to B: I see that you are holding the chair with your hands and that you are breathing fast. I get the impression that you are afraid.
Therapist to patient B: What is happening now that you are hearing this? What do you feel in your body?
B: I feel pain in my arms. I want to run away. I think this is terrible.
Therapist: Hmm, you feel more pain and you think, 'This is terrible', and you want to leave.
B: Yes, this is obviously nothing for me to be in the spotlight like this.
Therapist to patient B, about patient A: Now focus your attention on how she (patient A) is sitting. What do you notice?
B: She looks straight at me, she feels strong inside and probably thinks I am very pathetic.
A: I'm also getting stuffy now. I'm also finding this quite exciting. I'm not thinking at all, 'How pathetic she is'. I'm thinking, 'How exciting this is for her . . . and for me'.

9.3.12   Naming interaction patterns

The therapist can name interaction patterns, e.g. 'I notice that when A gets feed-back, she often falls silent and signals non-verbally: "Leave me alone."' Many group members respond to this by verbally encouraging her to do something any-way, to which she responds by becoming even quieter. The therapist can ask the group: 'Is this pattern recognisable?' If the group and the patient in question agree, the therapist can ask the patient: 'What happens to you when you get feedback? What do you notice in your body?'

The therapist explores with group members the underlying mental states in pat-terns of response, such as, 'Could it be that A is scared and therefore quiet, and then others worry and start pulling on her?' The therapist always makes it clear that his observation and punctuation of events is his own perspective. He then makes it clear that the intention is for the group members to explore for themselves what patterns are occurring in the group and whether they are recognisable to others. The naming of interaction patterns can in turn trigger new patterns of response, which we then name again. Asen and Fonagy (2012) call this approach the use of 'a men-talizing loop'. Only when a pattern of interaction is clear to the group members and sufficient attention has been given to the physical sensations and internal reactions that occur as a result, can we ask patients: 'Does this pattern occur at home?' If the patient confirms that it does, we could ask, for example: 'Can you try to handle this also differently at home?'

9.3.13   Validating differences

Our intention is to teach patients that they can understand events and private experiences in different ways. The therapist shows that differences are impor-tant, for example by saying: 'Some of you tend to ignore fatigue and think, "Just carry on, don't pay attention". Others, on the other hand, think, "This is going completely wrong", are afraid and think, "I have to keep a very close eye on it". I find it valuable to note that each of you, when faced with fatigue, comes up with his own response'. We emphasise the subjectivity of physical sensations and inner experiences. We show interest in differences and mark them as valu-able. It is also our intention to mark and validate differences between two group members. For example, during the group interaction we might say: 'What strikes me is that you (group member A) feel dizzy and think "I'm not doing well", while you (group member B) notice that your hands are shaking and you feel tears of sadness coming'.

The therapist tries to make it clear that different experiences of the same event can coexist and contribute to body-oriented mentalizing and problem solving. In the case of mutual misunderstandings or problems, it may be possible to empha-sise: 'Perhaps it is not as simple as that there is only one point of view. We all experience a different part of this situation. These differences in our experiences are important precisely because they contribute to the overall picture of this situ-ation'. A well-known group phenomenon is that the group overly seeks harmony by always trying to agree with each other. In this process, people are overly nice to each other and a false harmony is created. People are afraid that otherwise the group will fall apart, or that they themselves will be excluded from the group. Then it is our task to recognise these phenomena and discuss them with the group, looking for diversity of experience and validating differences.

9.3.14 Transparency

The principle of therapists being therapeutically transparent about their physical sensations and inner experiences (see Section 5.3) also applies to group therapists. For example, one might say: 'I feel a lump in my throat and notice that I feel sorry for you now that you are telling us how alone you feel'. In the presence of group members, therapists can also be transparent about their interactions with each other. This is done with the intention of demonstrating body-oriented mentalizing in interaction with others. For example, one therapist might say to the other: 'As you speak, I notice that I am getting sleepy and want to lean back in my chair, and that I am having difficulty following you. I wonder: what exactly are you trying to say? Could you say it again, but in a different way?' The other therapist can then respond, for example, with: 'I think it is good of you to say that. I can understand your reaction. In fact, while I was talking about this, my mind was elsewhere. I was still thinking about the beginning of this session and how it actually started unexpectedly for me'.

Mutual transparency also relates to disagreements between therapists. We can respectfully and openly disagree with our fellow group therapist and question each other about it, e.g.: 'I don't think that. I'm not worried that she (a group member) is not in control of herself and will take too much medication later. On the contrary, I feel calm and think that she knows exactly what is good for her. Can you tell me a little more about your worries?' Trying to understand each other is much more useful here than stubbornly trying to stick to the same line. We can also be transparent about our feelings about group phenomena that block body-oriented mentalizing in the group. For example, if the group is repeatedly judging newcomers as incompetent, we can say: 'I notice that this bothers me and it literally gives me the creeps. I see it happening but I am not sure how to change it. Is there anyone who can help?'

9.3.15 Dealing with the past

The here and now is central to B-MBT, with occasional forays into the recent past. However, we keep an eye on each patient's background to make sure that they are not acting it out in the group. A young man with severe headaches and a history of being bullied tells the group his story. The group then wants to protect him in situations in the group that even slightly resemble bullying. This can strongly influence the development of the group, because almost everyone takes on the role of protector again and again during the meetings. We can think of this as transference and counter-transference or enactment at group level.

The therapist can say that he notices this over-protection and ask the group members to explain the background to their reaction. Body-oriented mentalizing in the group provides a way out of the mutual tension of transference and counter-transference. The therapist can also take the lead in this if the enactment also affects him and he also wants to overprotect the patient. We can use the methodological focus described in Section 7.7. For example, the therapist can use an 'I' message to say that he notices that he often gets a lump in his throat when the patient is criticised, then he becomes sad and wants to protect the patient. The other therapist can involve other members of the group in discussing the enactment. What do they recognise? What do they experience when they hear it? Working out transference and counter-transference phenomena between patient and therapist in the group can have a strong model function and trigger a lot in the other patients. But it has its limitations. It can put too much emphasis on one participant. It can also take up more time than is available in the group session, and other patients and other issues need to be addressed too. For persistent enactments with the therapist, we may also choose to work through these in individual sessions.

9.3.16   Addressing prejudice

During group therapy on emotionally charged topics, patients can quickly run into their sensitivities. They will be upset by the behaviour of others, which is a reason to stop and think about it. If patients have strong prejudices against others, we should make this a topic of therapy. Attention should certainly be paid to group members who repeatedly state that they do not want to interact with someone else in the group during sessions, or cannot wait for that other person to leave the group.

Persistent prejudices such as 'she's just an avoidant' will be noticed and addressed by the therapist. For example, he might say: 'I notice that you regularly state that A is an avoider, as if this were an indisputable reality. Prejudices leave little room for views of A other than that she is an avoider. Would you (B) articulate this in a different way? In a personal way? For example, by saying to her: "When you were silent just now, when you were asked something, I noticed that I got excited, and I had the thought: she's making it easy for herself to avoid . . ."' After B has verbalised this to A, the therapist can invite A to respond. Prejudices about fellow patients do not have to be part of a negative group atmosphere. Group members may place someone in the 'non-assertive' category and then, when criticised, always defend them in a well-intentioned way. This however deprives this group member of the opportunity to share their own experiences. Again, the therapist will intervene and point out to the group members their prejudice, the behaviour involved (speaking for someone else) and its long-term effects, such as, 'She is not given the opportunity to learn to articulate her own bodily sensations and inner experiences such as her feelings and wishes'.

9.3.17   Dealing with patients who drop out due to stress or physical discomfort

Patients with severe PPS may (want to) leave the group during the session because of physical discomfort, such as increased pain, fatigue or loss of a bodily function, or because of high-running emotions. For example, a patient may suddenly get up and leave the group saying, 'I don't feel well'. Usually, the patient goes away to relax outside the group or to do something that might reduce the physical symptoms or intense emotions. They often return afterwards if this has been agreed with them beforehand.

Whatever the reason, it is important that one of the therapists intervenes. We may decide to go to the patient, see how things are going and discuss with them what they need to come back to the group. We make it clear that the person needs to come back when the physical discomfort or agitation has subsided. The physical discomfort or excitement does not have to be completely gone in order to return. After all, it is the intention of the therapy to reflect on this in a body-oriented way in the group. Next, it is important to consider the departure of the group member as an important event and to discuss it with the other participants by 'stop and go back'. For example, we can say: 'Let's go back to the moment she left the group. What did you notice about yourself when she left? What did you feel physically? And emotionally?' Group members are then given the opportunity to respond, for example with, 'She was very quiet' or, 'It made me tense. I found it annoying and difficult'.

When the patient who has left returns, the therapist summarises what was said during the patient's absence. The patient who has left is given the opportunity to reflect on what happened just before she left. For example, she might say that when a member of the group remarked that he disliked people who were passive, she related this to herself. For her, the tension made her feel dizzy, she was afraid of fainting and so she quickly left the group room to get some fresh air. Afterwards, the conversation continues in a body-oriented mentalizing, interactive atmosphere, and attention can gradually shift back to the here and now.

9.3.18   Debriefing

Therapists should review a group session with each other to keep the methodological side of B-MBT high. In the debriefing, we can give each other feedback on which interventions helped the group with body-oriented mentalizing and which did not. We can also reflect on when we were in a body-oriented mentalizing mode and when we were not: 'Do you think I was still body-oriented mentalizing? At what moment do you think I was?' The therapists also give each other feedback on their modes of (non-)mentalizing. In doing so, they follow feedback rules such as:

- Specify the situation in the group
- Specify the colleague's behaviour
- Name his or her bodily expressions and statements

- Say which elements of (non-)body-oriented mentalizing in the other's behaviour and interventions you thought you recognised

The intention is not to get into a debate about 'the truth'. The therapist presents his feedback as his subjective perception (via an 'I' message) and not as the only possible option. After all, everyone has their own interpretations and perceptions. If possible, the support of a colleague who was not present at the group session can help to organise and receive mutual feedback.

9.4   Conclusion

In this chapter we have described two types of group-based B-MBT treatment: the education and skills group, and the psychotherapy group. The intention is to run these groups alongside a non-verbal group therapy and individual therapy, if possible. Because the patients have similar problems, an atmosphere of mutual support, commitment and recognition quickly develops in the group. In the education and skills group, this has the advantage of quickly creating a safe, pedagogical group atmosphere in which understanding of the problems and body-oriented mentalizing succeed better than in individual counselling alone. In the psychotherapy group, the atmosphere of support and safety creates the opportunity to experience true body-oriented mentalizing. In the psychotherapy group, as in everyday life, complex interpersonal situations arise in which body-oriented mentalizing is important for balanced physical and mental functioning.

Chapter 10

Systemic therapy

10.1 Systemic therapy

10.1.1 Systemic therapy for PPS

PPS go hand in hand with profound changes in the relationship and family climate (Decraemer & Reijmers, 2017). The disruption of emotional balance that occurs with PPS, the changes in behaviour and the associated stress are often experienced by families and couples. Involving family members, partners and other system members in the treatment gives all parties the opportunity to express and exchange uncertainties in dealing with the patient and their problematic situation. This enhances relationships, communication and functioning as a family, couple or larger part of the system. There is a consensus that the body should be at the centre of any systemic therapy for PPS from the beginning (Decraemer & Reijmers, 2017). Regardless of the school of systems theory, the systemic therapist focuses on the bodily experience of everyone present. Systemic therapy for PPS makes bodily responses a shared topic of conversation in order to increase body awareness. This can be done through questions such as, 'What are you experiencing in your body right now?' or through mirroring such as, 'I see you frowning and leaning back in your chair'. It can also be done with more creative methods, such as asking each participant to choose an object that represents their body from a box of many objects and having each person briefly talk about it. As system members of patients with PPS may not be used to body-oriented questions, these can increase tension and lead to drop-out. The gradual introduction of body-oriented questions is then recommended.

10.1.2 Systemic therapy and mentalization

Systemic therapy that integrates body-oriented mentalization can largely be compared to mentalization-based therapy for families (MBT-F). This is aimed at family members of children, adolescents and patients with personality problems (Asen & Fonagy, 2012). One can also involve system members other than family members in such a therapy, such as neighbours, friends, colleagues or other

DOI: 10.4324/9781003637486-13

carers, if they are in close contact with the patient. Systemic therapy based on body-oriented mentalizing introduces, much more explicitly than MBT-F, the body as a medium for emotions and affective communication. Systemic therapy based on body-oriented mentalizing uses a number of general systemic therapeutic principles (see Table 10.1), including those of MBT-F (Asen & Fonagy, 2012; Asen & Midgley, 2019).

10.2   Body-oriented mentalizing in systemic therapy

Attention to bodily signals that indicate mental states, in self and others, is essential for healthy interactions in the system, while high-quality systemic interactions are also necessary for good body-oriented mentalizing. Systemic therapy for patients with PPT and their loved ones based on B-MBT is about the system learning to cope together with the uninvited guest of PPS in the relationship (van der Werf, 2018). Because of the endless search for solutions to the physical symptoms, the emotional exchange in the relationship may have disappeared over time. Restructuring the connection between family members involves learning to name

Table 10.1 Systemic therapeutic principles in body-oriented mentalizing with systems.

The body as a medium: The willingness to explore bodily sensations and be open to see the body as the medium for emotions and affective communication.

Open to discovery: An attitude in which the individual is genuinely interested in the physical sensations, thoughts and feelings of others.

The opacity of mental states: The open acknowledgement that one will never know the exact nature of the inner world of others, but can only guess.

Reflective contemplation: A flexible, relaxed and open mental attitude that replaces the controlled and obsessive pursuit of exactly knowing how others think and feel.

Perspective taking: Accepting that the same phenomenon or process can look very different from different personal perspectives.

Forgiveness: Understanding the actions of others by understanding and accepting their underlying mental state.

Impact: How do one's thoughts, feelings and actions affect others?

An attitude of trust: The ability to adopt an attitude of trust in others.

Modesty and an attitude of 'not knowing': A willingness to be surprised and to learn from others, regardless of status.

Awareness of inner conflict: Being 'attuned' to people's conflicting thoughts and feelings.

Playfulness and humour (self-mockery): The ability to be light-hearted and to laugh at oneself with others.

Willingness to change turns: The ability to 'give and take' in interactions.

Belief in changeability: The belief that the inner self and related physical experiences can change or be changed, and a sense of optimism about the therapeutic enterprise.

Taking responsibility: Accepting responsibility for one's own actions.

physical and inner experiences that are normally not considered during interactions. This allows the patient and the system to find each other again and reshape their need to be meaningful to each other.

In B-MBT systemic therapy, we integrate the systemic approach with the concepts, theory, and treatment principles and methods discussed earlier in this book (especially in Chapter 4, Chapter 5 and Chapter 7). We assume that when body-oriented mentalizing is (temporarily) absent in system interactions, there is a greater likelihood of mutual problems in coping with emotions and physical symptoms. This is particularly true when system members have difficulty with body-oriented mentalizing during adverse and stressful family interactions. This inability affects the sense of mutual safety needed to be aware of one's own bodily sensations, emotions, thoughts, tendencies and needs in contact with system members.

Systemic therapy based on body-oriented mentalization ultimately helps to:

- Raise awareness of one's own and others' physical and inner experiences
- Improve awareness of interconnectedness and (in)appropriate patterns of interaction
- Enhance attachment in relationships
- Strengthen the ability to regulate one another's emotions
- Improve mutual communication and increase the ability to solve problems together

In this way, members of the system, including the patient, are given different ways of dealing with long-term physical complaints, and the sense of competence to understand and help each other is strengthened. Body-oriented mentalizing can be used in systemic therapy for severe PPS to discuss issues such as:

- Mutual misconceptions and misunderstandings
- Accepting limitations
- Setting mutual boundaries
- Dealing with the unpredictability of physical symptoms
- Touch and sexuality
- Shared rules, norms and values for dealing with illness, physical limitations and emotions

The therapist encourages body-oriented mentalizing once the interaction has been stripped of the personal exchange of bodily sensations and inner experiences. We make it clear to system members that the physical sensations and inner reactions of others are important. In promoting body-oriented mentalizing, we need to maintain a balance between following the natural interactions of system members and intervening to promote change. We do this using the therapeutic stance and basic techniques described in Chapter 4, Chapter 5 and Chapter 7, and keeping in mind the systemic principles in Table 10.1. The following section lists points of attention for body-oriented mentalizing in systemic therapy.

10.2.1   Providing information

System members can be educated, possibly in groups, about:

- PPS and common misconceptions
- The biopsychosocial model
- The intersubjectivity of experience
- What body-oriented mentalizing is (a patient information folder like in Appendix A.1 can contribute to this)
- The quality of attachment relationships
- Other therapy-related issues

For more information on educational topics, see also Section 4.7.

10.2.2   Increase willingness to reflect on interaction

There may be a homeostasis in which the members of the system have no requests for relational help. In this case, we as therapists do not have to be reluctant to suggest relational topics of conversation ourselves. For example, we first ask questions about the current interaction between the patient and his or her significant others. These include:

1. What goes well and is helpful?
2. What goes less well and is not helpful?
3. What are the possibilities to improve the interaction, especially in terms of helping each other, emotional exchange and closeness?

We can ask and discuss these questions. But we can also have members of the system talk to each other about an issue that is topical, personal and relevant to them, and get a picture of the three areas of concern mentioned earlier. In this way we validate what is still going well. This 'social reanimation' again offers new perspectives within systems and increases the willingness to reflect on the physical and emotional side of interaction.

10.2.3   Stopping the conversation

The therapist stops a conversation when there is too little body-oriented mentalizing communication, such as emotionless stories or repetitive conversations that lead nowhere. We can then stop the conversation using 'stop and stand still' and 'stop and go back' (see Section 5.2.16 and Section 5.2.17) to clarify each person's physical and inner response. For example, the therapist might ask the system members, 'What are you experiencing in your body right now?' or, 'What is going through your mind right now?' In this way, new perspectives become clear to system members, making everyone's behaviour more understandable.

10.2.4 Reading each other's physical expressions

To encourage contact about physical sensations and emotions, the therapist asks members of the system to 'read each other': to focus on the other person's physical expression and what it says about their inner self. For example, we might ask: 'As you look at your daughter's body posture now, what emotions does she express for you?' Here the therapist emphasises that, while emotions are a way of affective communication, we can never know someone's physical experience and inner reaction with complete certainty. We can only make well-considered guesses about what other people are thinking and feeling. If someone finds it difficult to guess what another system member is thinking or feeling, the therapist can ask other system members to try.

10.2.5 Empathising with each other's situation

The therapist can ask system members to change perspective and put themselves in the other person's shoes, e.g.: 'If you were to imagine you were her, what would you experience in your body and what thoughts or emotions would you notice in yourself as a result?' If necessary, the therapist can emphasise the difference between what a member of the system would experience in a situation (e.g. feeling stressed), and what the other person (e.g. the patient) is now experiencing (e.g. abdominal pain). After all, empathising with another person also means recognising and accepting that the other person may have different physical and emotional reactions to your own.

10.2.6 Encouraging body-oriented mentalizing sequences

When practising body-oriented mentalizing communication, we aim for sequences of reciprocal communication:

Therapist: Now that you hear that mother has a headache, what does that make you feel inside?
Son: I find that sad.

The therapist can then ask the mother about her physical sensations and her inner reaction to hearing her son's reaction, and so on.

10.2.7 Noticing patterns of interaction

The therapist tries to identify interaction patterns in terms of irritation, misunderstanding, disbelief, confusion or frustration. In particular, he will name patterns that are not normally thought about, such as:' I notice that when A (the son, a patient with chronic back pain) talks about how difficult it is for him to study because of the back pain, father starts sighing and staring out the window, and mother gets tears in her eyes. Has anyone else noticed this? Did I see that right?' These are mainly interaction patterns in which people unintentionally can reinforce each other's negative behaviour. Severe PPS also includes common clinging and withdrawal, the fight and flight movements (van der Werf, 2018). When naming and recognising reaction patterns, the systemic therapist will focus on each person's physical and mental experience with a pattern of communication. The aim is to make communication more transparent and to translate it into underlying feelings and attachment needs. Once the system members have identified their patterns of interaction, and everyone's personal, physical and inner reactions to them have been discussed, the focus can shift to looking at other ways of interacting. For example, we can ask system members how they can change the interaction pattern if it threatens to reoccur at home.

10.2.8   Validating differences

During systemic therapy sessions, system members can learn that everyone can understand situations differently, that physical sensations and inner experiences are subjective. That's why we show interest in differences and value them. To the mother of a young daughter with chronic fatigue, the therapist can say: 'What strikes me about you is that when your daughter expresses her fatigue, you feel tired and powerless and think there is no solution. This triggers something else in the father'. The therapist turns to the father: 'Then you feel a lot of restlessness in your legs, you feel impatience and anger, and you think she should try harder'. The therapist keeps trying to make it clear that different experiences of the same phenomenon can coexist. Or they can even complement each other. Respecting each other's differences can be the starting point for improved communication and problem solving.

10.2.9   Recognising and marking body-oriented mentalizing

The therapist will indicate when he notices that one or more members of the system are clearly engaging in body-oriented mentalizing. He may praise the skill demonstrated, e.g. 'I like to notice that you are really reflecting on what you are experiencing physically and emotionally and sharing it with each other'. Highlighting effective body-oriented mentalizing helps system members to notice and expand moments of body-oriented mentalizing themselves.

10.2.10   Therapist transparency

The therapist is open about his own mental and physical state and how the interaction of the system members affects him. For example, to the father mentioned earlier, whose daughter is being treated for chronic fatigue, he might say, 'I notice that you are quite raising your voice now that she mentions she is so tired again, and I hear that you think she should stop this "whining". I notice that I feel tension in my neck and shoulders, that I feel myself getting restless, and that I think this is quite an intense reaction to a daughter'. The therapist will then consider the implications of his self-disclosure. He might ask the father, 'What are you experiencing inside and physically right now, listening to what I am saying?' To avoid the father dropping out after such a self-disclosure, the therapist can show understanding for the father's experience: 'I can also imagine how difficult it is for you to hear all the time how tired your daughter is'.

10.3   Conclusion

Systemic therapy based on body-oriented mentalizing for people with severe PPS and those directly involved, like their loved ones, may help improve their ability to communicate with each other and strengthen attachment relationships. Therapists can pay attention to whether members of the system, including the patient, are sufficiently attuned to their own and others' physical and mental reactions. If this is decreasing, we stimulate body-oriented mentalizing, as described in this chapter. Here we can name patterns of interaction and explore the underlying emotions, needs and ideas in a relational context. The therapist is open about his own physical and mental state in a pedagogical way and he is aware of the impact of self-disclosure on members of the system. Further research is needed to determine whether this approach is effective not only within B-MBT multidisciplinary treatment but also as a stand-alone systemic therapy. For now, body-oriented mentalizing can be considered a potential component of any systemic therapy for (severe) PPS.

Chapter 11

Multidisciplinary treatment

11.1 The multidisciplinary team

One of the most effective forms of B-MBT for PPS is the multidisciplinary treatment. Several disciplines work together as much as possible 'without partitions'. This prevents somatic, psychological and social specialists from approaching PPS separately from each other and only from their own area of expertise. A division between disciplines can exacerbate the problems, whereas combined treatments of PPS have been shown to have a greater effect than stand-alone treatments (Kamper et al., 2014). In multidisciplinary B-MBT, different disciplines strive for maximum therapeutic integration at different levels, such as psychological and somatic, verbal and non-verbal, individually or in groups, and with family and other directly involved parties. In doing so, each discipline naturally retains its own professional responsibility to work from their own professional standard.

The experience of the author and the contributors to this book is in the treatment of severe PPS in (highly) specialised mental health care. A multidisciplinary team in such a setting may consist of, for example: physicians such as general practitioners, rehabilitation physicians, internists, neurologists or psychiatrists; psychologists; psychotherapists; systemic therapists; (psychosomatic) physiotherapists; (psychosomatic) exercise therapists; occupational therapists; psychomotor therapists; occupational therapists; art therapists; music therapists; drama therapists; mental health nurses and social workers.

Multidisciplinary treatment does not necessarily mean that all elements of B-MBT are provided in the same setting. In this case, optimal interdisciplinary coordination is essential.

Several aspects of multidisciplinary B-MBT will be described in this chapter.

11.2 Willingness to work from the B-MBT vision

Consistent multidisciplinary treatment using body-oriented mentalizing as a guide requires that all team members have a correct understanding of the B-MBT (treatment) vision and endorse it. One should, for example, also assume the importance of the quality of attachment relationships and the inextricable link between the

DOI: 10.4324/9781003637486-14

physical, inner and social aspects of PPS. In addition, team members should be aware of the treatment principles (see Section 4.8), the therapeutic stance (see Section 4.6) and the basic interventions (see Chapter 5). The willingness of all team members to accept the patient's current physical symptoms and to help them to cope with the symptoms is crucial. The primary aim of B-MBT treatment is not to reduce symptoms and pursue behavioural change. This has often been done with previous therapies, such as cognitive behavioural therapy, which was not effective enough and reason for referral to B-MBT.

Team members should not only express the B-MBT vision in words, but also put it into action, otherwise team members may work against the body-oriented mentalizing processes. For example, if the aim is for a patient to learn to perceive and tolerate her own physical and mental tensions, interventions aimed at directly reducing anxiety may disrupt the treatment process. This can happen, for example, when the doctor prescribes additional medication to be taken when tension or physical symptoms occur. And it may happen when a team member uses distraction techniques in the case of increasing tension in the same patient, without body-oriented mentalizing. Wanting to help patients with symptom-relieving medication or exercises is a normal human tendency, also among team members, and is often also in line with the patient's request for help and perceived in line with the suffering. During B-MBT, symptom-relieving measures can only be used with the aim of bringing the patient back to his tolerance zone. The aim then is to restore body-oriented mentalizing, not to avoid, eliminate and reduce body signals and complaints. If one uses symptom-reducing interventions with no other goal than symptom reduction, then there is a high probability that both the patient and the therapist will fall into a body or teleological mode, which can work against B-MBT treatment. It is therefore important to check regularly during team consultations or team supervision whether a body-oriented mentalizing approach from an accepting attitude towards physical complaints is still sufficiently present in the team.

11.3   Competence

The fact that the vision of B-MBT should be reflected in the professional behaviour of all disciplines does not necessarily mean that one has to apply B-MBT exclusively. Not all therapists need to be pure B-MBT psychotherapists. Sometimes it is sufficient to keep the B-MBT vision in mind in one's interventions and to choose methods from one's own discipline that are compatible with B-MBT. For all disciplines, if one wants to integrate B-MBT into one's own field, one should acknowledge the B-MBT treatment principles and develop B-MBT core competencies to develop a minimum level of competence.

We can distinguish the following four levels of competence:

1. A correct understanding of B-MBT
2. Knowledge and skills in basic techniques through a general B-MBT basic course and/or a course in integrating B-MBT basic techniques into the treatment techniques of one's own discipline

3. Additional knowledge and skills through a B-MBT advanced course or a Mentalization-Based Therapy (MBT) course
4. Level 3 knowledge and skills with prior training as a clinical psychologist, psychotherapist, psychiatrist or other mental health specialist who can also lead an B-MBT team

Training for multidisciplinary teams usually goes up to level 2. Team members who wish to become B-MBT therapists in the strict sense (levels 3 and 4) usually do this in addition to a team training. The development of competence in B-MBT does not end with a one-off training or the completion of an advanced course. Team members are encouraged to have an ongoing willingness to improve their skills and understanding of B-MBT. Regular peer intervision/supervision regarding body-oriented mentalizing skills can support and strengthen this willingness (see Section 11.7.1).

11.4   Mutual alignment

Mutual task alignment is central to the vision of B-MBT treatment. This requires flexibility and interdisciplinary professional empathy. Team members must also be able to omit or postpone interventions in their own area of expertise. It is clear that a fourth level practitioner has a role to play in translating the patient's themes into B-MBT processes. In order to maintain the substantive balance in the treatment, we must prevent the psychological perspective from becoming too dominant in other disciplines and thus causing all team members to do the same thing. Different disciplines may each have their own emphasis in the treatment. Some examples:

- *Physicians*, such as general practitioners, rehabilitation physicians, internists, neurologists or psychiatrists: Education on the continuous interaction between body and mind, such as the functioning of the stress system, chronic pain and the biology of the attachment system; body-oriented mentalizing when considering somatic examination or medication and when monitoring and evaluating its effect.
- *Psychologists and psychotherapists*, including psychiatrists: Provide verbal individual and group psychotherapy and work with enactments and trauma.
- *Non-verbal therapists*, such as (psychosomatic) physiotherapists, exercise therapists, occupational therapists and psychomotor therapists: Strengthen body awareness and use this ability to dose and build up physical activities.
- *System therapists*: Stimulate the body-oriented mentalizing capacity of the patient and system members, with attention to attachment strategies within the system.
- *Art therapists*: Encourage artistic expression of inner processes, with symbols and metaphors, in relation to the body.
- *Nurses and sociotherapists*: Encourage body-oriented mentalizing in self-care or in asking others for help. They can help with body-oriented mentalizing in everyday life, in the therapy group and in building valuable daily activities.

- *Social workers*: Encourage body-oriented mentalizing in everyday life outside the hospital.

Because of the typical perspective of each discipline, regular reflection on interdisciplinary coordination and delineation is necessary. The quality of the alignment largely determines the effectiveness of the treatment. Multidisciplinary alignment may include the following questions:

- How can we use findings from one discipline to the therapies by other disciplines?
- In which specific therapeutic situations does body-oriented mentalizing decrease and when does it increase? And with which therapist or discipline does this happen? How can we take advantage of this?
- Which topics are covered by different disciplines and do they form enough of a coherent whole?
- To what extent does the patient show different themes or behaviours with different disciplines or practitioners, and how do we form these aspects into a coherent whole with the patient in treatment?
- In which therapy does transference/countertransference play the biggest role and what can we do with it?
- Are there any splits within the team that reflect the patient's issues?

11.5   Dealing with a somatic or mental crisis

During therapy, acute somatic crises may occur which we may or may not be able to adequately explain, medically or somatically. For example, patients may acutely experience severe chest pain, suddenly experience severe attacks of abdominal pain, or unexpectedly experience paralysis. Suddenly, team members' attention naturally turns to the medical outcome of the crisis. For example, a patient experiences acute severe chest pain during group therapy and is very stuffy. The ward physician refers her to the emergency department of a nearby general hospital. An ambulance takes her to the hospital. All team members are concerned and anxiously await the results of tests at the hospital. The severity of a somatic crisis is likely to cause a stress response in team members, with a focus on the results of medical or somatic examinations and the physical condition of the patient.

Patients in a state of severe imbalance with severe somatic symptoms will often be inclined to look only at somatic factors ('Did I do anything physically wrong?') and not at what they have experienced mentally or socially. It is the responsibility of the team to identify the possible factors from a broad biopsychosocial perspective, and such a broad multifactorial inventory forms the basis for further treatment policy. The team members must also switch back to body-oriented mentalization as quickly as possible, both individually and with each other ('What physical and mental reactions does this crisis evoke in me?'). Especially in times of somatic crisis in one or more patients, it is important to make team decisions from a body-oriented mentalizing stance, rather than just from a somatically solution-oriented approach.

We should also agree among ourselves who will look back on the crisis situation with the patient experiencing the somatic crisis on his return via 'stop and go back'.

If none of these scenarios happens, parallel processes may take place in the patient group. They become even more single- focused on the physical aspects of their problems, with a further decrease in body-oriented mentalizing. Even in the case of a mental crisis of one or more patients, such as severe acute suicidality, it is important for team members to maintain a broad perspective. In addition to the patient's mental state, what have we recently noticed about the somatic and social aspects of the patient's functioning? How can we continue to mentalize in a body-oriented way amongst each other? Once the crisis is over and both patient and practitioner are back within their tolerance zones, who will engage in body-oriented mentalizing with the patient about the most striking things or impactful situations from the crisis using 'stop and go back?' Often a crisis has both somatic and mental aspects. Even then, the aim is for team members to be aware of the somatic, psychological and social factors at play and how they fit into the phase and developments of the treatment.

11.6   The therapist-patient match

In B-MBT, more than in other forms of therapy, we assume that a good patient-therapist relationship (attachment) is crucial for learning body-oriented mentalizing. The quality of the therapeutic relationship experienced by the patient does not depend solely on the professional actions of the therapist. The combination of the two styles of attachment is a strong determinant. Is there a match in this area or not? The patient's perception of the therapeutic relationship is a regular topic of discussion in therapy. In the treatment plan meeting that the patient attends, one can evaluate how both the patient and the therapists experience their therapeutic relationship. Different therapeutic relationships, for example, the relationship with both the senior psychiatrist and the student nurse, can be topics of discussion. For example, the patient may get on better with a student nurse than with an experienced psychiatrist. It may then be better for the psychiatrist to leave certain interventions to the student nurse, while they regularly discuss how the therapy is progressing.

In case of a strained therapeutic relationship with a patient, we should always also consider a background of transference, counter-transference, 'enactment' or possibly past trauma. We should explore, in consultation with the patient, which therapy addresses these sensitivities and whether the patient is willing to discuss them further with the therapist in question.

11.7   Consultation with colleagues

Consultation with colleagues in the form of peer intervision, group supervision and case conferences is inseparable from B-MBT. Again, it is important that the emotional safety is such that team members dare to explore and share their personal physical and inner experiences in working with patients. B-MBT only has a chance of success if the organisation/institution provides opportunities for safe B-MBT consultation among colleagues and emphasises its importance. Peer intervision and case conferences are described in Section 11.7.1 and Section 11.7.2. Guidance here is preferably in the hands of an experienced staff member trained in level four B-MBT (see Section 11.3).

11.7.1 Peer intervision

The aim of peer intervision is professional exchange and mutual support in the practical implementation and maintenance of the B-MBT vision. It aims not only to promote the competence of the team members, but also to promote a B-MBT atmosphere in the team. Topics for peer intervision can be in the area of methodological and motivational aspects of working with B-MBT. Examples of common topics are:

* Dealing with one's own aversions to certain patients
* Recognising counter-transference
* Assessing the way patients mentalize in certain therapies
* Remaining sufficiently body-oriented mentalizing in one's own therapy
* Dealing with barriers to intervention
* Dealing with group phenomena (e.g. excessive mutual help in order to avoid irritations)

When discussing the motivational and methodological aspects of B-MBT, the aim is to use expertise and experience and to give constructive feedback. Personal experience of working with B-MBT and intercollegiate exchange receives explicit attention. It is intended that peer intervision meetings will take place on a regular basis, e.g. once a month. To ensure confidentiality and a safe atmosphere, a small group (about four to ten participants) with a fixed composition is preferred. It is also recommended that the participants have similar competences, such as having attended a basic course in B-MBT. The programme of a peer intervision session could be as follows:

1. Discuss everyone's experience of working with B-MBT. Questions might include: How does it feel to work with B-MBT? What are the barriers and facilitators?
2. Distil common bottlenecks in applying B-MBT.
3. Bring to life a case that reflects the common bottleneck, e.g. with role play, audio or video recording.
4. Reflecting on one's own (body) signals and inner experiences evoked during part 3.
5. Based on the personal experiences, identify possible options in dealing with the bottleneck applying B-MBT.

6. Take an inventory of individual learning points: each team member formulates personal points of interest for future body-oriented mentalizing with patients and shares them with the other participants.

11.7.2 Case conference

In case conferences, participants reflect on a patient's situation in the light of a question such as, 'How can treatment be made more effective?' or 'Why is the patient's physical condition deteriorating so much?' B-MBT provides the context. Known components of case discussion are:

1. Selection of the case
2. Formulation of a question
3. Clarification of the question
4. Mutual exchange of observations and information related to the question
5. Keeping the patient in mind while doing body-oriented mentalizing
6. Analysis of the problem in light of B-MBT treatment principles and everyone's experience in part 5
7. Identification of any points of attention for improvement or treatment
8. Conclusions and intentions

In a B-MBT case conference, the analysis of the problem or question focuses on the nature of the patient's inability to mentalize in a body-oriented way. With whom and when does the patient struggle with it? How does it manifest itself? What mode of non-body mentalizing is the patient in then? What helps to promote body-oriented mentalizing in the patient? During further reflection, team members consider questions such as, 'Are we still responding to the patient from a symptom-accepting and body-oriented-mentalizing stance or are we in a teleological, solution-focused mode? What is the patient's view of the therapeutic process and where does transference/counter-transference occur?'

Part 5 of the case conference is essential to incorporate subjective experiences of team members when identifying areas for improvement. This part of the case conference helps the participants to change their subjective impressions of the patient, to empathise with the patient's situation through a change of perspective and, on this basis, to arrive at possible areas for improvement. The person leading the case conference can go through the following steps with the participants:

- Focus your attention on your body. Feel the contact of your feet with the floor and your legs and back with the chair.
- Bring awareness to your breathing.
- Imagine the patient in a situation where the problem occurs.
- What do you notice about the patient when you think about him or her? What physical expressions do you notice and what thoughts, feelings, tendencies and other internal reactions do you think the patient has?

- What do you experience yourself when you think of the patient in the given situation? What physical sensations do you notice in yourself? What are your inner reactions, thoughts and feelings?
- Now imagine you are the patient in the given situation. What do you experience? What physical sensations do you experience? What emotions, thoughts, tendencies, memories, etc. arise?
- Focus your attention again on the fact that you are sitting here in this chair, feeling the contact of your feet with the floor and your legs with the chair.

Each person then shares their experience of the different steps of the exercise with the other participants. This sharing of body-oriented mentalizing about the patient can provide surprising new insights into the treatment. The facilitator sums up the experiences and asks the question: 'What do these experiences say about the question of this discussion? And what are the possible solutions?'

Box 11.1   Case conference fragment: Body-oriented mentalizing during case conference

A young woman with severe chronic fatigue makes little progress during treatment. During the case conference, in the debriefing of the body-oriented mentalizing exercise on the young woman, team members' experiences included the following:

- I notice how fragile she looks and how much I worry about her.
- I saw in my mind's eye her thin wrists and thought maybe she has problems with eating.
- When I put myself in her shoes, I feel anxious and detached from the world.
- When I put myself in her shoes, I feel tired and worried at the same time, and then I think, 'Am I doing it right?'

On the basis of the exercise and the rest of the case conference (case conference fragment in Box 11.1), team-members decide to discuss with the patient: her possible difficulties with eating and weight, her fear of failure, and how she perceives contact with fellow patients and team members. Practising body-oriented mentalizing with a change of perspective during a case conference not only leads to new points of intervention for treatment, but also evokes empathy for the patient. This can strengthen the process of mutual body-oriented mentalizing between patient and therapists. Often the relationship between team members and the patient changes for the better after such a team exercise. Team members who are having considerable difficulty with a particular patient can also focus on the following questions during the case conference:

- In which situation does body-mentalizing stop in this patient?
- What physical and mental reactions do I experience in the problem situation?
- What physical signals and inner experiences do I see in the patient in the problem situation?
- In which mode of non-mentalizing is the patient in the problem situation?
- What image do I have of myself in the problem situation?
- What image do I think the patient has of me in the problem situation?
- Which division of roles between me and the patient dominates the problem situation?
- What is my mode of non-mentalizing in the problem situation?
- Is my physical and mental reaction to the patient a familiar one for me? Do I recognise this reaction from previous situations? Is there perhaps a counter-transference here?
- Can I perhaps look at the problem situation differently and react differently myself?

Working through these questions together develops a shared awareness of transference, counter-transference and 'enactment' and where they occur. This allows team members to make choices about where, when and who will work on the enactment with the patient.

11.8   Body-oriented mentalizing within the team

Providing care to patients with severe PPS can easily get stuck in a non-mentalizing, rationalising or solution-focused atmosphere. Because of the worrying nature of their physical or mental condition and the complex nature of their problems, team members collectively fall into a teleological mode of approaching and solving problems without adequate reflection on their own and others' physical and mental states. In an atmosphere of decisive and goal-oriented action, team members may begin to hide their insecurities or fears and strive to appear competent. Or worse, team members begin to compete with each other for competence. They believe that doubt, 'not knowing', feeling down or afraid is not appropriate now. After all, they think, other team members don't show this either. If this mechanism occurs more often, the treatment becomes less mentalizing. It can lead to a lack of job satisfaction, fatigue, burnout or other health problems among team members.

Body-oriented mentalizing within the team is not only important in the case of a patient's worrying condition or a crisis situation (see Section 11.5); it is a permanent integral part of B-MBT. This starts with a team atmosphere of unconditional acceptance of each other's bodily sensations, feelings and thoughts, as well as openness to experiencing frustration, uncertainty and failure, etcetera. In a body-oriented mentalizing interaction, team members can ask themselves the following questions:

1. When discussing patients, am I aware of my physical and mental reactions and those of other team members? And do I communicate about it?

2. Do I pay attention to team interaction in the here and now?
3. Do I accept differences between myself and colleagues in the experience of treatment, patients and team atmosphere? Do I communicate about it?
4. Can I experience my prejudices about team members or other frames of reference as thoughts rather than reality?
5. Do I recognise my role in this team without identifying with it?
6. Am I open to feedback on my performance from colleagues? And do I myself give feedback to others with an 'I' message, reflecting about my physical sensations and inner experiences in contact with them?

In team interactions, we can use the B-MBT framework to pay attention to behavioural, emotional and cognitive processes in one or more team members or within the team itself. We can look at:

• A (non-)body-oriented mentalizing mode
• Mutual exploration of physical and inner reactions
• Mutual transparency
• Mutual exchange through feedback
• Recognition of repetitive mutual reaction patterns
• Recognition of individual traumatic experiences
• Recognition of traumatic experiences of the team as a whole

Doing a shared experiential exercise, such as a mindfulness exercise focusing on bodily sensations and inner experiences, at the beginning of a team meeting has several advantages:

• It makes team members more familiar with using B-MBT principles in sessions with patients.
• It creates a body-oriented mentalizing atmosphere in the here and now.
• It strengthens the bond between team members through the shared experience.
• It can be a good starting point for a discussion about body-oriented mentalizing.

In short, B-MBT is not only suitable as a multidisciplinary treatment method. It can also clarify and support the processes of teams and team members so that they are flexible, motivated and effective.

11.9 Dealing with splits

As a response to individual patients with PPS using splitting as a defence mechanism, splitting can also occur as a group dynamic within the multidisciplinary team. In this case, the team itself becomes polarised, with members unconsciously splitting into opposing subgroups, often around different perspectives on patient care, theoretical frameworks or professional roles. This process can be further fuelled by unresolved tensions, emotional pressures, or the complexity of working with patients with complex problems like severe PPS.

A cohesive team that has mastered the art of mutual body-oriented mentalizing is also resilient to splits. Splits in a team can significantly reduce a team's effectiveness. We can best describe impending splits as inherent to the work, so that they can be recognised and addressed in time through team reflection. Acknowledging the split can be the starting point for renewed mentalizing in a body-oriented way. Here we can then make the physical and inner background of each person's opinion or positioning mutually understandable and, with respect for everyone's experience, seek a communal approach to treatment.

11.10   Conclusion

This chapter has focused on the functioning of the multidisciplinary team. A safe team with good cohesion is the basis for effective B-MBT teamwork. Team members are trained in B-MBT, work from the same treatment principles as far as possible and use B-MBT interventions appropriate to their own area of expertise. They always coordinate their own interventions with those of other team members and the patient. Team members recognise that it is not just about the content of the treatment plan but also about the quality of the team interaction and the therapeutic relationship. Our effective collaboration with the patient depends, in part, also on a good match between our own attachment style and that of the patient.

Peer intervision, case conference and group supervision are necessary components of team collaboration. Mutual body-oriented mentalizing is important for the quality of treatment and for a healthy, motivating working atmosphere. It is also important for dealing with splitting phenomena within teams. Finally, as an addition to the factors included here, the consistency and coherence with which we apply multidisciplinary treatment over time is also crucial for effective multidisciplinary B-MBT treatment (Bales, 2019).

Appendices

A.1 Patient information leaflet

Table A.1 Patient information leaflet.

What is body-oriented mentalizing?

Learning to be aware of your body and mind is an important part of the treatment. We call this 'body-oriented mentalizing'. What exactly is this? It starts with the ability to notice body signals, such as tension in your muscles or a heavy feeling in your legs. Body-oriented mentalizing means that you can experience these signals from your body and realise that they may be related to inner experiences such as emotions, thoughts, memories or tendencies. For example, if you notice that your muscles are tense, you can ask yourself, 'What is happening to me inside right now?' Physical sensations are often inextricably linked to inner experiences. When you think about something that moves you, you might feel a lump in your throat, or your limbs might shake when you are frightened by something. Body-oriented mentalizing, then, is sensing that physical and inner experiences are interconnected.

Body-oriented mentalizing also helps you to better understand the physical expressions of others. For example, you hear a car door slam in the street. You turn towards it and see a man searching his pockets and apparently not finding what he is looking for. He starts pacing, stamping his feet on the ground and putting his hands to his head. You automatically conclude that the man is frustrated because he has left his keys in his car, and he urgently needs to leave. This behaviour would be quite astonishing if we could not do body-oriented mentalizing: if we could not understand the physical manifestations of an inner reaction in ourselves and in the other person. Body-oriented mentalizing is a universal human ability.

All people can do it to varying degrees. Many people experience noticing each other's physical and inner experiences as personal contact. A personal relationship with the other person is therefore an important part of body-oriented mentalizing.

What does body-oriented mentalizing have to do with long-term physical complaints?

If you have distressing long-lasting physical symptoms, such as pain, fatigue or muscle failure symptoms, you may react with stress or anxiety. If the stress becomes too high, you may feel less comfortable with loved ones. The reassurance that normally comes from their presence decreases. You may avoid loved ones or demand their attention excessively, which can make your situation worse. With stress and problems in dealing with others, your capacity for body-oriented mentalizing also diminishes. This may have the following consequences:

(Continued)

- *Impaired perception of body signals*: For example, you work hard and don't notice how heavy your body feels, or that you're tired and you don't feel that your muscles hurt very much. This can make physical symptoms worse.
- *Impaired awareness of your needs*: Despite feeling tired, you continue to work hard and don't realise that you need to sit down and have a rest from time to time. This can make physical symptoms worse.
- *Not being able to recognise emotions*: You are no longer aware of certain emotions. You feel your heart beating faster and blood rushing to your head, but you don't realise that this is a sign that you are angry. You feel increasingly angry, sad, anxious or tense, but you don't realise it. This can make physical symptoms worse.
- *Worrying more*: You start to worry more and more about the physical symptoms and your health. You fear a serious illness and think a lot about the physical causes of your symptoms. Worrying causes more stress and more physical symptoms.
- *Social problems*: You can no longer express well what you are experiencing physically and internally. Others do not understand you and all sorts of communication problems arise. This often leaves you feeling 'unseen', 'unappreciated', lonely and angry, which can increase physical symptoms.
- *Increased avoidance behaviour*: In the long run, you tend to automatically avoid physical symptoms more and more, for example, by not doing activities that cause pain, or by overexerting yourself in all kinds of situations. You no longer consider what you are actually experiencing physically and internally. This may also worsen physical symptoms.

To reduce these effects of distressing physical symptoms and associated stress, conscious reflection on body and mind, i.e. body-oriented mentalization, is essential.

What do you notice about it when you are in therapy?

Body-oriented mentalizing is something we usually do automatically. We don't have to think about it. Just as you don't have to be a linguist to use language to have a conversation, you don't have to know exactly what mentalize in a body-oriented way is. But if you have serious, long-term physical symptoms, you can benefit greatly from conscious body-oriented mentalizing. By paying attention to your physical and inner reactions, you can better align your behaviour with your personal perceptions. This increases your capacity for self-healing.

We believe that we learn to better body-oriented mentalize in contact with others, like with therapists, group members, partners, family members and friends. During treatment you will be asked to open up to what you experience in contact with your fellow patients and therapists. What do you notice when you are being treated with body-oriented mentalization? Therapists will regularly:

- Ask you about your bodily sensations and your inner experiences in relation to them
- Tell you what bodily sensations and inner experiences they think they perceive in you (mirroring), so that you become more aware of them
- Ask you to reflect on and say something about what you are experiencing physically and mentally in contact with other patients (in group therapy) or people directly involved
- Tell you what bodily sensations, feelings, thoughts and images they themselves experience in contact with you

– Asking you how you experience contact with him/her and encouraging you to give a sincere answer

Therapists help you to increase your capacity for body-oriented mentalizing. But it also requires self-efficacy. The idea is that you make a conscious commitment to recognise body signals and to feel what physical experiences are telling you. This is not always easy. Sometimes it works and sometimes it does not. But over time, you will come to recognise what is good for you, and you will be better able to deal with persistent physical symptoms.

A.2 Signals of body-oriented mentalizing

Table A.2 Signals of body-oriented mentalizing.

Key signals of body-oriented mentalizing

– Be able to recognise physical signals and inner experiences in oneself and others
– Demonstrate an open, inquiring attitude towards one's own and others' physical signals and inner experiences
– Demonstrate empathy for one's own and others' physical signals and inner experiences
– Recognise the subjective nature of bodily sensations and inner experiences and that they are not 'absolute truths'
– Tolerate bodily signals and inner states, even if they are unpleasant or painful
– Accept the dynamic nature of bodily signals and inner experiences
– A willingness to look beyond practical somatic solutions to bodily experiences
– Congruence between non-verbal and verbal expression
– Thoughtful, inquiring, nuanced reflection on bodily cues and inner experiences of self and relevant others
– Be able to talk about bodily and inner experiences in the here and now
– Use rich, affective, flexible language about bodily cues and inner experiences of self and relevant others
– Show autobiographical continuity: show no conspicuous gaps in recollection of physical and emotional experiences
– Make connections between physical sensations and inner experiences, such as emotions, and demonstrate this verbally and non-verbally
– Recognise that inner experiences may be opaque or unconscious
– Have multi-faceted opinions on their own and others' physical and inner experiences
– Demonstrate the ability to adopt different perspectives on one's own and others' bodily and inner experiences
– Demonstrate openness to others' views of bodily and inner experiences and tolerance for different opinions
– Showing interest in other people's bodily signals and inner experiences and how they interact with one's own bodily signals and inner experiences
– Mildness: tolerating and forgiving one's own mistakes and those of others
– Show compassion: viewing oneself and others from a compassionate perspective
– Demonstrate and understanding of social causality: recognising that one's own perceptions are influenced by the perceptions of others and vice versa
– Show willingness to engage in nuanced, open, verbal exchanges with others about physical and inner experiences

A.3 Signs of non-body-oriented mentalizing

Table A.3 Signs of non-body-oriented mentalizing.

Key signs of non-body-oriented mentalizing

Body mode

- Primarily concerned with physical sensations
- Feelings are experienced purely physically and not understood as a mental experience
- Physical discomfort is experienced without any mental representation
- Only have few words for a physical or mental experience
- Response to others is mainly in a non-verbal way
- Respond primarily to non-verbal communication
- Experiencing physical sensations in a concrete, literal way
- Unable to see a broader psychological or social context
- Direct action based on physical sensations
- One cannot imagine that stress or emotions are involved in the case of a physical symptom
- Not thinking things through and reacting directly and impulsively in response to a physical complaint
- High level of arousal, without realizing that this has to do with stress or strong emotions
- Very low arousal without awareness of the absence of tension
- Implicit desire to be taken care of by a caregiver (substitute for former caregiver)

Teleological mode

- Strong focus on the physical/observable: 'I only believe it when I see it', 'Only what I see is real'
- Strong belief in biological causes ('somatic attributions'); strong belief in physical labels and biological causes and solutions
- Viewing the body as a 'thing' that needs to be repaired
- Transforming inner experience directly into action: e.g. anger is directly transformed into beating or running away
- Prefer actions over words: 'Actions speak louder than words'
- Focus only on tangible results, not on feelings, thoughts, wishes, dreams, etc.
- Don't let relationships count unless there is a practical benefit
- Seeing others mainly as a source of practical solutions (for physical problems), without seeing them with their own physical sensations and inner experiences
- Not seeing one's own psychic contribution to the outcome of an interaction
- Being coercive and manipulative; therapist is pressured to do something
- Making dramatic statements about bodily signals and inner experiences in order to coerce others into action
- Being preoccupied with rules, do's and don'ts
- Thinking that only actions with physical consequences can change symptoms

(Continued)

Table A.3 (Continued)

Equivalence mode

- Finding it very difficult to change perspective; only one reality is possible: 'I am right'
- Hyperembodiment:
o Being overwhelmed by painful physical experiences, emotions or thoughts that threaten one's sense of self: 'one loses oneself'. Common overwhelming feelings include: shame, fear, anger, gloom, emptiness, feeling bad, suspicion, powerlessness
o Equating physical and inner experiences to reality: 'I feel sick, therefore I am sick'. Thinking you have a serious illness is the same as being seriously ill, or equating the pain of rejection to physical pain
- Fundamentally misunderstanding physical and mental processes, rejecting and disregarding scientifically based information about body and mind
- Experiencing feelings and bodily signals as unbearable
- Having no words for (the connection between) body signals and inner experiences
- Believing knowing what others are thinking and feeling
- Attacking, defending and withdrawing
- Narcissistic mindset: 'What I think and feel is most important. Others are irrelevant'
- Body absolutism: Black and white perceptions: 'My body is totally sick'
- Being confused
- Condemnation and disapproval of own and others' experiences
- Aggression towards one's own and others' bodily cues and inner experiences
- Preoccupation with rules, commandments and prohibitions and taking them literally, leaving no room for flexibility, 'play', humour or putting things into perspective
- Many misunderstandings with others

Pretend mode

- Empty, meaningless words and phrases: endless chatter about nothing, 'babbling', 'psychobabble'
- Copying others' mental formulations, using therapy language
- Incongruence: Verbal expression does not match body language
- Overly detailed reporting of physical and inner experiences
- Cognitive hypermentalization: Excessive intellectualising and rationalising
- Explaining and expounding a lot without contact with one's own physical and inner experiences
- Overly rich and complex but confusing descriptions of body signals and inner experiences
- Blaming others for own physical and inner experiences
- Few reports of inner experiences
- Distancing oneself from bodily signals and inner experiences of oneself and others
- Talking a lot about 'there and then'
- Talking a lot about others
- Talking a lot about external circumstances such as diagnoses, medication, medical procedures or appearance
- Talking in a detached, unemotional way

A.4 Physical signals of inner experience

Table A.4 Physical signals of inner experience.

Examples of common physical signals of (intense) inner experiences

- Local signs: Tingling, lump in the throat, headache
- A general physical feeling: Heaviness or exhaustion
- Muscle tension: Tense parts of the body, such as hands, arms, neck or shoulders
- Posture: Sitting bent over or upright, active or relaxed
- Movement or tendency: Moving a leg back and forth, restless sudden movements, large violent or quiet small hand and arm movements, such as squeezing hands
- Facial and eye expressions: Tense or relaxed facial muscles or half-closed eyes
- Changes in voice use
- Consciousness: Diminished awareness or passing out/fainting or the opposite: excessive alertness
- Bodily processes: Sweating, changes in breathing, shivering, trembling, changes in skin colour, feeling hot, dizziness, cramps, congestion, nausea and vomiting
- Physical changes: Increased tiredness or changes in body temperature
- Sensitivity to stimuli such as sound, smell, light, etc.

A.5 Traces of non-(body-oriented) mentalizing during non-verbal expressions

The tables that follow list examples of common traces of non-body-oriented mentalizing in non-verbal therapies such as art, music, movement and posture therapies. These traces can be recognised during an exercise aimed at expressing the inner life without words. For the other characteristics of non-(body-oriented) mentalizing, see Table A.3 in these appendices.

Table A.5.1 Traces of non-(body-oriented) mentalizing in artistic expressions.

Examples of traces of non-(body-oriented) mentalizing in artistic expressions

Body mode

- Focus on sensations (such as colour, texture, pressure, temperature, muscle activity) rather than symbolism/meaning/emotion
- Repetitive forms from need for repetitive body movements without explanation (such as strokes or scratches)
- Strong physical involvement or aversion (pressing hard, wiping, using fingers, using large strokes, using physical force, pushing aside) without assigning meaning other than physical
- Not able to explain choice of materials and shapes

(Continued)

Table A.5.1 (Continued)

Teleological mode

- Focused on concrete results ('I'll probably feel better after this'; 'I'll do some sculpting because then I'll have a present for my mother'; 'I'm not satisfied until a given task is finished'
- Difficulties with abstraction or symbolism ('I don't like vague things')
- Frustrated by imperfection, may erase or discard work ('This doesn't make sense'; 'Leave it, it's a failure')
- Takes part only when clearly instructed to portray or get something concrete out of it

Equivalence mode

- Seeing art as an exact representation of the inner and experiencing this as absolute truth ('This drawing is my inner world')
- Rigidity, overwhelming images, little room for change ('This is just the way my life is now and no different, a terrible dead end')
- Cannot see alternative interpretations ('There is no point in looking at it differently, because this is just the way it is')
- Change feels like a denial of reality and of oneself ('There's no other way'; 'This is the way it is'; 'This is who I am')
- Intense emotional involvement without playfulness
- Totally absorbed in artistic expression ('This is totally and completely exactly my feeling. I really can't get away from it'!)

Pretend mode

- Art can appear playful, exaggerated or imitative, but without connection to emotion
- Style, colour or theme changes abruptly and without consistency ('Yes, it was all black at first, but then boom—all bright red. Why not?')
- Focus on aesthetics or technique rather than personal expression ('Look how perfectly straight those lines are. It always has to look tight to me')
- Imitating others or a well-known work of art without any meaning of their own ('I like what my friend does in this case, so I've imitated it')
- Taken from social expectations rather than authentic experience ('That's how you're supposed to draw a sad child'; 'That's what I learned from my teacher at school')

Table A.5.2 Traces of non-(body-oriented) mentalizing in musical expression.

Examples of traces of non-(body-oriented) mentalizing in musical expression

Body mode

- Musical expression without reflection on the inner self
- Making music is mainly a physical effort
- Focus mainly on sound sensations (volume, rhythm, vibration) without reflection on emotion or symbolism
- Repetitive patterns with strong physical emphasis (powerful drumming, hitting the keys hard, singing loudly), without further explanation
- Musical changes reflect physical states (e.g. playing softer when exhausted or harder when having energy) rather than a conscious emotional expression

Teleological mode

- Music is approached technically, precisely and purposefully ('I have to play this correctly')
- One wants to convey a message and evoke feelings in others ('All I want is for others to feel exited')
- Difficulties with abstract or emotional musical interpretations ('How do I play something sad?')
- Frustration when music does not live up to expectations ('This is bad! It's not at all the way others like to hear it')
- Playing or singing only when there is a clear purpose ('I'm singing to improve my technique')

Equivalence mode

- Music reflects emotions as absolute truth, without modulation or variation ('These sounds are who I am. If you don't understand them, you don't understand me')
- Sound can be overwhelming, repetitive or rigid ('Every time I play, the same thing happens. I can't do it differently')
- Difficulty with alternative forms of musical expression ('When I try something different, it feels completely wrong. It's not me')
- Strong emotional investment in the music, becoming totally absorbed in it ('These sounds swallow me whole')

Pretend mode

- Superficial personal musical meaning ('I just do it, nothing special')
- Is playful but lacks deep emotional connection ('It's just kind of fun to do it that way')
- Changes style or mood abruptly without clear underlying feelings or explanation ('Yes, that's right, sometimes I play hard, then soft, but it doesn't really mean anything')
- Focuses on entertainment, performance or imitation rather than authentic expression ('I like to sing exactly like Tom Jones. He is my hero')

Table A.5.3 Traces of non-(body-oriented) mentalizing in movement and posture expressions.

Examples of traces of non-(body-oriented) mentalizing in movement and posture expressions

Body mode

- Little awareness of the emotional significance of movement or posture
- Many unintentional, automatic movement impulses and sudden changes of posture without reflection
- Movement patterns are repetitive, stiff, chaotic or tense, and posture does not modulate with interaction
- Movements and postures are directly affected by physical tension or arousal, such as constantly moving limbs, difficulty sitting still or just being stunned, shifting or fidgeting a lot, or suddenly running away; failure to communicate what is happening internally

Teleological mode

- Movements and postures are functional or purposeful ('I move a lot so that my fitness doesn't deteriorate. Does this exercise also help with shaky hands?')
- Resistance to expressive commands ('Why should I wave my arms?')
- Emotions that are only visible through very clearly visible physical actions and postures (punching when angry, stiffly crossed arms when irritated) or to get something done or to trigger something in others
- Frustration when movement/posture has no direct physical/emotional effect ('And now I'm sitting quietly for once and I still can't relax'!)

Equivalence mode

- Movement and posture are immediate, intense, complete and unchangeable in the service of an emotion (e.g. when feeling trapped: completely stiffened or frozen movements) ('This is not a posture I choose. This is just how it is now')
- Little flexibility or playfulness ('When I feel like this, my body has to be like this. There's no other way')
- Can refuse to adjust movement or posture because it feels like denying one's own inner reality ('This is how it feels and this is how it is, so I can't change my movement/posture now')
- Strong identification with a movement or posture ('This is how I am')
- One may be sceptical or dismissive of interventions ('Oh no, that's not for me at all. I'm not like that')

Pretend mode

- Movement style and posture are imitative, theatrical or exaggerated, with no real connection to one's own emotions ('OK, it looks fierce in your eyes, but I don't really feel that much about it. I'm doing this because that's how others do it')
- Adopts posture and movements in accordance with social expectations ('That's how you're supposed to do it, right?')
- Can suddenly change styles ('I just vary a bit, try a bit, nothing else)'
- Difficulties with authentic physical expression ('I don't feel anything special. It's like acting')

A.6 Overview of B-MBT education and skills group meetings

Table A.6 Overview of B-MBT education and skills group meetings.

Overview of 24 weekly sessions of a B-MBT education and skills group

Meeting	Theme of education	Experiential exercise	Homework
1	Design of the group therapy	Getting acquainted, discussing treatment frameworks, group rules, trust, atmosphere	Complete questionnaire on personal goal of treatment
2	Body-oriented mentalizing, attachment and PPS	Focus attention on body signals and notice three of them and name them in turn, sitting in a circle	Read patient leaflet (see Appendix A.1)
3 and 4	Noticing and naming body signals	Notice and name body signals when looking at pictures and listening to music	Once a day, consciously notice and report body signals
5	Mindfulness	Mindfulness body scan; exercise in displaying body signals with colours in a drawing of the human body	A short mindfulness exercise every day; one-time display of body signals with colours in a drawing of the human body
6	Emotions (and its functions) and other inner experiences	Brief mindfulness exercise; brainstorm together about common emotions; name three familiar emotions, along with related thoughts, images, memories and desires	A short mindfulness exercise every day; noticing body signals, emotions and other inner experiences in a pleasant and an unpleasant situations
7 and 8	The physical side of emotions and other inner experiences; opening up versus closing down to one's own physical and mental reactions	Short mindfulness exercise; notice the body sensations when thinking back to a situation with anger and with joy; practice noticing and writing down your own physical and mental reactions when you think back to an emotional situation	A short mindfulness exercise every day; think back to an emotional situation and note your own physical and mental reactions to it; read an information leaflet about the physical side of inner experience

(Continued)

Table A.6 (Continued)

Overview of 24 weekly sessions of a B-MBT education and skills group

Meeting	Theme of education	Experiential exercise	Homework
9	Tolerance zone ('window of tolerance'), tension, hyper and hypoarousal	Brief mindfulness exercise: recognise and record levels of tension using a tension thermometer	A short mindfulness exercise every day; reading the 'window of tolerance' leaflet; reflect on a situation in which you found yourself outside your 'window of tolerance'
10	(Non-)mentalizing modes; body-oriented mentalizing in case of physical complaint	Short mindfulness exercise; brainstorming about internal reactions when being aware of physical complaints; reflecting on a recent situation where body-oriented mentalizing failed	A short mindfulness exercise every day; bring awareness to and write down physical and inner experiences in a situation where body-oriented mentalizing did not work
11	Implicit versus explicit body-oriented mentalizing; perception of bodily symptoms as interplay of physical and mental aspects	Brief mindfulness exercises; noting inner reactions to current physical complaint	A short mindfulness exercise every day; writing a letter to yourself about the physical symptoms you are experiencing: this involves describing thoughts, feelings, needs, tendencies, images and memories associated with the physical complaint
12	Attachment and its connection with coping with physical and mental reactions	Brief mindfulness exercise; brainstorming about 'what is attachment'; exercise: 'Still face' (not reacting to each other) and noticing your own physical and mental reaction to it; exercise: 'Friendly face' and notice physical and mental reaction when someone listens to you friendly and attentively	A short mindfulness exercise each day; observing and noting what the family norm is/was in the family of origin regarding illness and physical complaints

(Continued)

Table A.6 (Continued)

Overview of 24 weekly sessions of a B-MBT education and skills group

Meeting	Theme of education	Experiential exercise	Homework
13 and 14	Interaction styles; internal working models of attachment	Brief mindfulness exercise; be aware of physical sensations and inner reactions when thinking of an important person in your personal life	A short mindfulness exercise every day; fill in a questionnaire about your interaction style
15	Education for system members also attending the session. Topics: PPS and the biopsychosocial model; body-oriented mentalizing; the importance of involvement, helping and non-helping actions; getting to know therapists	Experience-based exercise for system members	A short mindfulness exercise every day; have an open conversation with a person who is important to you about the impact of your physical symptoms on your relationship
16	Where is your attention in contact with others?	Brief mindfulness exercise; recognise your own physical and mental reactions in conversation with a groupmate	A short mindfulness exercise every day; looking back on a conversation with another person and asking yourself the question, 'Where was my attention focused on? On myself or on the other person?' What bodily signals, emotions, thoughts, needs, desires or memories occurred to you in the conversation? Write them down
17	Experiencing boundaries	Short mindfulness exercise; think back to a situation where you received a request and your physical and inner response to it	A short mindfulness exercise every day; think back to a situation this week in which you received a request. Reflect on your physical and mental reactions and your inner tendency to say 'Yes' or 'No' and what you actually did

(Continued)

Table A.6 (Continued)

Overview of 24 weekly sessions of a B-MBT education and skills group

Meeting	Theme of education	Experiential exercise	Homework
18 and 19	Committed action	Short mindfulness exercise; mutual sharing of current valuable activities (committed action) and the physical sensations and inner experiences involved; identifying committed action that you would like to do more often	A short mindfulness exercise every day; doing a committed action once and noticing the physical sensations and inner reactions you experience
20 and 21	Support system function	Brief mindfulness exercise; mapping the support system	Do a short mindfulness exercise every day; undertake valuable action with someone from the support system and become aware of your physical and mental experiences and your interaction style
22 and 23	The signalling plan with the stress thermometer	Brief mindfulness exercise; inventory of measures to regulate stress in order to return to body-oriented mentalization	Do a short mindfulness exercise every day; make a signalling plan; discuss this plan with someone in your system who supports you and discuss how someone can help when you can no longer body-oriented mentalize
24	Ending, evaluation and closure	Brief mindfulness exercise; individual practice in looking back on therapy; evaluative group discussion; completion of evaluation form	

A.7 Contact

For information on research, education and training: Altrecht Psychosomatiek Eikenboom
Address: Vrijbaan 2, 3705 WC Zeist, the Netherlands
Telephone: 030–6965600
E-mail: psychosomatiek@altrecht.nl
Website: https://www.altrecht.nl/topggz-psychosomatiek-eikenboom

To contact the author:
E-mail: j.spaans@hccnet.nl
Website: https://jaapspaanspsycholoog.nl

References

Akwa GGZ, Alliantie kwaliteit in de GGZ. (2018). *Zorgstandaard somatisch onvoldoende verklaarde lichamelijke klachten (SOLK)*. Retrieved June 4, 2020, from https://www.ggzstandaarden.nl/zorgstandaarden/somatisch-onvoldoende-verklaarde-lichamelijke-klachten-solk

Allen, J. G., Fonagy, P., & Bateman, A. W. (2008). *Mentalizing in clinical practice*. American Psychiatric Publishing.

American Psychiatric Association. (1994). *Diagnostic and statistical manual of mental disorders* (4th ed.). American Psychiatric Publishing.

American Psychiatric Association. (2014). *DSM–5. Handboek voor de classificatie van psychische stoornissen*. Boom.

Anzieu, D. (1994). *Le penser. Du Moi-peau au Moi-pensant*. Dunod.

Asen, E., & Fonagy, P. (2012). Mentalization-based family therapy. In A. Bateman & P. Fonagy (Eds.), *Handbook of mentalizing in mental health practice* (pp. 107–128). American Psychiatric Publishing.

Asen, E., & Midgley, N. (2019). Working with families. In A. Bateman, & P. Fonagy (Eds.), *Handbook of mentalizing in mental health practice*. (Chapter 8). American Psychiatric Association Publishing.

A-Tjak, J. G. L., Davis, M. L., Morina, N., Powers, M. B., Smits, J. A. J., & Emmelkamp, P. M. G. (2015). A meta-analysis of the efficacy of acceptance and commitment therapy for clinically relevant mental and physical health problems. *Psychotherapy and Psychosomatics*, *84*, 30–36.

Bales, D. (2019). Partial hospitalization settings. In A. Bateman & P. Fonagy (Eds.), *Handbook of mentalizing in mental health practice*. American Psychiatric Publishing.

Baron-Cohen, S. (1991). Precursors to a theory of mind: Understanding attention in others. IN *Natural theories of mind: Evolution, development and simulation of everyday mindreading* (Vol. 1, pp. 233–251). Springer.

Bartholomew, K., & Horowitz, L. M. (1991). Attachment styles among young adults: A test of a four-category model. *Journal of Personality and Social Psychology*, *61*, 226–244.

Bateman, A., Bales, D., & Hutsebaut, J. (2020). *Quality manual for MBT*. Anna Freud Centre. www. annafreud.org

Bateman, A., & Fonagy, P. (2004). *Psychotherapy for borderline personality disorder*. Oxford University Press.

Bateman, A. W., & Fonagy, P. (2006). *Mentalization-based treatment for borderline personality disorder: A practical guide*. Oxford University Press.

Bion, W. R. (1970). *Attention and interpretation*. Tavistock Publications.

Boon, S., Steele, K., & van der Hart, O. (2012). *Omgaan met traumagerelateerde dissociatie: Een vaardigheidstraining voor patiënten en hun therapeuten*. Pearson.

Bowlby, J. (1951). *Maternal care and mental health* (Vol. 2). World Health Organization.

Bowlby, J. (1969). *Attachment and loss: Vol. 1: Attachment.* Hogarth Press, Institute of Psychoanalysis.

Bowlby, J. (1973). *Attachment and loss: Vol. II: Separation, anxiety and anger.* Hogarth Press, Institute of Psychoanalysis.

Bowlby, J. (1988). *A secure base: Clinical applications of attachment theory.* Routledge.

Brennan, K. A., Clark, C. L., Shaver, P. R., Simpson, J. A., & Rholes, W. S. (1998). *Attachment theory and close relationships.* Guilford Press.

Brown, R. J. (2004). Psychological mechanisms of medically unexplained symptoms: An integrative conceptual model. *Psychological Bulletin, 130*, 793–812.

Bucci, W. (1997). *Psychoanalysis and cognitive science: A multiple code theory.* Guilford Press.

Burton, C., Fink, P., Henningsen, P., Löwe, B., Rief, W., & Euronet-Soma Group. (2020). Functional somatic disorders: Discussion paper for a new common classification for research and clinical use. *BMC Medicine, 18*, 1–7.

Calsius, J., De Bie, J., Hertogen, R., & Meesen, R. (2016). Touching the lived body in patients with medically unexplained symptoms: How an integration of hands-on bodywork and body awareness in psychotherapy may help people with alexithymia. *Frontiers in Psychology, 7*, 179610.

Cassidy, J., & Kobak, R. R. (1988). Avoidance and its relation to other defensive processes. In J. Belsky & T. Nezworski (Eds.), *Child psychology: Clinical implications of attachment* (p. 300–323). Lawrence Erlbaum Associates.

Choi-Kain, L. W., & Gunderson, J. G. (2008). Mentalization: Ontogeny, assessment, and application in the treatment of borderline personality disorder. *The American Journal of Psychiatry, 165*, 1127–1135.

Cittern, D., Nolte, T., Friston, K., & Edalat, A. (2018). Intrinsic and extrinsic motivators of Attachment under active inference. *PLOS One, 13*(4), Article e0193955.

Conway, A. M., Nordon, I. M., Hinchliffe, R. J., Thompson, M. M., & Loftus, I. M. (2011). Patient-reported symptoms are independent of disease severity in patients with primary varicose veins. *Vascular, 19*(5), 262–268.

Craig, A. D. (2010). The sentient self. *Brain Structure and Function, 214*, 563–577.

Creed, F., Henningsen, P., & Fink, P. (Eds.). (2011). *Medically unexplained symptoms, somatisation and bodily distress; Developing better clinical services.* Cambridge University Press.

Crucianelli, L., & Filippetti, M. L. (2018). Developmental perspectives on interpersonal affective touch. *Topoi*, 1–12.

Damasio, A. (2010). *Het zelf wordt zich bewust: Hersenen, bewustzijn, ik.* Wereldbibliotheek.

Davies, J. M. (2004). Whose bad objects are we anyway? Repetition and our elusive love affair with evil. *Psychoanalytic Dialogues, 14*(6), 711–732.

Debbané, M., & Nolte, T. (2019). The neurobiology of mentalising. In A. Bateman & P. Fonagy (Eds.), *Handbook of mentalizing in mental health practice* (Chapter 2). American Psychiatric Association Publishing.

Decraemer, K., & Reijmers, E. (2017). Systeemtherapie. In J. A. Spaans, J. van Rosmalen, Y. van Rood, H. E. van der Horst, & S. Visser (Reds.), *Handboek behandeling van somatisch onvoldoende verklaarde lichamelijke klachten* (pp. 417–430). LannooCampus.

Dehue, T. (2014). *Betere mensen. Over gezondheid als keuze en koopwaar.* Atlas Contact.

den Boer, C., van Eck van der Sluijs, J. F., & van der Feltz-Cornelis, C. M. (2017). Organisatie van zorg. In J. A. Spaans, J. van Rosmalen, Y. van Rood, H. E. van der Horst, & S. Visser (Reds.), *Handboek behandeling van somatisch onvoldoende verklaarde lichamelijke klachten* (pp. 77–88). LannooCampus.

Dendy, C., Cooper, M., & Sharpe, M. (2001). Interpretation of symptoms in chronic fatigue syndrome. *Behaviour Research and Therapy, 39*, 1369–1380.

de Roos, C., & van Rood, Y. (2017). *Eye movement desensitization* and reprocessing. In J. A. Spaans, J. van Rosmalen, Y. van Rood, H. E. van der Horst, & S. Visser (Reds.),

Handboek behandeling van somatisch onvoldoende verklaarde lichamelijke klachten (pp. 337–350). LannooCampus.

De Waal, M., Arnold, I., Eekhof, J., & van Hemert, A. (2004). Somatoform disorders in general practice: Prevalence, functional impairment and comorbidity with anxiety and depressive disorders. *British Journal of Psychiatry, 184*, 470–476.

De Wilde, P. (2015). Leven met een chronische lichamelijke aandoening. Over het restaureren van identiteit. *Systeemtheoretisch Bulletin, 33*, 3–20.

Dosamantes-Beaudry, I. (2007). Somatic transference and countertransference in psychoanalytic intersubjective dance/movement therapy. *American Journal of Dance Therapy, 29*(2), 73.

Dozier, M., & Kobak, R. R. (1992). Psychophysiology in attachment interviews: Converging evidence for deactivating strategies. *Child Development, 63*(6), 1473–1480.

de Drachler, M., Leite, J. C., Hooper, L., Hong, C. S., Pheby, D., Nacul, L., Lacerda, E., Campion, P., Killett, A., McArthur, M., & Poland, F. (2009). The expressed needs of people with chronic fatigue syndrome/myalgic encephalomyelitis: A systematic review. *BMC Public Health, 9*. https://doi.org/10.1186/1471-2458-9-458

Dunbar, R. I. (1998). The social brain hypothesis. *Evolutionary Anthropology: Issues, News, and Reviews, 6*(5), 178–190.

Ebert, A., & Brüne, M. (2018). Oxytocin and social cognition. *Current Topics in Behavioral Neurosciences, 35*, 375–388.

Eisenberger, N. I., & Lieberman, M. D. (2004). Why rejection hurts: A common neural alarm system for physical and social pain. *Trends in Cognitive Sciences, 8*(7), 294–300.

Eisenberger, N. I., Lieberman, M. D., & Williams, K. D. (2003). Does rejection hurt? An fMRI study of social exclusion. *Science, 302*(5643), 290–292.

Elster, J. (1999). Emotion and addiction: Neurobiology, culture and choice. In J. Elster (Ed.), *Addiction: Entries and exits*. Russell Sage Foundation.

Enzlin, P., & Pazmany, E. (2006). Wanneer lust verwordt tot last. Over de invloed van chronische aandoeningen op partnerrelaties. In L. Migerode & J. van Bussel (Reds.), *Als liefde alleen niet volstaat* (pp. 154–172). LannooCampus.

Feldmann-Sinnige, M., Pielage, S., & van der Sluijs, J. V. E. (2023). Body-oriented mentalization based therapy in severe somatic symptom disorder. *Tijdschrift voor Psychiatrie, 65*(9), 542–548.

Fonagy, P., & Adshead, G. (2012). How mentalization changes the mind. *Advances in Psychiatric Treatment, 18*(5), 353–362.

Fonagy, P., & Allison, E. (2014). The role of mentalizing and epistemic trust in the therapeutic relationship. *Psychotherapy, 51*, 372–380.

Fonagy, P., & Bateman, A. W. (2006). Mechanisms of change in mentalization-based treatment of BPD. *Journal of Clinical Psychology, 62*(4), 411–430.

Fonagy, P., Gergely, G., Jurist, L. J., & Target, M. (2002). *Affect regulation, mentalization, and the development of the self*. Other Press.

Fonagy, P., & Luyten, P. (2009). A developmental, mentalization-based approach to the understanding and treatment of borderline personality disorder. *Development and Psycho Pathology, 21*(4), 1355–1381.

Fonagy, P., & Target, M. (1996). Playing with reality I: Theory of mind and the normal development of psychic reality. *International Journal of Psychoanalysis, 77*, 217–223.

Fonagy, P., & Target, M. (2000). Playing with reality: III. The persistence of dual psychic reality in borderline patients. *International Journal of Psychoanalysis, 81*(5), 853–873.

Fonagy, P., & Target, M. (2008). Attachment, trauma, and psychoanalysis: Where psychoanalysis meets neuroscience. In E. L. Jurist, A. Slade, & S. Bergner (Eds.), *Mind to mind: Infant research, neuroscience, and psychoanalysis* (pp. 15–49). Other Press.

Fonagy, P., Luyten, P., Moulton-Perkins, A., Lee, Y. W., Warren, F., Howard, S., & Lowyck, B. (2016). Development and validation of a self-report measure of mentalizing:

The reflective functioning questionnaire. *PLOS One.* https://doi.org/10.1371/journal. pone.0158678

Fonagy, P. E., & Bateman, A. W. (2019). Introduction. In A. Bateman & P. Fonagy (Eds.), *Handbook of mentalizing in mental health practice* (Chapter 1). American Psychiatric Publishing.

Fotopoulou, A., & Tsakiris, M. (2017). Mentalizing homeostasis: The social origins of interoceptive inference. *Neuro-Psychoanalysis, 19,* 3–28.

Fraley, R. C., Hudson, N. W., Heffernan, M. E., & Segal, N. (2015). Are adult attachment styles categorical or dimensional? A taxometric analysis of general and relationship-specific attachment orientations. *Journal of Personality and Social Psychology, 109*(2), 354.

Freud, S. (1905). Fragment van de analyse van een geval van hysterie. In *Ziektegeschiedenissen* (Vol. 2, 1980). Uitgeverij Boom.

Freud, S. (1915). Triebe und Triebschicksale. *Internationale Zeitschrift für (ärztliche) Psychoanalyse, III,* 84–100.

Freud, S. (1923). The ego and the id. In *Standard edition* (Vol. 19, pp. 1–59). Hogarth Press.

Friedman, L. (1988). *The anatomy of psychotherapy.* Analytic Press.

Frijda, N. H. (1988). *De emoties.* Bert Bakker.

Friston, K. J. (2017). Self-evidencing babies: Commentary on "mentalizing homeostasis: The social origins of interoceptive inference" by Fotopoulou and Tsakiris. *Neuropsychoanalysis, 19,* 43–47.

Gergely, G. (2007). The social construction of the subjective self: The role of affect-mirroring, markedness, and ostensive communication in self-development. In L. Mayes, P. Fonagy, & M. Target (Eds.), *Developments in psychoanalysis. Developmental science and psychoanalysis: Integration and innovation* (p. 45–88). Karnac Books.

Hafkenscheid, A. (2014). *De therapeutische relatie.* De Tijdstroom.

Hafkenscheid, A., & Rouckhout, D. (2009). Circumplex structure of the impact message inventory (IMI-C): An empirical test with the Dutch version. *Journal of Personality Assessment, 91*(2), 187–194.

Hambrook, D., Oldershaw, A., Rimes, K., Schmidt, U., Tchanturia, K., Treasure, J., Chalder, T. (2011). Emotional expression, self-silencing, and distress tolerance in anorexia nervosa and chronic fatigue syndrome. *British Journal of Clinical Psychology, 50,* 310–325.

Hansen, L., Chang, M. F., Hiatt, S., Dieckmann, N. F., Mitra, A., Lyons, K. S., & Lee, C. S. (2022). Symptom classes in decompensated liver disease. *Clinical Gastroenterology and Hepatology, 20*(11), 2551–2557.

Harris, R. (2010). *Acceptatie en commitment therapie in de praktijk. Een heldere en toeganke- lijke introductie op ACT.* Hogrefe.

Havsteen-Franklin, D. (2019). Creative arts therapies. In A. Bateman & P. Fonagy (Eds.), *Handbook of mentalizing in mental health practice* (2nd ed., Chapter 11). American Psychiatric Publishing.

Hayes, S. C., Luoma, J., Bond, F. W., Masuda, A., & Lillis, J. (2006). Acceptance and commitment therapy: Model, processes and outcomes. *Behaviour Research and Therapy, 44*(1), 1–25.

Hayes, S. C., & Smith, S. (2005). *Get out of your mind and into your life: The new acceptance and commitment therapy.* New Harbinger.

Henningsen, P. (2018). Management of somatic symptom disorder. *Dialogues in Clinical Neuroscience, 20*(1), 23–31.

Henningsen, P., Zipfel, S., & Herzog, W. (2007). Management of functional somatic syndromes. *The Lancet, 369*(9565), 946–955.

Houtveen, J. (2009). *De dokter kan niets vinden. Het raadsel van medisch onbegrepen onverklaarde lichamelijke klachten.* Bert Bakker.

Houtveen, J., van der Sluijs, J. V. E., Herremans, P. J., & Geenen, R. (2025). Treatment-related changes during and after inpatient treatment for refractory somatic symptom disorder or functional neurological symptom disorder: Testing the applicability of a new approach for analyzing routine outcome monitoring data. *Journal of Psychiatric Research, 185*, 138–145.

Houtveen, J. H., van Broeckhuysen-Kloth, S. A. M., Lintmeijer, L. L., Bühring, M. E. F., & Geenen, R. (2015). Intensive multidisciplinary treatment of severe somatoform disorder: A prospective evaluation. *Journal of Nervous & Mental Disease, 203*, 141–148.

Huber, M., Knottnerus, J. A., Green, L., Horst, H. van der, Jadad, A.R., Kromhout, D., Leonard, B., Lorig, K., Loureiro, M. I., Van Der Meer, J. W., & Schnabel, P. (2011). How should we define health? *British Medical Journal, 343*, d4163.

Huismans, S. (2017). *A taxonomy of the components of body-oriented mentalization in somatic-symptom and related disorders as perceived by experienced clinicians: A concept-mapping study* [Master's thesis Clinical and Health Psychology]. University Utrecht.

Janssens, K. A. M., Houtveen, J. H., Tak, L. M., Bonvanie, I. J., Scholtalbers, A., van Gils, A., & Rosmalen, J. G. M. (2017). A concept mapping study on perpetuating factors of functional somatic symptoms from clinicians' perspective. *General Hospital Psychiatry, 44*, 51–60.

Jurist, E. (2022). Mentalizing from/to/with the body. In *Psychoanalysis and the mind-body problem* (pp. 186–203). Routledge.

Kabat-Zinn, J. (1990). *Full catastrophe living: Using the wisdom of your body and mind to face stress, pain and illness.* Delacorte.

Kalisvaart, H., van Broeckhuysen, S., Bühring, M., Kool, M. B., van Dulmen, S., & Geenen, R. (2012). Definition and structure of body-relatedness from the perspective of patients with severe somatoform disorder and their therapists. *PLOS One, 7–8*, E42534.

Kalisvaart, H., van Busschbach, J. T., van Broeckhuysen-Kloth, S. A., & Geenen, R. (2018). Body drawings as an assessment tool in somatoform disorder. *The Arts in Psychotherapy, 59*, 46–53.

Kalisvaart, H., & Van der Maas, L. (2017). Bevorderen van Lichaamsbewustzijn met lichaamsgerichte therapie. In J. A. Spaans, J. van Rosmalen, Y. van Rood, H. E. van der Horst, & S. Visser (Reds.), *Handboek behandeling van somatisch onvoldoende verklaarde lichamelijke klachten* (pp. 377–386). LannooCampus.

Kamper, S. J., Apeldoorn, A. T., Chiarotto, A., Smeets, R. J., Ostelo, R. W., Guzman, J., & van Tulder, M. W. (2014). Multidisciplinary biopsychosocial rehabilitation for chronic low backpain. *Cochrane Database of Systematic Reviews.* https://doi.org10.1002/14651858. CD000963.pub3

Karterud, S. (2015). *Mentalization-based group therapy (MBT-G): A theoretical, clinical, and research manual.* Oxford University Press.

Karterud, S., & Bateman, A. W. (2012). Group therapy techniques. In A. Bateman & P. Fonagy (Eds.), *Handbook of mentalizing in mental health practice* (pp. 81–105). American Psychiatric Press.

Kaufman, G. (2013). Wie vangt mij op? Behandeling van conversiestoornissen in de groep. *Groepen, 8*(4), 36–46.

Kooiman, C. G., Klaassens, E. R., van Heloma Lugt, J. Q., & Kamperman, A. M. (2013). Psychometrics and validity of the Dutch experiences in close relationships–revised (ECR–R) in an outpatient mental health sample. *Journal of Personality Assessment, 95*(2), 217–224.

Kooiman, C. G., & Koelen, J. A. (2012). Gehechtheid en somatisatie. *Tijdschrift voor Psychotherapie, 38*(4), 291–309.

Kroenke, K. (2003). Patients presenting with somatic complaints: Epidemiology, psychiatric co-morbidity and management. *International Journal of Methods in Psychiatric Research, 12*(1), 34–43.

Lapsley, D., & Woodbury, R. D. (2016). Social cognitive development in emerging adulthood. In J. Jensen Arnett (Ed.), *The Oxford handbook of emerging adulthood* (pp. 142–159). Oxford University Press.

Levenson, J. L. (2008). Psychological factors affecting medical condition. *Psychiatry*, 1754–1772.

Levine, P. A., & Frederick, A. (1997). *Waking the tiger: Healing trauma: The innate capacity to transform overwhelming experiences.* North Atlantic Books.

Lieberman, M. D. (2007). Social cognitive neuroscience: A review of core processes. *Annual Review of Psychology, 58*, 259–289.

Lind, A. B., Delmar, C., & Nielsen, K. (2014). Struggling in an emotional avoidance culture: A qualitative study of stress as a predisposing factor for somatoform disorders. *Journal of Psychosomatic Research, 76*, 94–98.

Löwe, B., Toussaint, A., Rosmalen, J. G., Huang, W. L., Burton, C., Weigel, A., Levenson, J. L., & Henningsen, P. (2024). Persistent physical symptoms: Definition, genesis, and management. *The Lancet, 403*(10444), 2649–2662.

Luyten, P. (2014). Persistente somatische klachten: Nieuwe inzichten vanuit dialoog met de neurowetenschappen. *Tijdschrift voor Psychoanalyse, 20*(4), 266–276.

Luyten, P., & Fonagy, P. (2015). The neurobiology of mentalizing. *Personality Disorders: Theory, Research, and Treatment, 6*(4), 366–379.

Luyten, P., & Fonagy, P. (2019). Mentalizing and trauma. In A. Bateman & P. Fonagy (Eds.), *Handbook of mentalizing in mental health practice.* (Chapter 5). American Psychiatric Association Publishing.

Luyten, P., Van Houdenhove, B., Lemma, A., Target, M., & Fonagy, P. (2012). A mentalization-based approach to the understanding and treatment of functional somatic disorders. *Psychoanalytic Psychotherapy, 26*(2), 121–140.

MacLean, P. D. (1990). *The triune brain in evolution: Role in paleocerebral functions.* Plenum Press.

Marty, P. (1968). A major process of somatization: The progressive disorganization. *International Journal of Psychoanalysis, 49*, 246–249.

Marty, P., & de M'Uzan, M. (1963). La pensée opératoire. *Revue Française de Psychanalyse, 27*, 345–356.

McGlone, F., Wessberg, J., & Olausson, H. (2014). Discriminative and affective touch: Sensing and feeling. *Neuron, 82*(4), 737–755.

Mehling, W. E., Wrubel, J., Daubenmier, J. J., Price, C. J., Kerr, C. E., Silow, T., Gopisetty, V., & Stewart, A. L. (2011). Body awareness: A phenomenological inquiry into the common ground of mind-body therapies. *Philosophy, Ethics, and Humanities in Medicine, 6*(1), 6.

Neumann, I. D. (2008). Brain oxytocin: A key regulator of emotional and social behaviours in both females and males. *Journal of Neuroendocrinology, 20*(6), 858–865.

Newton, B. J., Southall, J. L., Raphael, J. H., Ashford, R. L., & LeMarchand, K. (2013). A narrative review of the impact of disbelief in chronic pain. *Pain Management Nursing, 14*(3), 161–171.

Nicolai, N. (2017a). *Emotieregulatie als basis van het menselijk bestaan: De kunst van het evenwicht.* Bohn Stafleu van Loghum.

Nicolai, N. (2017b). Enactments, impasses en empathische breuken in psychoanalytische psychotherapie. *Tijdschrift voor Psychoanalyse, 23*(4), 264–276.

Nijenhuis, E. R. S. (2000). Somatoform dissociation: Major symptoms of dissociative disorders. *Trauma and Dissociation, 1*, 7–32.

Nijenhuis, E. R. S., Spinhoven, P., Van Dyck, R., Van Der Hart, O., & Vanderlinden, J. (1996). The development and psychometric characteristics of the somatoform dissociation questionnaire (SDQ-20). *Journal of Nervous and Mental Disease, 184*(11), 688–694.

Ogden, P., & Fisher, J. (2017). *Sensorimotor psychotherapy interventies voor traumaverwerking en het herstel van gehechtheid.* Uitgeverij Mens.

Ogden, P., Pain, C., & Fisher, J. (2006). A sensorimotor approach to the treatment of trauma and dissociation. *Psychiatric Clinics of North America, 29*, 263–279.

Olde Hartman, T. C., Blankenstein, A. H., Molenaar, A. O., Bentz van den Berg, D., van der Horst, H. E., Arnold, I. A., & Woutersen-Koch, H. (2013). NHG Standaard somatisch on- voldoende verklaarde lichamelijke klachten (SOLK). *Huisarts en Wetenschap, 56,* 222–230.

Oldershaw, A., Hambrook, D., Rimes, K. A., Tchanturia, K., Treasure, J., Richards, S., & Chalder, T. (2011). Emotion recognition and emotional theory of mind in chronic fatigue syndrome. *Psychology & Health, 26,* 989–1005.

Ormont, L. R., Hunt, M., & Corman, R. (1964). *The talking cure.* Harper and Row.

Pielage, S., & Spaans, J. (2019). '*Stilstaan bij lichaam en geest'. Een ambulante groepstherapie van 18 bijeenkomsten op basis van lichaamsmentalisatie bevorderende therapie (L-MBT) voor patiënten van Altrecht Psychosomatiek Eikenboom.* Interne publicatie.

Porges, S. W. (2011). *The polyvagal theory: Neurophysiological foundations of emotions, attachment, communication, and self-regulation* (Norton Series on Interpersonal Neurobiology). WW Norton & Company.

Renik, O. (1993). Countertransference enactment and the psychoanalytic process. In M. J. E. Horowitz, O. F. Kernberg, & E. M. Weinshel (Eds.), *Psychic structure and psychic change.* International Universities Press, Inc.

Roelofs, K., & Spinhoven, P. (2007). Trauma and medically unexplained symptoms: Towards an integration of cognitive and neuro-biological accounts. *Clinical Psychology Review, 27,* 798–820.

Rogers, C. (1951). *Client-centered therapy.* The Riverside Press.

Rutten-Saris, M. (1990). *Basisboek Lichaamstaal.* Van Gorcum/Dekker & van de Vegt.

Safran, J. D., & Muran, J. C. (2000). *Negotiating the therapeutic alliance: A relational treatment guide.* Guilford Press.

Satpute, A. B., & Lieberman, M. D. (2006). Integrating automatic and controlled processes into neurocognitive models of social cognition. *Brain Research, 1079*(1), 86–97.

Schaefer, M., Egloff, B., & Witthöft, M. (2012). Is interoceptive awareness really altered in somatoform disorders? Testing competing theories with two paradigms of heartbeat perception. *Journal of Abnormal Psychology, 121*(3), 719–724.

Schmeets, M., & van Reekum, A. (2007). Infantonderzoek en neurowetenschappen. In E. H. Eurelings-Bontekoe, W. M. Snellen, & R. Verheul (Eds.), *Handboek persoonlijkheidspathologie* (pp. 21–36). Bohn Stafleu van Loghum.

Schore, A. N. (2011). The right brain implicit self lies at the core of psychoanalysis. *Psychoanalytic Dialogues, 21*(1), 75–100.

Schultz-Venrath, U. (2023). *Mentalizing the body: Integrating body and mind in psychotherapy.* Taylor & Francis.

Senger, K., Schröder, A., Kleinstäuber, M., Rubel, J. A., Rief, W., & Heider, J. (2022). Predicting optimal treatment outcomes using the personalized advantage index for patients with persistent somatic symptoms. *Psychotherapy Research, 32*(2), 165–178.

Shai, D., & Belsky, J. (2011). When words just won't do: Introducing parental embodied mentalizing. *Child Development Perspectives, 5*(3), 173–180.

Siegel, D. J. (1999). *The developing mind. Toward a neurobiology of interpersonal experience.* Guilford Press.

Skaderud, F., & Fonagy, P. (2012). Eating disorders, In A. Bateman & P. Fonagy (Eds.), *Handbook of mentalizing in mental health practice* (pp. 347–383). American Psychiatric Press.

Spaans, J. (2017). Lichaamsgerichte mentalisatiebevorderende therapie. In J. A. Spaans, J. van Rosmalen, Y. van Rood, H. E. van der Horst, & S. Visser (Eds.), *Handboek behandeling van somatisch onvoldoende verklaarde lichamelijke klachten* (pp. 321–336). LannooCampus.

Spaans, J. (2020). *Lichaamsgericht mentaliseren. Gids voor de klinische praktijk.* Tielt. LannooCampus.

Spaans, J., & van der Boom, K. J. (2017). Theoretische modellen. In J. A. Spaans, J. van Rosmalen, Y. van Rood, H. E. van der Horst & S. Visser (Reds.), *Handboek behandeling van somatisch onvoldoende verklaarde lichamelijke klachten* (pp. 51–64). LannooCampus.

Spaans, J., & van der Boom, K. J. (2018). Stand van zaken bij somatisch onvoldoende verklaarde lichamelijke klachten. Verbeteren van de effectiviteit van cognitieve gedragstherapie. *Gedragstherapie, 51,* 246–266.

Spaans, J. A., Koelen, J. A., & Bühring, M. E. F. (2010). Mentaliseren bij ernstige onverklaarde lichamelijke klachten. *Tijdschrift voor Psychotherapie, 36*(1), 5–21.

Spaans, J. A., Veselka, L., Luyten, P., & Bühring, M. E. F. (2009). Lichamelijke aspecten van mentalisatie: Een therapeutische focus bij ernstige onverklaarde lichamelijke klachten. *Tijdschrift voor Psychiatrie, 51,* 239–248.

Steinbrecher, N., & Hiller, W. (2011). Course and prediction of somatoform disorder and medically unexplained symptoms in primary care. *General Hospital Psychiatry, 33,* 318–326.

Stern, D. N. (2004). *The present moment in psychotherapy and everyday life* (Norton Series on Interpersonal Neurobiology). WW Norton & Company.

Stonnington, C. M., Locke, D. E., Hsu, C. H., Ritenbaugh, C., & Lane, R. D. (2013). Somatization is associated with deficits in affective theory of mind. *Journal of Psychosomatic Research, 74,* 479–485.

Subic-Wrana, C., Beutel, M. E., Knebel, A., & Lane, R. D. (2010). Theory of mind and emotional awareness deficits in patients with somatoform disorders. *Psychosomatic Medicine, 72*(4), 404–411.

Tak, L., & van Geelen, S. (2017). Kenmerken en voorkomen. In J. A. Spaans, J. van Rosmalen, Y. van Rood, H. E. van der Horst, & S. Visser (Reds.), *Handboek behandeling van somatisch onvoldoende verklaarde lichamelijke klachten* (pp. 33–49). LannooCampus.

Tak, L., van Rood, Y., & Spaans, J. (2017). Educatie. In J. A. Spaans, J. van Rosmalen, Y. van Rood, H. E. van der Horst & S. Visser (Reds.), *Handboek behandeling van somatisch onvoldoende verklaarde lichamelijke klachten* (pp. 159–172). LannooCampus.

Taubner, S., Kessler, H., Buchheim, A., Kächele, H., & Staun, L. (2011). The role of mentalization in the psychoanalytic treatment of chronic depression. *Psychiatry: Interpersonal & Biological Processes, 74*(1), 49–57.

van der Boom, K. J., & Houtveen, J. H. (2014). Psychiatrische comorbiditeit bij ernstige somatoforme stoornissen in de derde lijn. *Tijdschrift voor Psychiatrie, 56,* 743–747.

van der Kolk, B. A. (2014). *The body keeps the score: Mind, brain and body in the transformation of trauma.* Penguin UK.

van der Maas, L. C. C., Köke, A., Pont, M., Bosscher, R. J., Twisk, J. W. R., Janssen, T. W. J., & Peters, M. L. (2015). Improving the multidisciplinary treatment of chronic pain by stimulating body awareness: A cluster-randomized trial. *Clinical Journal of Pain, 31,* 660–669.

van der Werf, N. (2018). Relaties helen creëert helende relaties. EFT bij mensen met ernstige SOLK. In J. de Graaf & J. Zoetmulder (Eds.), *EFT in uitvoering—Een casusboek* (pp. 273–289). Stichting EFT.

van Overwalle, F., & Baetens, K. (2009). Understanding others' actions and goals by mirror and mentalizing systems: A meta-analysis. *Neuroimage, 48,* 564–584.

Verfaille, M. (2018). *Mentalizing in arts therapies.* Routledge.

Vlaeminck, H. (2005). Het ecogram als röntgenfoto van het netwerk bij psychische problemen. *Tijdschrift voor Welzijnswerk, 29*(266), 13–23.

Waller, E., & Scheidt, C. E. (2006). Somatoform disorders as disorders of affect regulation: A development perspective. *International Review of Psychiatry, 18*(1), 13–24.

Waller, E., Scheidt, C. E., & Hartmann, A. (2004). Attachment representation and illness behavior in somatoform disorders. *The Journal of Nervous and Mental Disease, 192,* 200–209.

Wallin, D. J. (2010). *Gehechtheid in psychotherapie*. Uitgeverij Nieuwezijds.

Weiland, A., van de Kraats, R. E., Blankenstein, A. H., van Saase, J. L., van der Molen, H. T., Bramer, W. M., van Dulmen, A. M., & Arends, L. R. (2012). Encounters between medical specialists and patients with medically unexplained physical symptoms; influences of communication on patient outcomes and use of health care: A literature overview. *Perspectives on Medical Education, 1*(4), 192–206.

Winnicott, D. W. (1960). The theory of the parent-infant relationship. *International Journal of Psychoanalysis, 41*, 585–595.

Zevalkink, J. (2007). De bril van nu: Het in kleuren van het heden door ervaringen uit het verleden. In J. Zevalkink & Q. van Dam (Reds.), *Tegenwoordigheid van geest. Het actuele moment in een psychoanalytische behandeling*. Van Gorcum.

Acknowledgements

The daily work with colleagues and patients at the highly specialised treatment and research centre Altrecht Psychosomatiek Eikenboom in the Netherlands was a great inspiration for the development and implementation of B-MBT over the years. It also motivated me to write articles about body-oriented mentalizing and, eventually, this book. Psychiatrist Martina Bühring, the medical director at the time, played an important role from the very beginning. In 2006, she and the psychiatrist Ariëtte van Reekum arranged our consultation in London with Peter Fonagy and Anthony Bateman, the developers of MBT. Encouraged by this consultation, we began to develop B-MBT for patients with severe PPS. The work and courses of Fonagy and Bateman continued to encourage us in this process.

Researchers Dr Saskia van Broeckhuysen, Dr Jan Houtveen and Professor Dr Rinie Geenen (University of Utrecht) supported several studies and publications in the field of body-oriented mentalizing. In this way, they provided the indispensable link between clinical B-MBT and science.

In addition to the works of Peter Fonagy and Anthony Bateman, the articles and books of David Wallin, Patrick Luyten, Jon Allen, Pat Ogden, Nelleke Nicolai, Marianne Verfaille and Ulrich Schultz-Venrath were a great source of inspiration for the writing.

My dear partner Dubravka Spaans-Knezic provided constructive comments to the entire manuscript. In this book, she was again that constant, loving, patient, wise source of inspiration and support for me at home.

My good friend Fred Verdoorn (psychologist) gave his courageous professional opinion on the subject and the writing process during many walks.

Several colleagues within Altrecht Psychosomatiek Eikenboom were critical co-readers of (parts of) the manuscript. In no particular order they are: Stanneke Lunter (psychiatrist), Kees Jan van der Boom (clinical psychologist), Suzanne Pielage (clinical psychologist), Shiva Thorsell (clinical psychologist), Myriam Lipovsky (internist/psychotherapist), Hanneke Kalisvaart (psychomotor therapist, researcher), Peter Visser (systems therapist), Claartje Verheul (psychosomatic physiotherapist), Sanne Huismans (psychologist), Pieter Jan Herrenmans (clinical psychologist) and Lotta de Beus (art therapist). Kees Jan van der Boom (clinical psychologist) not only provided constructive comments throughout the manuscript, but also made a major contribution to the drafting of Chapter 2. Stanneke Lunter (psychiatrist) also did more than co-read: she coordinated the feedback from all the co-readers and brought it together into a usable whole.

Lauren Redhead, editor at Routledge|Taylor & Francis, trusted me to write this English update of the Dutch book *Lichaamsgericht mentaliseren.* Together with her colleagues, she edited the book and provided valuable guidance and support during the process.

My sincere thanks go to all those mentioned here.

Finally, I would like to acknowledge the use of the AI-powered translation and writing program DeepL Pro Advanced + Write Pro (version February–April 2025), which supported the early stages of the English version of this book. I reviewed and edited the AI-generated translations for fidelity to the original and clarity, accuracy and consistency—both in language and in content.

Jaap Spaans

Index

For Product Safety Concerns and Information please contact our EU representative GPSR@taylorandfrancis.com
Taylor & Francis Verlag GmbH, Kaufingerstraße 24, 80331 München, Germany